AMERICAN TURNAROUND

AMERICAN TURNAROUND

Reinventing AT&T and GM and the Way We Do Business in the USA

ED WHITACRE

FORMER CEO, AT&T AND GENERAL MOTORS
WITH LESLIE CAULEY

**BUSINESS
PLUS**

NEW YORK   BOSTON

Business Plus
Hachette Book Group
237 Park Avenue
New York, NY 10017

www.HachetteBookGroup.com

Printed in the United States of America

RRD-C

First Edition: February 2013
10 9 8 7 6 5 4 3 2 1

Business Plus is an imprint of Grand Central Publishing.
The Business Plus name and logo are trademarks of Hachette Book Group, Inc.

The Hachette Speakers Bureau provides a wide range of authors for speaking events. To find out more, go to www.hachettespeakersbureau.com or call (866) 376-6591.

The publisher is not responsible for websites (or their content) that are not owned by the publisher.

Library of Congress Cataloging-in-Publication Data
Whitacre, Edward E., 1941–
     American turnaround : reinventing AT&T and GM and the way we do business in the USA / Ed Whitacre ; with Leslie Cauley.—1st ed.
         p. cm.
     Includes index.
     ISBN 978-1-4555-1301-7 (hbk.)
     1. Whitacre, Edward E., 1941–   2. Chief executive officers—United States—Biography.   3. AT & T—Management.   4. General Motors Corporation—Management.   5. Industrial management—United States.   I. Cauley, Leslie, 1957–   II. Title.
     HC102.5.W476A3 2013
     338.7'629222092—dc23
     [B]

                                                                            2012021819

To my wife and daughters,
Linda, Jessica, and Jennifer

Contents

Author's Note

If you'd asked me when I was a high school senior what was in my future, here's what I would have told you: I planned to go to work for the railroad and stay there until I retired. Growing up, I just assumed that was how my life would go.

I come from a long line of railroad people: My daddy—his name was Edward Earl Whitacre, that's whom I'm named after—dropped out of high school to take a job with the railroad and worked there fifty years. His daddy did the same thing. So did the other men in my family. There are no silver spoons in my background. We had farmers, a part-time rancher, an Air Force navigator, a high school football coach, and a town blacksmith in our family. But the railroad, well, that was almost a calling. Being a part of America's railroad tradition was a real point of pride in our family. And it always will be.

But as it turned out, I did not go to work for the railroad. Instead, and much to my own surprise, I wound up becoming the chairman and CEO of two of the biggest companies in the world, AT&T and General Motors. I spent forty-four years with AT&T—I worked my way up from student engineer. And GM—I wound up there at the request of the White House in 2009, right after the company got out of bankruptcy. I had just retired from AT&T, and like everybody else in America I was saddened and somewhat mystified by GM's collapse: *How could GM management allow this to happen?* That's the question I kept asking myself walking in the door at GM, and I kept asking that question—and lots of others, especially of senior management—the entire time I was there. I am a private man by nature, which is one reason I've never said much publicly—in fact, I spent most of my career avoiding microphones and interviews, and for the most part was successful. I'm also not the kind to talk about myself. That sort of thing has always embarrassed me, to be perfectly honest. And it still does. So I will admit to you up front that I approached this entire book-writing idea with a little—maybe a lot of—trepidation.

But after much thought and reflection, I decided that a book would be a good way, maybe the only way, for me to thank and publicly acknowledge a lot of people who have helped me along the way. And since I just recently turned seventy, I figured I should probably do that sooner rather than later. These people didn't just help me personally; they also helped build and contributed to the success of businesses that positively affect lives and the whole of America. I'm very proud of what we accomplished together, sometimes under the roughest of circumstances—GM jumps to mind. My experiences at AT&T and GM reminded me every single day, in big and small ways, just how good American workers are, and why they're so important to the long-term success of this country.

And so I finally decided to write this book. There's a lot in here about me, because, well, this is my life and these are my experiences. I did my best to tell the story straight—pulling punches and tap-dancing around tough subjects just aren't my way. But I'm also going to talk a lot about other people, as I just mentioned, and about the management principles that have guided me and shaped me for more than four decades now.

And I've written about some other things, too, like the idea of destiny, which is directly tied to a cherished and time-honored notion in this country: the American Dream. The rail-road business is still in my blood—it's a part of who I am, and where I come from, and I'm very proud of that legacy. But life took a very different turn, and as a result I experienced things, and learned things, that would have seemed almost impossible to me when I was growing up. Who would have ever predicted that I would become the chief executive...of anything? Not me, certainly. But that's how it is in America: If you can dream it, or even be open to the possibilities, you really can live it.

So how does a guy make the leap from a railroad family in Ennis, Texas, to become the CEO of not just one but *two* iconic American businesses? I have no idea, to be honest—some days I still can't believe all this stuff happened to me. But it did, and this is my story.

Ed Whitacre
Fall 2012

AMERICAN TURNAROUND

CHAPTER 1

"The Economy Got Us"

Bolt holes.

That was the main concern, the only concern, really, of one senior executive at General Motors right after the company emerged from bankruptcy. The White House had just appointed me chairman, so I was asking senior management to talk to me about their concerns, as well as their future hopes for the company. That was this manager's response to my query: that he only cared about one thing, "making sure all the holes are in the right places."

I had no idea what he was talking about, to be perfectly honest. I was new to GM and didn't know a lot about cars. But I figured this must be important, otherwise he wouldn't have been making such a fuss. So I asked him to explain.

Turned out, he was referring to the placement of holes for bolts on the car chassis as it rolled through the assembly line. This person—a senior manufacturing executive—said it was a constant struggle for him to get the people responsible for drilling the holes to put them in the right places. Without proper alignment, he explained, the bolts, which hold the chassis and other components to the frame, don't go in the way they're supposed to. He was really fired up about this bolt-hole thing, I could tell, because the more he talked about it, the more worked up he got.

I did my best to keep a poker face on, but inside my reaction was pretty much this: *Wow*. I mean, c'mon, "Government Motors" was now the biggest failure in America, taxpayers were upset because they were footing the $50 billion bailout tab, employees were upset because they weren't sure if they'd have a job three months out, the longtime CEO had just been shown the door, sales were anemic, dealers were filing lawsuits left and right, and all of this was making the future of America's number one carmaker a question mark at best. And the only thing this guy cared about, or worried about, or wanted to talk about, was *bolt holes*?

And yet this was the state of General Motors right after bankruptcy. It was as if the entire Chapter 11 proceeding had just been some sort of messy misunderstanding. *Not our fault. Not our problem.* That was the general feeling and attitude inside GM's Detroit headquarters. Even worse, there was little sense of urgency that I could detect; no larger sense of purpose. The "new" GM was just like the old GM, except it was smaller and had $50 billion in taxpayer money to keep it going for a while. It was a big slug of money, in absolute terms. But not a lot for a $150-billion-a-year enterprise like GM that burns through billions in expenses every single month. If GM management continued down the same path, with no course correction or strategy, it could easily run out of money again. That would put the company right back where it started: in bankruptcy, looking for a financial lifeline. The American people had generously stepped up the first time with $50 billion. GM might not be so lucky the second time around.

But to hear GM management talk—and I was getting an earful as the new chairman—the collapse wasn't their fault. It was due to some combination of bad luck, bad timing, and bad circumstances. In other words, bad management had nothing to do with it.

"The economy got us," one executive told me. His comment stayed with me, like gum stuck on the bottom of a shoe. I will always remember that quote.

All across the company, I soon discovered, managers had whole sacks of excuses and justifications as to why they thought GM had gone off the rails so hard: The union got us, gas prices got too high, the Japanese yen went soft—I heard that one a lot—the list went on and on. One executive told me—with a completely straight face—that the only reason GM went broke was because "we didn't sell enough cars and we ran out of money." I thought he was kidding. He wasn't. The focus on bolt holes was indicative of the problem: Management had zero sense of urgency or accountability. Senior managers also had little interest in discussing possible solutions, because in their minds nothing was wrong or needed fixing.

I had a lot of "wow" moments those first few days. A lot of that had to do with GM's organizational chaos—there really was no plan, or strategy. One person—a very senior executive—spent the better part of an hour just trying to explain to me exactly what he did at GM. And the more he talked, the more nebulous his job sounded. By the time he finished I came away feeling that this guy really didn't have anything to do—and he was supposedly in charge of a big piece of GM's business. (Wow moment!) That meeting ended and I still didn't know exactly what that guy did. And I'm pretty sure he didn't, either. Most troubling to me, none of this seemed to bother him, or even occur to him. For him, I guess, it was just another business-as-usual day at America's largest automaker.

He wasn't the only one like that. When I started asking people whom they reported to—a relatively simple question, you might think—nobody really seemed to know. People would give me a name, then another name, and then give me another name a few minutes later after they'd thought about it some more. Before long I got the idea that people on the senior management team, who were responsible for running the most important parts of GM—design, development, manufacturing—were having to interact with just about everybody at GM. Or with nobody if they didn't feel like it. In other words, there were no clear lines of authority or responsibility, so nobody was really in charge or accountable if things went wrong. The problem, I soon discovered, went all the way to the top of the executive chain.

My takeaway from all this?

Well, from my perspective, you didn't have to be a car expert to figure it out: The economy didn't get GM. Mismanagement did. And in truth, I can't say I was surprised. I sort of assumed, before I ever showed up, that I was going to find a lot of management stuff there I didn't like. My logic was pretty simple: For GM to get itself in that big of a mess—bankrupt, bad relations with labor, demoralized workforce, no clear strategic path—there must be something terribly, and fundamentally, wrong at the top. My gut told me that much. And my conversations with senior managers those first few days, with all their talk about the economy, gas prices, and bolt holes, confirmed my suspicions real quick.

If I sound like a guy who's prone to make snap judgments, well, maybe I am. But those judgments are based on gut instincts about people, management, and the state of American business that took me a lifetime to develop. And I'm right at seventy as this is being written, so you can draw your own conclusions about that.

I'm a Texan by birth and wiring—I was born and raised in Ennis, Texas, just outside Dallas. I have a strong Texas drawl, or so I've been told. I don't hear it myself—that's just the way I talk. I have a long independent streak—this I do know. For me, giving something a shot and failing is always far better than not even trying. I'm not sure if that's the Texas in me or just the way I was brought up. But I do know this: Risk is a fundamental part of life. Try to run from it too hard and you'll never accomplish anything that really matters to you; openly embrace it and you can sometimes achieve amazing things—in business, and in life. That's not to say that you won't fall on your butt once in a while. You will, I promise. But you'll also learn some valuable lessons that you can use and apply to the next mountain you try to climb. Do that often enough and you'll build confidence. You may also wind up doing things, and accomplishing things, you never thought possible.

Take me, for instance. I'm a guy who grew up thinking I'd never leave Ennis. Always figured I'd work for the railroad just like my daddy—he was an engineer with the old Southern Pacific Railroad. He loved that railroad, worked there fifty years. Instead, and very much to my own surprise, I went on to run two of the biggest companies in the world: AT&T and General Motors. I'm still not sure how that happened, to be honest. But it did. Along the way I think I learned an awful lot about management and about people, which is 99 percent of management when you get right down to it. And yes, I fell on my butt once in a while, no question. But I never stayed down for too long.

Before I got to General Motors I was the chairman and CEO of AT&T, based in my adopted hometown of San Antonio, Texas—that's about as far away from Detroit as a guy can get, in more ways than one. AT&T today is the largest telecommunications company in the world. It didn't start out that way. When I became CEO in 1990, the company—it was then called Southwestern Bell—was a $9-billion-a-year "Baby Bell" that provided local phone service in five states in the Southwest. By the time I retired in 2007, we had global revenue of around $120 billion. We still provided local phone service in those five Southwest states. But we also owned three other Bells—four if you include Southwestern Bell—the largest wireless business in America, a growing cable TV business, and AT&T, whose name we adopted in

2005. In addition, we had exclusive US rights to the Apple iPhone, which revolutionized the wireless business, and a bunch of international assets.

None of this is magic.

It's called *management*. At AT&T, I had a great team of dedicated managers—people like Jim Kahan, my longtime deal guy; Charles Foster, our top operations person for many years; Jim Ellis, the general counsel; and Stan Sigman, who brilliantly managed our wireless business. We had a clear vision of our future, and a road map for how we planned to get there. But the real reason we were successful at AT&T—the *only* reason, really—was because we had great people. I'm referring to all the men and women who get up, every single day, and come to work to do all the things that allow a business to function. Think about this: CEOs don't make or produce anything—when I was at AT&T, I didn't install phones (though I know how to), and when I was at GM, I didn't make cars (still not a clue). Employees do all that. That's why it's so important to have an engaged and enthusiastic workforce, because with an engaged and enthusiastic workforce, miracles really are possible. Just look at GM today.

That brings me to one of my favorite subjects: the state of American business. There's a lot of talk these days about how America has lost it—that we've lost our edge and can't compete globally. I think people who say that don't know what they're talking about. They have either never worked in industry, or never been around people so they don't know what a valuable asset we have out there, in terms of the spirit, the depth, and the capability of American workers. Workers here are imbued with that uniquely American spirit that says: *We can do anything. We're the best. We're the most enthused. We're the most capable.* Our approach has always been: *Give me a challenge and I'll tackle it; show me a mountain and I'll climb it.*

I saw it at AT&T, and I saw it again at General Motors—

not when I first got there, but later. When I first showed up in Detroit employees were feeling beaten down and defeated, and I really couldn't blame them because they'd been through hell and back. But we did some things to help change that around, and I'll be talking about how we did that a little later. But my larger point is this: *People are the number one asset of any business.* The number one asset; and if you only get one takeaway from this book, I hope it is that. Because if you don't get that aspect right—the *people* part—you will fail. That's a good segue to get back to where I started, talking about General Motors.

Now, I'm sure the economy had some impact on GM's collapse, because it caused people to buy fewer cars. And the bump up in gas prices—that probably didn't help, either, because it resulted in higher demand for smaller, gas-efficient vehicles, which was not GM's strength at the time. But I never thought for a moment those were the underlying reasons for GM's collapse. I mean, just look around—Ford had made it. Nissan was doing fine. Volkswagen was doing fine, and it operates in a global economy. Toyota, Honda, Mercedes-Benz, lots of others—all fine. And they were dealing with the same tough economy as GM. But you sure didn't see any of them flying the white flag, did you? So for GM to stand up and say "the economy got us" was a bunch of baloney—because the economy didn't get any of those other car manufacturers.

Good managers sometimes make bad decisions, no question. But good managers don't make bad decisions *consistently*. They also don't stay wrong for long. If something's not working, a good manager will spot it pretty quickly, and figure out something to get it back on track. Bad managers, they tend to sit pat and do nothing because they're worried about making a mistake. Or they make bad decisions, over and over again, until small problems begin to fester to the point that they become big ones. Or—and this is classic—they blame bad outcomes on things outside their control, like the economy or the Japanese yen, so they can throw up their hands and say: "Not my fault."

Bad management is easy to spot, because companies eventually go broke, lag behind, or become extinct. Consider the sad case of MCI. For years—decades—MCI was America's number two long-distance company, right behind AT&T. MCI's management clung tight to its long-distance crown. So tight that it missed a critically important business shift: the growing threat of wireless to the traditional long-distance business. MCI's management was seemingly unconcerned, and here's why: As of 1990, there were only five million wireless subscribers in the United States—not enough to worry about, or so MCI thought. So management sat pat on MCI's long-distance assets...for years. Meantime, the number of wireless subscribers in the United States continued to grow, quarter by quarter, and year by year. By 2000 there were one hundred million wireless subscribers in America, with no sign of a slow-up in sight. That got MCI's attention. But by then it was too late. All the best wireless properties (spectrums, operating licenses, and so on) were long gone. MCI's days, at that point, were numbered. It later was acquired by WorldCom, ran into a bunch of accounting problems, and landed in bankruptcy court.

MCI eventually got free of all that and went back to selling long-distance, just like it always had. But it didn't matter. Thanks to the fast rise of wireless and flat-rate calling plans, calls were just calls. With no wireless assets to fall back on, MCI had no way to grow revenues. That meant it had no future. MCI's long-distance assets were later acquired by Verizon. As this is being written in 2012, there are more than 327 million wireless subscribers in the United States, and the number keeps rising thanks to the proliferation of cool new wireless devices. A lot of people nowadays own more than one, which is why there are now more devices than people in the United States. (Current US population: around 315 million.)

The moral of this story: Managers aren't caretakers. You're not supposed to maintain the status quo, or ride an asset down into the dirt until nothing's left. Just because your business is humming now doesn't mean it will be doing so five years from now, or even a year from now, let alone a decade out. Good managers know that *change* is the only constant in business, so they actively *manage* their businesses—smartly, aggressively, and as humanely as possible. That last part—the people part— that's the most important of all. Managers have huge influence and huge obligation here, because they're the ones who make hiring and firing decisions, help create corporate cultures. They also help inspire—or beat down—employees. Or worse, they just forget about the human part. Growth doesn't work that way. That sort of approach, in combination with management blinders—or ignoring market signals until it's too late—is a surefire way to crater your business.

GM's experience is instructive. Hard to believe now, but back in the 1960s General Motors controlled nearly 50 percent of the US car market. Think about that: One out of every two vehicles sold in America had a GM nameplate on it—Chevy, Buick, et cetera. Daunting numbers, especially if you're a competitor. But Toyota, Honda, and other global brands decided to give it a go anyway. They didn't make much headway, at least initially. In 1965 Toyota controlled only about 0.1 percent of the US car market.

Then came the '80s, and things started to shift for GM. Inexplicably, the company that brought the world such classics as the 1955 Chevy—still regarded as one of the finest car designs ever—started churning out a bunch of ill-conceived, poorly designed cars that nobody wanted, and nobody bought. Emblematic of the era was the Cadillac Cimarron. A Caddie in name only, this car had clunky styling, four cylinders, and a four-speed manual transmission. *Time* magazine named the Cimarron one of the fifty worst cars of all time. (Wrote *Time*: "Everything that was wrong, venal, lazy and mendacious about GM in the 1980s was crystallized in this flagrant insult to the good name and fine customers of Cadillac.") Other GM cars on the "50 Worst" list included the ninety-horsepower Camaro Iron Duke (1982), the Cadillac Fleetwood V-8-6-4 (1981), and the Corvette 305 California (1980), which featured a three-speed *automatic* transmission. That gave GM's ultimate muscle car "acceleration comparable to a very hot Vespa." *Time* blamed the Fleetwood's famously bumpy ride—it was prone to buck, jerk, and make funny noises—on the car's "Titanic engine program," a V-8 that could power down to a V-4 to conserve energy.

GM's design problems continued throughout the '80s and into the '90s. Toyota and other global brands brilliantly capitalized. They started showing up with consistently well-designed cars that looked good and drove well, and also offered solid value. After a while—this was a slow evolution, not an instant revolt—they got traction with American car buyers, and their market share started to grow. And GM? Owing to a bunch of factors—lousy cars, first and foremost—its market share started eroding. In the meantime, the world did not stand still—it never does. A few recessions came and went, the Japanese yen bounced around, and gas prices did what they did. Consumer tastes changed. Auto trends changed.

In 2008, after years of steady declines, the unthinkable finally happened: Toyota bypassed GM to become the world's largest carmaker. By a nose—Toyota's global market share that year stood at 12.5 percent, versus 12.4 percent for GM. But the larger message wasn't lost on anybody. At the same time, the spike in gas prices, coupled with the recession and some other factors, caused demand for cars in the United States to drop like a stone. And that 50 percent market share? It was down to 22 percent, and still falling. That's when things turned desperate for GM. Since it wasn't selling enough cars and trucks to pay its bills, the company started burning through its cash reserves—$19.2 billion in 2008 and another $10.2 billion in the first three months of 2009. At the end of that short period of time, GM's cash was all gone—it was flat broke.

That's when the wheels came off the bus.

On June 1, 2009, GM filed for Chapter 11 bankruptcy court protection. In its formal filing to the court, GM listed liabilities of $172 billion and assets of just $82 billion. GM shares, which lost 95 percent of their value between 2000 and 2009, were instantly rendered worthless. The economy didn't do that to GM. The union didn't do that to GM. And the Japanese yen certainly didn't do that to GM—GM's management did that to GM. They just never had the smarts or the guts or whatever you want to call it to make a course correction to give GM a shot at a better future. Or if they did it wasn't dramatic enough to alter the path going forward, because we all saw what happened—GM went bust. That's when the federal government stepped in, with the noble goal of avoiding a financial calamity on the order of the Great Depression. In the end, the government—this was a bipartisan effort that started with President Bush and continued with President Obama—handed over taxpayer money to help GM get through bankruptcy. Absent that $50 billion cash infusion GM, in all likelihood, would have been forced to liquidate—the assets would have been carved up and sold off to the highest bidder.

Personally, I did not want to contemplate an America—or a world—without General Motors. Part of my reasoning is purely emotional: GM is a major part of America. I mean, really, GM *is* America. Its contributions as a carmaker and designer—the '80s and most of the '90s notwithstanding—are legendary. For examples, look at the 1955 Chevy, 1959 Cadillac, and 1967 Corvette. Add in too many great trucks to name; I'm a longtime GMC guy myself. Also legendary are its contributions as a corporate citizen. During World War II, GM converted major production facilities to the Allied effort; it delivered billions of dollars in aid over the course of the war—airplanes, tanks, machine guns, even shells. GM's dedication to country means something to me. Means something to a lot of Americans, I suspect.

That's not to say that legacy alone is enough reason to save GM, or any company, for that matter—it's not. Throughout history, lots of great companies have felt the pain of time and change: AOL, Motorola, Western Union—at one time it was one of the largest companies in the world—and many others. The old AT&T, known affectionately by those of us who worked there as "Ma Bell," got dismantled by the federal government in 1984, and that was a century-old business whose roots trace back, quite literally, to the invention of the telephone. In each of these cases companies got outrun by technology, outgunned by competitors, and in some cases just beat up by the clock. That's what happens if you're in business long enough—the world changes. And if you don't change along with it, you're going to have trouble. Charles Darwin said it best: Adapt or die.

General Motors clearly did not adapt. But just let it die? That was never a good idea, in my view. Forget history. Forget the legacy. And forget all those cool cars. (And trucks.) Just focus on the economic reality: GM was, and still is, America's largest manufacturer. That makes it the face, and anchor, of our manufacturing base. That's why I supported the bailout 100 percent, because I felt that we could not afford to lose a manufacturer of GM's size and importance. GM supports nearly one million jobs, directly and indirectly. It's also the backbone of the US auto industry, which supports eight million jobs overall. And all those jobs have real people attached to them—people with mortgages to pay, kids to send to college, and families to support. We'd already lost steel, electronics, and a couple of other big industries. If autos went out, we'd never again be taken seriously as a major manufacturer. There would have been no recovery from that—ever.

On the other hand, a strong and standing General Motors sent a powerful message: *We are America. We stick together. We can do anything.* The American Dream is all about second chances, beating the odds, and, let's be honest, winning. When we get knocked down, we don't stay down long—we get back up. We think our way around problems, and if that doesn't work, we'll think some more, and try something different. Never say die; it ain't over till it's over; remember the Alamo—you get the idea. That's our legacy as a country, and our shared DNA as a population. GM is imbued with that same spirit, which is one reason it has always stood out among the world's leading carmakers. No knock on Ford or Chrysler; they're both world-class car companies. But General Motors is just special, in part because of its size, in part because of what it represents to this country. As goes General Motors, so goes America. You bet.

Washington got that. When the White House announced the government's decision to save GM, President Obama said the bailout was necessary to ensure that future generations "can grow up in an America that still makes things." It's a simple idea on its face—preserving an America that "makes things." But it's also an important and poignant notion, one that I happen to support. Today there are fewer manufacturing employees in the United States than there were in 1955. According to some industry estimates, more than nine million manufacturing jobs have been lost over the past twenty years—four million in the past decade alone. And the trend line is accelerating. Throwing GM on the trash heap, given all the jobs it supports, directly and indirectly, would have been industrial suicide.

But was GM fixable? It was a legitimate question given GM's shaky state right after it got out of bankruptcy. And I will confess here that I asked myself that very question many times. And

I found myself coming back to the same one-word answer every time: *Yes.*

Make that two words: *Hell, yes.*

My main source of optimism?

GM employees. People, like I said, are the number one asset of any business. Over the years—and I've had this confirmed a thousand times—I have learned that 99.9 percent of the people out there want the exact same thing: to feel good about their lives, to feel that they're not failures, to feel like they're contributing and are part of something that is having a positive impact on their kids and families. Everybody wants that. I do. You do. We all do. It's just part of the human condition. That inner need to contribute and be a part of something that is good and positive is a powerful force. And it can drive people to accomplish some pretty amazing things. Even impossible things, if you ask them in the right way.

General Motors didn't get to be the world's biggest carmaker for nothing, you know. It got that way because of the people it had working there—they had guts, good ideas, and a lot of talent. GM's people are truly the heart and soul of that company, and the union is a big part of that. But somewhere along the line, it seemed to me, GM employees forgot how special they are, and how talented they are, and how important they are, and always will be, to the success of that company. And the reason all that happened, I think—I know—is because GM's management let them down, and let them forget.

And that, to me, was the real shame of the bankruptcy. Not that GM went bankrupt, but that senior management let it happen. We're talking about a handful of people, basically, and they were ultimately responsible for the welfare of General Motors, and the welfare of the two-hundred-thousand-plus employees who depended on them to look out for the interests of the company, and the interests of the employee body, so that GM could keep going and growing. These senior managers were not bad actors, by any stretch. In most cases they devoted their lives and careers to GM. But the fact of the matter is, management lost control of the wheel at some point, and the sad result is that GM, under their charge and control, got put nose-first into the dirt.

The numbers tell the story: By the time I showed up at GM in 2009, GM hadn't posted a profit in five long years. But it did lose $82 billion and burn through all of its cash trying to stay afloat. The share price, which peaked at $90 in April 2000, went to less than $3. Employees didn't cause that to happen. Management did. Even in that tarnished state, the departing CEO, Rick Wagoner, continued to believe in GM: "Ignore all the doubters," he said. "Because I know GM is a company with a great future."

I agreed with him on that. And that's why I ultimately decided to go to General Motors: to see if I could help all those employees, and help save a company that is important to the future of America. I didn't know if I could pull it off. But I figured there was just one way to find out.

CHAPTER 2

Duty Calls

Life, when you really think about it, is basically just a series of key moments or turning points. And some of those moments, in the blink of an eye, can change your life forever. One of the moments for me arrived on what had been, up to that point, a very unmemorable day. I will always remember it.

It was March 25, 2009, a Wednesday. I'd been out all morning—doing what, I do not recall. I was driving into the office so I called my secretary, Marilyn Taylor, to let her know I was on the way. That's when Marilyn told me that Steve Rattner had just called and wanted me to call him back. And I remember thinking to myself: *Well, that's strange. Why would Steve be calling me?*

I had met Steve many years earlier—in the 1990s—when he was at Lazard Frères, the big investment bank in New York. Lazard was one of AT&T's longtime bankers, and Steve worked there, so that's how we met. Didn't know Steve too well, to be honest. At Lazard I mostly dealt with Felix Rohatyn, the managing director. Felix is famous for saving New York City from bankruptcy in the 1970s. He later became the US ambassador to France, which entirely tracks because Felix is a very worldly guy. But what Felix was best known for, and still is, is deal making—in Wall Street circles Felix was regarded as a deal maker's deal maker. And in the 1990s AT&T was doing a lot of that. Over the course of many deals—Felix helped us out on the $47 billion AT&T wireless deal, for instance—we got to be pretty good friends and stayed in touch. Steve and I, not so much. No good reason for that, we both just got busy with life, I guess. But I liked Steve just fine, always did.

When I got to the office, I called Steve back. His secretary put me right through. "So what's up?" I said, or something like that—I am recounting these conversations from memory, so the wording might not be exact. I hadn't talked to Steve in a couple of years and had no idea what to expect.

First thing Steve did was ask if I remembered him. Steve is one of those super-smart New York banking types. Polished, well spoken. Interesting background—he's a former reporter for the *New York Times*. So, yes, I remembered him. Then he started asking me what I'd been up to. *Not a lot* was the honest answer. I'd been retired from AT&T for about two years and was still trying to get used to not having to put on a suit and tie every day, which I'd done every day of my working life, pretty much, for forty-four years. I wasn't having much luck, but I was trying. I was also spending more time out at my ranch—I have a place about an hour outside San Antonio. I like to go there whenever I can with Lucille, my eleven-year-old chocolate Labrador. My wife, Linda, isn't particularly fond of the ranch, and I can certainly understand why she feels that way because it's basically in the middle of nowhere. But Lucille and I like it just fine. Anyway, I wasn't doing a whole lot right then, so that's what I told Steve.

After a few minutes, Steve said something like—and again I am paraphrasing—"So you know, Ed, I'm newly appointed as Car Czar to deal with the coming bankruptcy of GM and Chrysler."

I was not unfamiliar with Steve's Car Czar duties. I am a

longtime news junkie—you sort of get to be that way when you run a big publicly traded company like AT&T. A bad news story can upset investors and shave a billion dollars off your market cap pretty quick, so I always tried to stay on top of the headlines when I was running AT&T. And old habits are hard to break. I still watch the news most mornings when I'm having my coffee—except when it's duck season; then Lucille and I are usually out hunting. Right around this time you couldn't turn on the TV or pick up a newspaper without seeing some story about GM. Nobody had anything much good to say, because GM was basically flat broke. I knew from reading and watching the news that Steve was head of the auto task force—the formal name was the Presidential Task Force on the Auto Industry— that had been set up by the Obama administration to deal with the auto crisis. Since Steve was leading the group, a lot of media types had taken to calling him the Car Czar. Steve's number two was Ron Bloom, a former Lazard banker and restructuring specialist who'd just spent twelve years working with the steel- workers' union. Harry Wilson, another restructuring specialist and former Goldman Sachs banker, was also on the team; it had a dozen or so members in all. The Auto Team—or "Team Auto," as Steve liked to say—reported to Tim Geithner, the US Treasury secretary, and Larry Summers, chief economic adviser for the White House. President Barack Obama, who'd only been in office about two months at that point, had ultimate authority on everything.

The auto bailout had actually gotten started during the Bush administration, which stepped in with emergency funding right before President George W. Bush left office: around $13 billion for General Motors and $4 billion for Chrysler. (Ford ultimately said "no thanks" to a government handout.) Funding was pro- vided by the Troubled Asset Relief Program, known as TARP, which had been set up in the fall of 2008 to help deal with the mortgage crisis. A triggering event for creating the program was the fast dissolve of Lehman Brothers. Practically overnight, America's fourth-largest investment bank went out—it filed for bankruptcy in September 2008. Instantly twenty-six thousand people lost their jobs. Lehman turned out to be the canary in the coal mine. Before long, driven in part by the mortgage crisis, US banks and financial institutions were collapsing like lawn chairs. TARP authorized the Treasury Department to purchase up to $700 billion in troubled or "toxic" assets—meaning assets that nobody else wanted, at any price.

TARP funding was 100 percent taxpayer money, of course, so in theory at least all that money had to be paid back. Only, a lot of people thought that would never happen, especially in GM's case. One reason people thought that had to do with conventional wisdom, which had long held that people would not buy cars from a bankrupt car company. So even if GM managed to survive the bankruptcy process—and that was not a given—the aftershocks would surely kill the company anyway, or so the thinking went. The main problem with this theory? No major US carmaker had ever gone bankrupt, so nobody really knew how car buyers would react. They were all basically just guessing.

Anyway, I was sitting in my office, on the phone, listening to Steve rattle off all this stuff about his Car Czar duties and the sorry state of the auto industry when he said, almost casually, that he would like for me to think about becoming the chairman of General Motors. At first I thought I must've had cotton in my ears or something, because GM already had a chairman and CEO—Rick Wagoner. Surely I'd just misheard him. So I waited two beats and said to Steve: "Say that again?"

And damn if he didn't say it again.

"I'd like for you to think about becoming the chairman of General Motors," Steve told me. "We need somebody who has experience with big companies, experience with unions, a proven track record, and no association with the car industry." In other words, he said, getting straight down to business, "We'd like for you to become the next chairman of General Motors, Ed." As Steve explained it, Wagoner was about to step down because the White House felt a "new direction" was needed at GM, and the Auto Team agreed.

I didn't ask many questions about Wagoner, and to be honest I didn't have to. GM's financial performance pretty much said it all: GM shares lost more than 90 percent of their value on Wagoner's watch. GM also lost $82 billion and ran out of cash, and would have flatlined for good if the White House had not stepped in with emergency funding. Now GM was burning through that cash, which was all taxpayer money, at an alarming rate. I felt bad for Wagoner—no CEO ever wants to leave under a dark cloud like that. But I felt even worse for employees and shareholders, who were 100 percent dependent on management to keep the ship upright. GM's numbers staggered me. I simply did not understand how any management team could allow that to happen.

But the immediate question on the table—Would I consider becoming GM's chairman?—required no thought at all: *No, I would not.*

For one very simple reason: I knew nothing about cars. Zero. How could I even consider taking the reins of a company whose business I knew nothing about? GM was all cars, all the time—that was its one and only product. I knew telecom, not cars. How was that going to work? The short answer: It wasn't. Plus, I was retired. I'd put in my forty-four years and now I was on to the next chapter of my life. So that's basically what I told Steve: "I don't know anything about automobiles, I'm retired; the answer is no." Or words to that effect, but you get the idea. It occurred to me later, after we'd hung up, that I hadn't bothered to ask Steve a single question—I basically just turned him down flat. I figured that was pretty much the end of that.

But Steve called me back again the next day.

"You been thinking about our conversation?" he asked.

In truth, I had been thinking about it—and I still thought

the idea was utterly ridiculous. Because, as I said, and as I told Steve, I knew nothing about cars. Steve always was a good salesman—a lot of bankers are. So like any good salesman he just sort of breezed right past the "Not interested" part and started talking. Pretty soon, he was spinning all sorts of reasons why he thought I'd be perfect for GM: I have experience running big companies, I'm good with unions, I have deep management experience and experience with operating in a global market; the list went on.

The thing I was most concerned about—no car experience—Steve just brushed aside. Said I'd be bringing a "fresh perspective" to General Motors, which, according to Steve, had been stuck in a management rut forever. He also pointed out that it was a bunch of "car experts" who'd gotten GM in this mess in the first place, and I guess I really couldn't disagree with him there. I told Steve I'd think about it some more.

And that night I did think about it some more. But mostly what I thought was: *No way am I doing this.* In the back of my mind, I also thought Steve couldn't possibly be serious. I must've been seen as a shot in the dark, because surely there were better candidates than me out there, right? I didn't tell Steve any of this, just in case he was serious.

Steve called again the next day. Three days; three calls. This time he hit me in my soft spot: *patriotic duty.* "America needs you," Steve told me. "This is a great company, with great tradition and great history, but it's in real trouble financially. GM is probably going to go bankrupt, because its cash won't sustain the business. I'd really like for you to think about this, Ed." He got my attention with that.

"So this is public service, huh?"

I could tell that Steve could tell that he was getting to me—and he was.

"A total service for country," Steve said. "America needs you, Ed. Please think about this."

Steve was calling in from Washington, where he was holding round-the-clock meetings with GM executives. Things were about to come to a head. To get GM turned around, the Auto Team believed the company needed a steady hand at the top. I didn't disagree; my only question was whether I could credibly step into the chairman's role. We talked some more; Steve's patriotic pitch hit a nerve, no question. But this was a big, big decision, and I didn't want to make it in a moment when I was feeling rushed or emotional. I was heading out of the country for a few days—to Singapore, for an Exxon board meeting. I told Steve I'd think it over and call him when I got back.

Two days later—on Sunday, March 29—I took off for Singapore with my wife, Linda. That same day, Wagoner announced his intention to step down as chairman and CEO. In a prepared statement, Wagoner was brief and to the point: "On Friday I was in Washington for a meeting with Administration officials. In the course of that meeting, they requested that I 'step aside' as CEO of GM, and so I have."

Frederick "Fritz" Henderson, GM's president and chief operating officer, was immediately elevated to CEO. A long-standing GM board member, Kent Kresa, the former chairman and CEO of Northrop Grumman, was named interim chairman. The news swamped headlines around the world. A lot of people were surprised—many in America were outraged—that the Obama administration would involve itself so closely in the management of a big, publicly traded company like that. The perception that the government was now running GM got solidified when the Auto Team announced, later that same day, that most of GM's board would be replaced in the coming months. I was halfway around the world in Singapore but glued to the news. The headlines were all about GM, and all of them were bad.

I spent the next few days chewing on my conversation with Steve. The simple reality that I didn't know anything about cars still worried me. I mean, c'mon, a GM chairman with *no* car experience? Wagoner had three decades under his belt; Henderson was a twenty-five-year veteran. Almost every senior officer had deep industry knowledge and experience. Same for lower-level managers—the place was packed with car experts and car nuts, top-to-bottom. But Steve had a good point: "Car experts" had damn near killed that company. Maybe a "fresh perspective" would help. I figured it couldn't hurt.

The headlines were brutal. A lot of people were calling for the Obama administration to let GM go bankrupt and never come back—to just let it die. That's always a possibility in any bankruptcy situation. In bankruptcy, companies may liquidate, in which case they go away for good. Or if the firm is worth saving and all the interested parties can work out a deal—unions, bondholders, suppliers, those sorts—the company "reorganizes" into a new and hopefully better version of itself, then gives it another go.

People were also upset that General Motors might be in line for more TARP money, and I could certainly understand why, at least on one level. I mean, a 95 percent drop in the share price doesn't exactly give you confidence in the ability of a company to pull it out, you know? But I also thought $50 billion—which is how much GM ultimately got—was a drop in the bucket compared with the $182 billion the government gave AIG. And I still don't know exactly what AIG does, do you? It's a big insurance company, I know, but they don't produce any goods or services that I'm aware of.

GM, in sharp contrast, is a real company with real products. And it supports real jobs right here in America. So if you look at it in that context—and I do—spending $50 billion to save GM just wasn't that much. Take a shot and try to save GM, or stand down and know for sure that the US auto industry is going away for good, along with all those jobs? In my mind, it wasn't even a toss-up.

Steve's invitation was highly confidential, so I didn't discuss it with anybody. Except my wife, Linda—we've been married forty-seven years, she was my college sweetheart. Linda's been very supportive throughout my career. When I was coming up the line at AT&T we moved nineteen times—I kept getting promoted, so we kept having to move our family. Linda oversaw all that while also taking care of our two baby girls—they're both grown and married now. Linda never complained, even when we had to move to New Jersey. When I first told her about GM, she sort of smiled and said the same thing she's been telling me for more than forty years now: "I think you'd do a really good job. If you want to do this, go for it."

By the time Linda and I boarded the airplane in Singapore to fly back to Texas, my mind was pretty made up: I'd give it a try. The worst thing that could happen, I figured, was that I might not be successful. On the other hand, I just might. You never know until you try: That's how I've always lived my life, no reason to stop now.

Service to country. That's what I thought about the most. I've been very fortunate in my life. Damn lucky, in fact. So if my country wants my help, and is asking for my help, then by God I'm going to give my help to the best of my ability. I didn't know cars, true. But I did know that America didn't need another punch in the stomach. Not with record unemployment and the stock market jumping around like a Ping-Pong ball—up two hundred points one day, down four hundred the next, back up the day after that—it never seemed to stop. All that instability was contributing to a general sense of malaise in America, and the financial volatility was driving the common person out of the market. It's a scary thing when you can lose everything in a day, or make everything in a day. I know it was scaring me. If GM went through a painful bankruptcy restructuring, only to fail again due to weak or bad leadership, well, I didn't even want to think about that. If there was even an outside chance that I could help—and I was turning over some ideas in my head, forty-four years in business will do that to you—then why not give it a shot?

I was no spring chicken—sixty-seven. Not so old, but not so young, either. If the Auto Team really wanted me to take this on, it would have to be with the understanding that I would only stay long enough to get things fixed. Then I was heading back home. Life's short, you know, and it gets shorter the older you get.

I called Steve when I got back from Singapore and told him I'd do it. With one condition: I needed to be able to call my shots as I saw fit. No second-guessing. And no meddling. If I was going to sign on as GM's chairman with the express goal of fixing management—and that's what I was being asked to do—then I'd do my best to deliver. But I'd do it my way. I would listen to anything that anybody had to say. But ultimately, I'd make my own calls.

Companies aren't democracies; you can't run management by consensus. Somebody has to be in charge. And that person has to be willing and able to make hard decisions at times. It's a way of sending a message to the entire management team: *We have a vision, we have a plan, and we are executing on the plan. If you are not on board with the plan, for any reason, then you will be leaving. If you fall short for too long, then you, too, will be leaving.* And so on. Not quite "my way or the highway"—but close enough.

On the plus side, everybody knows what is expected of them, and what the potential penalties are for not meeting objectives. Sounds a little hard, I know, but clarity is key when it comes to managing a publicly traded company. And clarity had been missing at GM for far too long, which was one reason the place was such a discombobulated mess. That sort of dysfunction trickles down to employees—bad for morale, bad for production, bad for everything. On the flip side, if you can get management focused and hitting on all cylinders, it has a way of trickling down, too.

So that was my bottom line: I'll do this, but my way. Steve said okay, and that was pretty much that.

Shortly thereafter I had a few discussions with GM's interim chairman, Kent Kresa, about the timing of my formal appointment as GM's chairman. Kresa offered to spend a year or so in the job, to let me get up to speed. I had no interest in doing that—zero. Also did not have the time—my plan was to get in and out as soon as possible. I wasn't trying to build my résumé; I was just trying to get GM fixed. Kent said he understood, so we worked it out: I'd be chairman on Day One.

GM filed for Chapter 11 bankruptcy court protection on June 1, 2009. Eight days later, on June 9, my appointment was announced by the White House. I was the first non-GM person to serve as chairman in the hundred-year history of the company. Kent graciously agreed to stay on the board until his term expired at the end of the year.

As I expected, I immediately got a lot of criticism for not having any car experience. But of course it was absolutely true. No use trying to deny it. People poked a lot of fun at me over this, which didn't make me feel too good inside, I will admit. But it was what it was.

My game plan, to the extent that I had one, was pretty straightforward: Get in, immerse myself in management, assess the problem, fix the problem, then call it a day and get myself back to Texas. I wasn't looking to string this out. Like I said, I had a wife, family, four grandkids, and a really great dog waiting for me back home. But I also didn't think it was going to take that long, because GM's biggest problem—maybe its *only* problem—was management. And while I didn't know much about cars, I did know a little something about that.

Three days; three calls. That's all it took. Now I was heading to Detroit to become the chairman of General Motors. Me, a guy from Ennis, Texas, who didn't know a thing about cars. As I said at the beginning of this chapter, life—it can change on you just like that.

CHAPTER 3

"Government Motors"

General Motors emerged from bankruptcy in record time—just thirty-nine days from start to finish. Some people saw GM's fast rebirth as a victory, and in some ways I guess it was, because GM was still standing.

An even bigger victory, but one that people really didn't talk about, mostly because they were so focused on the miracle of GM's survival—and it was that—was the fact that the two-hundred-thousand-plus people who worked for GM still had jobs. All this was contingent on GM staying healthy, of course, and that was the armadillo in the room that nobody really wanted to talk about.

General Motors had a better balance sheet, sure. But it also had a tangle of new owners, a pervasive morale problem, and $50 billion in taxpayer money that had to be paid back. The car-buying public was still skeptical about whether GM would stick around, and employees, who were about as down and depressed as any workforce I'd ever seen, weren't far behind. That awful "Government Motors" name, a source of shame and embarrassment for many GM employees, was not helping. Meantime, the soft US economy was continuing to depress car sales, with no end in sight. So while the "new" GM was out of bankruptcy, it was not by any stretch out of danger.

Back in Detroit, GM's most senior managers weren't too worried. They'd all been through tough times before, so they were as confident as ever. That's what bothered me. The math was pretty simple: This was the same team that had driven GM into the wall, and they were still in the driver's seat, minus Rick Wagoner, the former chairman and CEO. But the rest of Wagoner's team, including his number two, who was now the CEO, was still pretty much intact. Nobody seemed too worried about that. But that's all I was thinking about.

How could the same management team that stood by while GM's stock price plunged more than 90 percent, stood by while the company racked up losses of $82 billion, stood by while the cash reserves got drained down to nothing, suddenly sprout wisdom and steer that company back to profitability again? The short answer: They couldn't. Because if that management team could have done that, I have to believe they would have done that at some point between $60 a share—which is what GM was trading for when Wagoner took over—and less than $3 a share. That's like asking a person who's never played the piano before to sit down and play you a little something from Beethoven. It just ain't happening.

Post-bankruptcy, GM's life was more complicated than ever. With most lenders, you can pay off the balance whenever you feel like it. Not in this case. Why: Only a small portion of the $50 billion in emergency funding, around $6.7 billion, was given to GM in the form of a loan, which accrued interest, just like any bank loan. We could pay back that part at our discretion. But the rest of the money, around $43 billion, got converted into a 61 percent ownership stake in GM, and only the government could decide when, and at what pace, those 912 million shares got sold. The net effect of all this: GM was no longer in control of its financial future—the US government was.

TARP money had other conditions. Example: The salaries

of top GM executives were now capped at around $500,000 a year. That sounds like a lot, and in absolute terms it is, especially when you consider that the median salary in this country is around $50,000 or so. But it's not so much when you consider that Ford and other carmakers that didn't have TARP money were paying double and triple that amount, in some cases, or even more. The net effect: GM couldn't compete for top outside talent, because it just couldn't pay. But on the plus side the talent pool at General Motors was deep and wide, and it was crammed with some of the brightest and most dedicated people you'll ever meet. So even if the current batch of top executives at GM wasn't right for the times, I figured there were plenty of rough diamonds scattered around the organization. It was just a matter of finding them.

GM, at that point, hadn't posted a profit in five years—it technically recorded a profit three years earlier, in 2006, after adjusting for special items. But the real show-and-tell moment is the "unadjusted" profit, and GM hadn't had one of those since 2004. If the company stumbled out of the gate, or showed signs of "business as usual," it could wind up digging a brand-new hole for itself—this was one of my biggest worries. The global media was analyzing every twitch GM made; car buyers and other carmakers were also tracking closely. So was Wall Street, the White House, and lots of other constituencies. Everybody wanted to know the same thing: Can the new GM make it? To start the long process of building confidence and restoring its tarnished name, management needed to craft a strong message and plan, one that was based on the reality of GM's new size and financial situation—not past glory days. Then they had to execute flawlessly. And they needed to do it *now*, not five quarters from now, or five years from now.

GM emerged from bankruptcy on July 10, 2009, a full three weeks ahead of expectations. I was in regular contact with board members, but had deliberately kept a low profile around GM's Detroit headquarters. I figured that was only proper. Plus, there really wasn't much I could do until GM got clear of Chapter 11. If GM had liquidated, that would have been it—all of the company's assets would have been sold off. In which case there would have been nothing for me to do except lament the passing of one of America's truly great companies.

The new GM was a lot smaller. Bankruptcy got rid of Hummer, Pontiac, and a couple of other brands, leaving it with just four nameplates: Chevrolet, Cadillac, Buick, and GMC. (Buick almost got shut down, but strong sales in China argued for keeping it.) The reorganization plan, which had been worked out among all the parties that GM owed money to, called for the US manufacturing workforce to shrink by more than a third. About 40 percent of GM's dealers also got handed their walking papers. Debt got slashed by 70 percent. And the executive ranks got thinned, from 1,300 to 1,100. A lot of other things got trimmed back, shut down, and reworked, and when it was all done the result was a slimmed-down company that was known, officially, as the "new" GM.

The new GM had a complicated ownership structure: 60.8 percent controlled by the US Treasury, 17.5 percent owned by a retiree trust fund affiliated with the United Auto Workers (UAW), and 11.7 percent owned by the governments of Canada and Ontario. About 10 percent was owned by Motors Liquidation Co.—that was the post-bankruptcy name of old GM, which still existed on paper. The old GM, which had always been traded on the New York Stock Exchange, was moved to the OTC after its bankruptcy filing; by then even those shares were no longer trading. Value at the time of suspension: around seventy-five cents a share. The new GM was not publicly traded at that point; its only shareholders were the big stakeholders I just listed, the biggest being the United States of America, which was really code for US taxpayers. The "Government Motors" name was a constant reminder of GM's compromised financial condition and history. Not that anybody at GM needed reminding.

With GM finally out of bankruptcy, I figured it was time to get myself on out to Detroit and get to work.

So, in mid-July, I headed out. On the flight to Detroit I had some mixed emotions, I will admit. On one hand, I felt excited to be going to GM, and very much hoped I could be helpful. But it was also a little scary. I didn't know a soul at the company. Didn't know cars. And hadn't stepped foot in Detroit in years. The last time I'd been there was to meet with Rick Wagoner, GM's then-CEO, in the dead of winter. GM owned a big stake in DirecTV, the satellite TV operator, and we at SBC Communications (formerly Southwestern Bell, later called AT&T) were interested in buying that interest. I was chairman and CEO, so I went along with my top deal guy, Jim Kahan, and our general counsel, Jim Ellis, to help pitch Wagoner on the idea. Wagoner was cordial. But he also seemed to think we couldn't afford that stake, which would have cost us a few billion or so. I assured him that financing was not an issue; that SBC had plenty of money and good credit. Wagoner and his chief financial officer—he was in the room, too—seemed unconvinced, like we were some small Texas company that couldn't play in GM's league. Or at least that's how it felt to me. I remember looking out the window in Wagoner's office—he had a corner office on the thirty-ninth floor that had a clear view of the Detroit River, which was frozen solid—and thinking to myself: *This meeting is going nowhere.* And it didn't.

Now Wagoner was gone and I was GM's chairman. The irony of all that was not lost on me as I made my way back to Detroit, and to that same building and corner office where that conversation had taken place. By then I'd already called on Wagoner to let him know I was going to GM. I put in that call right after the White House announced my appointment. I figured he already knew, but I also thought it was the respectful thing to do. Wagoner was cordial, but didn't have much to say, which I could certainly understand. So once again it was a very short conversation.

I touched down in Detroit and was met by a GM driver. We immediately headed downtown to the Renaissance Center, a mixed retail-and-office-space complex where GM's world headquarters is located. The building, nicknamed the RenCen, is impressively large: five and a half million square feet with seven towers, dozens of stores, four movie theaters, two foreign consulates, and a thirteen-hundred-room hotel that rises seventy-three stories. GM has almost four thousand people there; another four thousand or so work for other businesses. The place is a beehive of activity; people are always running around going somewhere. GM's offices are housed in a series of glass towers that have color-coded reception areas, connected by circular walkways and banks of escalators. The first time I went there, for that meeting with Wagoner, I remember thinking that the RenCen was the perfect metaphor for General Motors: overblown, overdone, complicated to the max. Walking into the RenCen again that morning, I had that same feeling all over again.

I made my way up to the thirty-ninth floor for my first meeting of the day, with GM's new CEO, Fritz Henderson. I was the "outside" chairman of GM—that's just a fancy way of saying that I was not an employee—so theoretically I had no day-to-day responsibilities. I say "theoretically" because my intention, all along, was just the opposite—to be a very involved chairman. Most outside chairmen preside over board meetings, and that's pretty much it. But I had not accepted the job to sit on the sidelines—I'd accepted with the understanding, and promise, that I'd do my best to help GM get turned around. And that's exactly what I intended to do.

Fritz was hunched over his desk working when I arrived. He welcomed me warmly and said he'd be most willing to help me find out anything I needed to know. I had never met Fritz, but I'd heard a lot of good things about him. People described him, universally, as a smart guy and very hard worker. He was also a devoted company man—he'd worked at GM his entire career, twenty-five years. Like other senior managers, Fritz's salary had been cut a couple of times—part of GM's cost-cutting efforts, this stuff had been going on for years. I respected his sense of duty and commitment. Fritz was relatively young, just fifty. Young to me, at least. When you're sixty-seven, everybody looks young to you.

I started out the conversation by asking Fritz how things were going—he said fine but busy. We also talked about his background: Fritz was the son of another GM company man, and he'd been born and raised in the Detroit area. So he had cars in his blood, you might say. Fritz had been working overseas in GM's global operations—did a good job, too, from what I understand—when Wagoner called him back to Detroit to help clean up GM's financial mess. Fritz was an encyclopedia of facts and figures. He also knew the global car business cold—he could quote numbers backward and forward, which was impressive.

But the CEO's job is about a lot more than numbers. You have to be able to lead and inspire people. You also have to be willing and able to make hard calls, even if it means moving out an executive who also happens to be your friend. (And if you work shoulder-to-shoulder with people long enough, they're all friends.) In addition—and this is really important—you have to be able to recognize, from somewhere within, when things aren't hanging together just right. All this tracks back to this thing we call "management," and that is squarely in the court of the CEO—to make sure his or her management team is delivering.

I had strong views as to what Fritz needed to do: To get GM back on track, and employees out of their funk and reengaged, he was going to have to communicate a clear and compelling vision to the entire company that people could believe in, and rally around. Hard financial targets needed to be established, and met. GM's days of just moving the pieces around the chessboard and making excuses when things didn't work out were over—the bankruptcy saw to that. I was on board as chairman and willing to help in any way he wanted, but it was up to Fritz, as CEO, to make sure his team delivered. Did Fritz have the management skills to pull that off? Listening to him talk that morning, reeling off all those facts and figures, I could only wonder to myself.

Fundamental to me is how a business is organized, so I asked for a copy of GM's organizational chart. Also known as "org" charts, these documents diagram how a business is laid out, who reports to whom, the interrelationships of different business units, that sort of thing. Big companies like AT&T and GM have multiple business units. Org charts help you keep track of all that. At AT&T, I always had org charts on hand, and I referred to them frequently when talking with direct reports, who also had copies—just to make sure we were all on the same page, literally and figuratively speaking.

But Fritz didn't have an org chart. He said GM had done away with them—to help save money, no doubt. Fritz said he was tracking everything in his head.

That was the first red flag.

Red Flag Number Two: Fritz had fifteen or twenty senior executives reporting to him directly. That's a *huge* number of direct reports. CEOs typically speak with their direct reports daily—it's one of the main ways you stay plugged in to what's going on in your business. I was mystified as to how Fritz found the time to talk with fifteen or twenty people daily and still deal with all the other things that were on his plate. GM, as I mentioned, had all that taxpayer money that had to be paid back, a crushing morale problem, a tarnished image, lots of other problems rattling around—and Fritz was the point person for all of it. How could he juggle all those balls and keep everything straight?

Since there was no org chart, I asked Vivian Costello, Fritz's assistant, to print out pictures of all the senior managers. I figured Fritz could just talk me through the details. I wanted to know about GM's business structure, and to get a firm understanding of the specific jobs and responsibilities of the senior management team: who was responsible for what, exactly, and how the various divisions stacked up from a reporting and organizational standpoint. So Vivian got me those photos, and Fritz and I started going through them.

And it was then that I got my first inkling of why we were in trouble. Fritz could not explain, in a clear, concise fashion, what these people did. Don't get me wrong, he had answers for all of it. And I have no doubt that Fritz knew, instinctively, exactly what these people were doing in their day-to-day business lives. But the descriptions he gave me were so general and so vague as to be completely meaningless. I'd say, "What does this person do?" And Fritz would respond, immediately, with a long explanation that didn't make any sense to me. And I was really leaning in and listening when he was talking, because I was *really* trying to understand the path he was taking me down. But the path, as best I could tell, went nowhere; it basically dead-ended. And that's how it went for the entire stack of pictures. By the time we got down to the last picture, I still had no idea how GM was structured or what his senior managers did, exactly.

Focus, it seemed to me, was the issue. I also thought the large number of direct reports—fifteen or twenty—could not be helping. I asked Fritz how he could handle all that. "I can take on more," he told me. There was not much I could say to that. Fritz was the CEO, and this was how he was running the company. So I said okay, and we moved on to other things.

That's not to say I was done digging around. I had two full

days of meetings scheduled in Detroit with all the top people—Fritz was just my first stop. So I figured I'd be getting some answers soon enough.

Next up was Bob Lutz, GM's vice chairman. Over the course of his long and storied career—Bob was seventy-seven when I met him—he'd held senior positions at the Big Three in Detroit, plus BMW. Bob, a former marine fighter pilot, was never a designer himself. But his passion for all things auto-related ran deep. Among his many accomplishments: bringing the Dodge Viper, one of the first V-10 cars in the world, to market. Built as a concept car, the original Viper had no door handles, roof, or roll-down windows. But it had major attitude and oozed cool. The Viper caused such a ruckus at its 1989 debut that it was rushed into production. Bob, then with Chrysler, oversaw the entire project. (Door handles, workable windows, and a removable roof were added to the commercial version.) The Viper was one of Bob's more memorable achievements, but he had many breakout moments over the years.

Lutz was firmly in residence at GM when I arrived. He'd retired several times over the years, but he'd been brought back by Wagoner as vice chairman to oversee the "creative elements" of products and customer relationships. Whatever that meant—I had no idea. So I asked Bob to fill me in. His description was pretty general, but the longer we talked the more I got the idea that Bob's main job at GM was to weigh in with advice and opinions about anything he wanted, anytime he felt like it. This arrangement, I soon discovered, also extended to GM board meetings. Bob regularly sat in on board meetings, even though he was not actually a board member himself. This was a highly unusual arrangement, so I asked Fritz why he allowed that. He said Bob often had helpful comments to make. Plus, Fritz said, Bob might not take it so well if he was uninvited. I did not know what to say to that.

That Bob got special treatment, in one respect, was not so

surprising. The car industry is full of colorful characters—that's just part of the glamour and mystique of the business. And these types are warmly embraced, and in some cases revered, by Detroit. Consider car designer Carroll Shelby, who recently passed away; he was 89. A former race car driver and test pilot, this guy is a certified legend in the car world. Shelby's GT350 Mustangs, created for Ford, defined the pony muscle car in the 1960s. (The Cobra 427, another Shelby creation and the inspiration for the Viper, continued the tradition.) The 1965 originals are coveted by collectors—only 522 were made—and expensive when you find them. Shelby's signature move is taking hunks of metal and turning them into street-legal dragsters. It was Shelby who helped turn the Viper into a slingshot with four wheels that could rocket from zero to sixty in 4.6 seconds. Top speed: 180-plus miles an hour. (Lamborghini, then owned by Chrysler, supplied the aluminum block truck engine that allowed the Viper to fry rubber in spectacular fashion.) Tom Gale, the design chief at Chrysler who sculpted the Viper's swoopy body design, is another Hall of Famer. He also gave life to the "cab forward" looks of the Ram truck and Plymouth Prowler.

In an earlier era, Harley Earl, the first vice president of design at General Motors, made a name for himself by pushing all sorts of styling boundaries. Among his many milestones: wraparound windshields, two-tone paint, sweeping tail fins, and the Corvette, which debuted in 1953 and has been going strong ever since. Earl was a flamboyant figure, and cultivated that image. His daily ride was the "Buick Y-Job," a 1938 concept convertible that featured fender extensions, disappearing headlights, flush door handles, electric windows, and other designer details that would not make their way into commercial production for many years. Earl's contemporary, Virgil Exner, senior designer at Studebaker and, later, Chrysler, also helped define that golden era of cars.

Automotive history is full of big personalities like that, and Bob Lutz, in the minds of many, was right up there. Media types loved Bob's colorful, off-the-cuff comments, and his habit of sometimes commuting to work in his own helicopter didn't hurt his cool car-guy image. Which was all well and fine except I didn't have a whole lot of use for colorful characters right then because we had a car company that needed fixing. How could Bob help? He knew just about everything there was to know about cars—and I figured there was value to that in a place like GM. But putting him in a power position over marketing, communications, and vehicle design, to me, was not the answer. Morale was lower than sludge, and constant reminders of past failures and past glory days—Bob was well versed in both— weren't helpful. So I pretty much knew, about five minutes into this conversation, that some changes were probably in order. As for Bob's habit of sitting in on GM board meetings, that was about to stop. Outsiders, including senior executives, are sometimes invited to give presentations during board meetings. But the meetings themselves are limited to board members only. That's no knock on Bob. That's just corporate protocol.

After Bob, I had a succession of meetings with the members of the senior management team. One by one, they came to see me, as I'd requested. And one by one we sat down and talked— about their jobs and responsibilities, about GM's problems, as they saw them, about anything they wanted to talk about, really. I began every conversation by posing a few simple, direct questions. Among them: *What do you do? Who do you work for?* and *What do you think went wrong at GM?* We talked about a lot more than that, of course, but those were my baseline questions, and conversations sort of meandered off in different directions from there.

Mostly, though, I just listened. These are some of the things I learned:

1. The place was far too complicated. Put a gold star by this observation, because this was my biggest takeaway by far. Noth-

ing at GM was simple or straightforward, and the complexity affected everything. Take basic job descriptions. When I asked people to tell me what they did, answers tended to be rambling and/or incredibly general, with no specificity or accountability. This really concerned me.

2. People seemed unclear, in many cases, as to how their particular business units interrelated to the rest of the team, and to GM broadly. Again, this suggested a lack of understanding about the basic organization of the global business. Since there was no org chart to refer to, people were basically going on their own understanding of GM's structure—and those understandings were not always in sync.

3. Managers, in most cases, reported to several bosses—or to nobody if they didn't feel like it, it seemed to me. So nobody was really accountable or responsible if things went wrong. On the flip side, managers were not clearly empowered to make decisions, making it difficult for them to take real ownership of problems, or solutions.

4. A few managers seemed like really bad fits for their jobs and needed to be repotted.

5. Some had clearly been in the saddle for way too long and needed a change of scenery.

6. Some needed to be moved out of GM entirely. People who hate their jobs, or constantly grouse about their jobs to other people, or threaten to leave if they are not given raises, which is what one individual at GM actually did, are not people you want in leadership positions. At least I don't. The message of senior managers was clear: GM's collapse was not our fault, not a thing we could have done about it. I probably don't need

to tell you what I thought about that, but I will anyway: Management is 100 percent responsible for what happens to a business. One hundred percent.

7. To remind you, GM's collapse was not an overnight occurrence. This had been building for decades. Yet management did not make a correction to alter the path going forward—or if they did it wasn't dramatic enough, because the path wasn't altered. Instead, they just kept going along the same curve, and they didn't bend that curve.

8. There was no identification of what we had to do going forward to get GM back on track, and there was little interest in even discussing this. That all tracked, I guess, because as far as they were concerned nothing at GM was broken, so what's to fix?

All of these meetings I have described, with the exception of the one with Fritz, took place in a big conference room that I was using as my makeshift office. In hindsight, it now seems a little odd that nobody ever offered to let me use a regular office. But I also think it was indicative of how I was generally viewed: as somebody who'd be in and out of Detroit in a flash, with no intention of doing any serious work while I was there. As I have explained, most times non-executive chairmen are not very involved in the companies they work with—those are often arm's-length relationships. So the fact that I was showing up and getting so involved, on its face, was most unusual. I suspect some of these senior managers thought I'd back off after a short while. But I knew walking in the door that I was just getting started.

I fully appreciated that I was an unknown quantity around the RenCen. I was from Texas, so I didn't sound like anybody from around there. I wasn't from the car world, so I didn't speak that language, either. And the government had just appointed me as chairman, so I had the double whammy of being a Washington appointee on top of all that. My takeaway was that senior management was going to tolerate me for the time that I was there, but otherwise they'd keep doing what they were doing, just like they'd always done. Everybody was really nice, like I said. But that vibe—*let's humor him until he goes back home*—was there, you could just tell. Or at least that's how it felt to me.

And I could certainly understand why they felt that way because, when you got right down to it, all that stuff was true. So I didn't get too upset. Except I did think to myself: *It's a mistake. You guys don't know what's going to happen here.* I was giving a lot of hard thought to every member of that GM management team, as well as the organizational structure of the company and how all those parts fit together, or didn't fit together. I didn't have a fix-it plan, at least not right then. But this much I did know: I wasn't going to pull out of there until GM was back on track and profitable again.

CHAPTER 4

Keep It Simple

I've been quoted as saying that a person is born with two ears and one mouth and should use them in that proportion. I'm not sure I ever said that, exactly that way. But I do believe that's true—people would be a lot better off, in general, if they talked less and listened more.

I'm not a big talker, in general. Except when I'm trying to work my way through a problem or situation—I did a lot of that at General Motors. Then I am prone to ask a lot of questions, some quite straightforward. I have my reasons: One, I'm a pretty direct person by nature, so I tend to get right to the point in a business conversation. Two, I think you can actually learn more that way. Direct questions almost force people to distill things down to a few sentences. To do that, they actually have to have a pretty good understanding of the subject they're talking about. Those who don't will often try to cover up that fact by giving long, rambling answers that go nowhere. Or they try to snowball you with all sorts of facts and figures that don't add up in your head. Some people are just less than stellar communicators, of course. So you have to use common sense when making these sorts of assessments. I don't think I'm such a good communicator myself, to be honest. But I am a pretty good listener.

Back at AT&T—I remember this well—I had a senior manager draw a complete blank one time when I asked him where the country of Ecuador is located. A curious question, you might say—also quite simple, at least on its face. But here was the situation: We were in a big strategy session, about a hundred people in the room, and this person—he was in international development—had all these world maps tacked up, color-coded flags stuck all over them showing where he thought we should be investing. Ecuador was one of his target markets.

For some reason—I don't know why, gut instinct, I guess—I just got the feeling that this guy didn't know what he was talking about. So I put my hand up and asked that question: "Where is Ecuador?" He didn't know—had no idea, in fact. He tried to make a joke out of it, and some people had a big laugh. But I sort of thought it was amazing that he didn't know where it was, because he wanted a substantial piece of business there. And the fact that he didn't know told me, instantly, that this person was not on top of his business, or properly engaged with the AT&T employees who supported the Latin American market, which, of course, includes Ecuador.

My larger point: *Basics do matter.* I didn't ask about Ecuador because I wanted to discuss world geography. I asked because I wanted to see if that person had command of the basics. And when you get right down to it, the basics, or fundamentals, are all that really matter in business: Revenues have to be higher than expenses; the people in your company—the employees, I mean—have to be feeling satisfied; and you have to take care of stockholders, who provide the capital that allows you to keep going, and growing. Management bears 100 percent responsibility for all this. It goes without saying that managers should be familiar with the basic facts of their business—like where Ecuador is located, if you happen to be looking to make a big investment there.

Keep it simple. That's one of my core philosophies, in business and in life. I've been preaching this for years—and I'm not the sort of guy who preaches about much. But I do believe in this idea strongly, based on many years of personal observation. If you don't keep it simple, you can get so tangled up in bureaucracy and weighed down by complexity that you'll get sidetracked and forget what you were trying to do in the first place. Process becomes the goal—not productivity.

Yet companies do that all the time. People gum up the machinery by adding layers of complexity—to management, operations, the communications function, organizational structure, internal programs, all sorts of things. Pretty soon you've got people running down all these rabbit trails, working on things that really aren't that important, while the things that *are* important, like your fundamentals, sit there and suffer. The net result: You lose focus, lose traction—you just lose, period. So always *keep it simple!*

There was nothing simple about General Motors. Everything had layers upon layers of complexity attached to it. Board meetings were representative of the problem. At AT&T our regularly scheduled board meetings lasted two or three hours, at most. At GM they could go on all day. That's a ridiculous amount of time, and I say that as a guy who's sat on a number of big corporate boards, including Exxon and Anheuser-Busch. Why'd GM do it that way? Because they could, I guess. Direct and to-the-point just wasn't part of GM's culture, so nobody ever questioned it. People who grew up in this culture viewed complexity as completely normal—they expected it, in fact. A *keep it simple* approach in that sort of environment—not so normal.

So I was only half surprised when top management was not clear in answering some very basic questions, like *What is your job? Who do you report to? How is General Motors organized?* and so on. These were simple questions on their face, yes, but they also went straight to the heart of GM's management and operational structure. Managers did their best to answer—this was a very nice group of people, also hardworking. And clearly knowledgeable about the car business. But this wasn't a popularity contest or a car trivia exercise. This was about getting GM back to profitability again. Management was the key to that, and Fritz and his team were flailing. There was no larger plan or strategy in play that I could detect, no sense of teamwork among top managers. It was like GM was a huge, rudderless ship.

The answers to my questions hinted at why: People were unable to talk about GM in a clear, concise fashion. Or to even describe their jobs and areas of responsibilities in a way that made sense. In some cases, answers just didn't add up. Other people were all over the map—it was almost like they were winging it. Most concerning to me, there was little agreement on the basics of the business—like how GM was organized, who reported to who, and the like. That confirmed what I'd suspected all along: Something was fundamentally broken at the top.

I didn't just talk to senior managers to get GM's temperature. I also talked to employees—the eyes and ears of every business. Employees are on the front lines every day, so they know, pretty much, how things are going. And if things aren't going so good, they can often tell you, with a high degree of accuracy, why that is. But you have to engage people and be willing to listen to what they have to say to find this stuff out.

When I was at AT&T, I used to talk to our people—our employees—all the time. I'd bump into people in the halls, elevators, the cafeteria when I was getting my lunch, in the garage when I was driving to the office in the morning, other places. I'd wander over and ask how they thought AT&T was doing and what we could be doing better; I'd ask about their jobs, their bosses, anything else that might be on their minds. Sometimes I'd call people up on the phone, or pop by in person, just to see what's up. Employees also called me. A lady called me one time to tell me about an insurance problem she was having. She couldn't get the medicine she needed because AT&T's health plan didn't cover it. I thought she had a good point, so I had a human resources person fix that—she got her medicine. Another time, a union guy called me up to let me know that AT&T was shutting down a local office in San Antonio, and planned to consolidate it with a bigger one in Dallas. He said the move was going to be quite a hardship. We talked about that and I decided he was right. We stopped that move.

I had those sorts of personal interactions constantly. And not just during office hours. One time I was driving somewhere with my older daughter, Jessica—she's a lawyer, smart as a whip—and I happened to see an AT&T telephone truck pulled over with a couple of guys standing around. So I wheeled over to see what was going on. Jessica thought it was pretty funny that I would do something like that, which was pretty funny to me, because I never gave it a second thought. I think it matters to people to have the chairman take the time to stop and talk with them, to let them know that they're important, they are contributing, and they're really part of this company—I know it did for me when I was coming along. And it still does something for me, because I always drive away from these sorts of exchanges feeling pretty good. Yes, I'm retired from AT&T now. But I still pull over sometimes when I see a telephone crew out working, just to see what's up.

I didn't know anybody at General Motors, because I was so new there, but I also figured there was one way to fix that: to start introducing myself. So that's what I did. I was still camped out in my conference room, so I'd start from there and just start walking. No destination in mind—I just walked around the Ren-Cen to see who I might bump into. I'd see somebody in the hall, or the elevator, or sitting in some office I happened to go by, and I'd hit the brakes and introduce myself.

I'd say something like, "Hi, my name's Ed Whitacre, and I

work at GM," then toss out a question: How's it going? How are you feeling about GM? Or something general like that to try to spark some conversation. Most times, that's all it took—people would start talking up a storm. Other times, people would get a little self-conscious, because maybe they had an idea about who I was, and that made them nervous. To help refocus things I'd ask about their job, or something to do with GM, and before long they'd get more comfortable and start talking.

I also spent a lot of time in the Food Court—that's a central dining area in the RenCen where a lot of employees go. I'd get my tray at lunchtime and stand in line with everybody else—I'm quite fond of Mexican, so I got that whenever I could—then I'd look for a table with people who looked like they might be from GM and ask if I could join them. Normally I wouldn't have horned in like that—I mean, people are trying to relax and have their lunch, and here I come along, you know? But I was on a mission, I guess you could say, so I pushed my way through and just did it. Sometimes I'd go sit at a table by myself, just to see if anybody would come over. Within a few minutes, somebody usually would. Most times, that would cause other people to come over, and before long I'd have a table full of people sitting with me, and pretty good conversation going about GM. I mostly listened.

People always seemed a little surprised that I'd be rambling around by myself, talking to people like that. I got the feeling that wasn't so typical for GM executives, especially at the more senior levels of the company. People didn't say that outright, but I could tell by the way they were looking at me—I could see it in their eyes: *Well, this is different.* Or something like that, you know? I never introduced myself as chairman. I would feel funny saying something like that to somebody, like maybe that made it sound like I thought I was better or more important. I don't feel that way, and I never think that. Even when I was at AT&T—and I was chairman and CEO there for seventeen years—I'd usually say that I worked for the company, and just leave it at that.

My "walkarounds" at General Motors turned out to be a good thing, because I wound up meeting a lot of people that way. I talked with security guards, secretaries, marketing types, engineers, new hires, midlevel managers, financial people, longtime GMers, lot of other types. I talked pretty regularly with the company drivers—one of them would usually pick me up at the airport when I flew into Detroit. (I usually drive myself whenever I go somewhere, except if I don't know my way around.) Most GM executives would get dropped off and head straight to the elevator to go up to their offices. I didn't do that. I'd see a couple of drivers huddled up talking, and I'd wander over. There was a certain edge to all this—people seemed to appreciate my interest, but I could also see in their eyes that they were sort of saying to themselves, *So what's up with this guy?* Can't say I blamed them, but that didn't stop me. Learned a lot from those drivers, I would add. Nice guys, well informed, too.

I also crossed paths with non-GM people. At the Food Court, I ate lunch one time with a bunch of consultants from Canada who happened to be in town for a big GM project. They never asked me what I did, so I never said. I spent the entire lunch, or most of it, anyway, just eating and listening to all of them talk. I also talked to people in the retail stores. One of my favorites was Jos. A. Bank, the clothing store for men. I bought a few shirts there and wound up meeting the manager, Tony—good guy. After that, I started swinging by on my walkarounds, just to see what's up. The one store I never visited was Verizon Wireless. No knock on Verizon, I'm just a dedicated AT&T guy, what can I say?

What did I learn from all these conversations? Plenty. I learned that employees were genuinely embarrassed by the GM bankruptcy; that it translated into an internal message for many—some felt this more deeply than others—that they, too, were failures. And that hurt people, made them feel bad and embarrassed, made them not want to face their friends and neighbors when they went home at night because they knew—everybody knew—that they were working for one of the biggest failures in America. People tried to put on a strong front, but I could see the hurt in their eyes, and hear it in their voices. And that was sad to see, especially because I knew GM's bankruptcy wasn't even their fault—it was management's fault. But the employees of GM didn't see it that way. All they knew was that the company they worked for, and in some cases had dedicated their lives to, had gone broke. And now they were having to live with the pain of that as well as the uncertainty it brought.

But I also saw this: Even though these people had been to hell and back, they weren't done—not even close. These people, these employees, wanted to prove to the world, and to themselves, I suspect, that they were not failures. That General Motors was a good company; that they could raise it back up and make it better than ever. The feeling was: *By God, just give us a chance to show America what we can really do.*

But people weren't so sure they'd ever get that chance because, from what they could see, it was "business as usual" at the new GM, which to them looked an awful lot like the old GM, only smaller. And that's why employees were feeling so down and depressed: because they had nothing to cheer about, nothing to believe in; nothing to look forward to. And the general sense of malaise that was hanging over the RenCen—you could feel the pall as soon as you set foot in the place—reflected that blue-on-black feeling.

Privately, I agreed with them: Nothing really had changed. GM was just as plodding, complex, and bureaucratic as it had ever been. And that "Government Motors" name was like a knife in the ribs to everybody who worked there—people just *hated* that. Yet if you talked with senior management—and I was doing a lot of that, too—everything was right on track. Everything was going good. Everything was fine.

Everything was not fine. If GM kept limping along like this, the company was never going to get itself turned around—I was 100 percent sure of this. The dilemma, for me, was what to do about it. Fritz had only been CEO for a short while, and I was most sympathetic to the difficult circumstances surrounding his appointment. But this was no time to be sentimental. Strong competitors like Ford and Toyota were piling on hard, the US economy wasn't getting any stronger, and gas wasn't getting any cheaper. GM's lineup of cars and vehicles was its strongest in years, but there were a few holes, the most obvious being gas-efficient vehicles. The Chevy Volt was getting a lot of buzz, which was good. But it was still more than a year away from commercial production, which was not so good.

Was senior management up to the challenge? There was no way to be sure right then, but the signs weren't looking so good.

A GM board meeting—my first since being named chairman—was coming up. I figured that would be as good a time as any to sit down with Fritz and talk about the direction of his team, and the direction of General Motors. The board meeting would provide a strong platform for him to lay out his plan in clear, concise terms. To do that, however, he needed to clarify his thinking and craft a convincing strategy. I was willing to help. But Fritz was the CEO, so it was up to him to make those calls.

Fritz was accustomed to GM board meetings that went on for much of the day. I planned to cut them to two or three hours, so he needed to tailor his comments, and thinking, accordingly. I did my best to prepare Fritz for what he could expect.

As was my habit, I got right to the point with Fritz: "Board members just want to know what's going on, what our plans are—and that's it," I told him. (As with other direct quotes, I am paraphrasing from memory.) GM's post-bankruptcy board, for obvious reasons, was most interested in the company's financial performance. So I told Fritz to stick to the basics: sales, revenues, the organizational structure coming out of bankruptcy, and any other information that directly related to the business fundamentals. I figured he could cover all of this in twenty minutes or so, allowing plenty of time for questions and answers. Fritz said okay, no problem.

Now, I am not the sort to repeat myself over and over when I am telling somebody something—I tend to say what I have to say, and then I stop talking. But in this case, because the stakes were so high—this was going to be an important meeting for Fritz—I thought a final reminder couldn't hurt. "Remember, keep it short," I told him—I could not have been any clearer. "I don't want this thing going on all day long."

Fritz did not exactly take my advice. Instead of keeping things right to the point, as I'd asked, his presentation turned into a long string of facts and figures that offered little insight into GM's financial health or global strategy. I listened, hopeful that he would switch and hurry it up—but that never happened. At the one-hour mark, Fritz was still talking. I was incredulous: Instead of making it look like he had a handle on things, Fritz's presentation did just the opposite. I could see that he was trying, really hard, to make a good impression. But it wasn't working. And he was losing board members fast—I could see it in their faces. All around the room, eyes were starting to glaze over. Some people fidgeted in their seats. After an hour and a half, I figured we'd heard enough. I cut Fritz off and told him to sit down.

Next up was Ray Young, GM's chief financial officer. His presentation was a version of the same thing—long, rambling, no real point. Instead of focusing on the fundamentals—here's how much money we made, here's how much we lost, and so on—he started talking about some obscure financial instruments that might have been interesting if you were an accountant. But it had nothing to do with the topic at hand: How's GM doing financially? A couple of the board members were really sharp on numbers, and they pretty much tore into him. I felt bad for Ray—he's a good guy and I liked him a lot. But his presentation, well, it was pretty much a disaster.

This entire scene was dripping with tension: Half the board members were brand new and didn't know each other. Half were holdovers from pre-bankruptcy, and a few were still smarting from Rick Wagoner's fast exit. Everybody appreciated Fritz's efforts, but some weren't so happy he'd been named CEO. A few thought he should have left with Wagoner. (I was not in that camp.) The fact that Fritz and I didn't know each other probably didn't help. Typically, the chairman and CEO have worked together for a while—years, in most cases. That tends to make for an easier rapport in the boardroom—between the CEO and chairman, and with board members, who are typically hand-picked by the chairman and CEO.

Nothing about this situation was normal. Out of the eight board members, I knew only two, really: Rob Krebs, the retired chairman and CEO of Burlington Northern Santa Fe, a big railroad outfit out of Fort Worth; and Pat Russo, the former chairman and CEO of Lucent, the telecommunications equipment maker, now known as Alcatel-Lucent. Right after I got named by the White House, I recruited both to fill board spots that had been vacated during GM's bankruptcy. I knew other board members by reputation, certainly, but had no personal relationships with them. But we all had one thing in common, at least: We wanted very much to see GM succeed, and were willing to devote considerable amounts of time and energy to help make that happen.

By then I'd been spending a little time getting to know Steve Girsky, the union's representative on the board. (A retiree trust fund affiliated with the United Auto Workers owned 17.5 percent of the new GM; Steve represented that interest.) Right after I got named chairman, Steve called me up in San Antonio and said he'd read in the papers that I didn't know anything about the car business. I told him that was all true. Steve, as it turned out, knew a lot about cars: He'd covered GM as an auto analyst for more than twenty years, so he was well versed in all things auto-related. Steve asked if he could come see me in San Antonio and have dinner. I said sure, and he flew out the next day.

Over dinner, Steve laid out everything that was wrong with GM. And according to Steve, just about everything at GM was in need of a serious overhaul, especially management. I mostly just sat and listened, which was pretty easy to do because Steve *really* likes to talk. We're about as different as two guys can get: I'm a slow-talking Texan and he's this mile-a-minute Yankee. Steve's also funny, bright, and seriously smart about the car business. And he was deeply passionate about saving GM. We got along, instantly.

In any event, GM's board meeting finally wrapped up. Then we went into an "executive" session, which is where non-employee directors—like Rob, Pat, and Steve—sit around and talk. I didn't try to gloss things over. My first observations, I told the group, were that GM was disorganized and management did not know what it was doing. Management didn't seem to have any sense of urgency or a larger mission. It was basically "business as usual," which was not acceptable. My conclusion: "I think we may have the wrong CEO." Heads nodded in agreement all around the room.

But I also didn't think it was fair to just bounce Fritz out. He'd only been on the job a short time, and he'd been appointed under difficult circumstances. "I think we should give Fritz a chance to prove himself," I told the group. I suggested giving him ninety days to get it together. I figured Fritz would show his hand in less time than that—probably in the first few weeks—but anything less than ninety days would have signaled a complete lack of faith. That wasn't fair to Fritz or good for GM. A lot of people were still upset about Rick Wagoner—he was a much-beloved figure around GM. About the last thing employees needed right then was to see yet another CEO walk out the door.

Some board members weren't so crazy about the ninety-day plan—they thought we should let him go right then. The fact that Fritz was part of the team that stood by and watched GM go up in flames just rubbed them the wrong way. My view: not fair. Fritz wasn't even in the country when a lot of those calls got made—he was over in Europe, running GM's operations there. But perception is reality, like they say.

One of the critics on the board was Dan Akerson. I didn't know Dan personally, but I did know him by reputation. Dan had a finance background and had worked at a string of companies over the years—MCI, General Instrument, Nextel, and Forstmann, Little, a private investment firm based in New York City. In 2003 he joined The Carlyle Group, a private equity firm based in Washington, DC, which is where he was when GM got into trouble.

Dan also had some experience with bankruptcy. Before Carlyle, he was the chairman and CEO of XO Communications, which went through a bankruptcy proceeding in 2002. (Dan was the CEO from 1999 to 2002.) He stayed on to help XO restructure, then joined Carlyle the following year. He was appointed to GM's board in July 2009, about the same time as Rob and Pat.

Dan was pretty vocal during the executive session. Said he thought GM was one of the worst companies he'd come across in his entire life. And he was not a fan of GM cars—he made that crystal-clear. Dan wasn't alone in his hard assessment of GM's product line. Other board members felt pretty much the same way.

And I could certainly relate to that sentiment, because GM had not been managed well. But that's also why we were all there: to help Fritz and his team get GM turned around. So that's what I basically told everybody: "Look, guys, you can talk about this all you want, but we've been sent here as a board to get this thing going, so I propose that we give Fritz ninety days to get himself and the company organized. Then let's see what happens." Nobody had any better ideas. So that's what we agreed to do—we'd give Fritz three months, essentially, to get his act together. This conversation did not last long, maybe fifteen minutes.

Right after the executive session ended, I headed up to Fritz's office to deliver the news.

He was there, waiting.

As is my habit, I got right to the point: "Fritz, the board has talked it over and the feeling is that we want you to have a fair try at this job. So we're going to set a specific time period—ninety days—to see how you do," I told him—and again I am paraphrasing from memory. "The board," I added, "genuinely wants you to succeed—I want you to succeed."

And all that was true—we wanted Fritz to succeed. Regardless of how he wound up in the job, he was now the CEO of General Motors. Nobody on the board was eager to go through the pain and drama of having to find a replacement, not with employee morale in the sinker and the eyes of the world watching. Me, especially. I liked Fritz a lot. And I greatly admired his work ethic. That he'd worked at GM his entire career, for me, was not a negative. I'd done the same thing at AT&T—worked there forty-four years, never even considered working anywhere else. I loved that company, still do. Just like Fritz loved General Motors. That's called *loyalty*. I respected Fritz's dedication and sense of duty.

But failure was not an option. GM was America's largest manufacturer and the backbone of the US auto industry. If the new GM faltered or reverted to its old ways for too long, the company could quickly find itself pushed into a corner again. Employees were my biggest concern. They had a lot of fight left in them, but that wouldn't last forever.

Was Fritz up to the challenge? It was time to fish or cut bait: If Fritz couldn't step it up, we'd find a replacement—it was that simple. As chairman, it was not my place to tell Fritz what to do or how to run GM. But I *really* wanted to help him, so I sort of did anyway.

"Here are some things we think you should do," I told him, then ticked off a couple of things board members would respond favorably to: "You should organize this place in a way that makes some sense and isn't harum-scarum all over the place. You should simplify wherever possible. And get a strategic plan for which way you're going to take this company. It doesn't have to be elaborate, but here are my priorities as CEO, number one, number two, number three, and so on"— and again, I am paraphrasing here. As an example, I said, one of his priorities might be, and probably should be, car dealers. During bankruptcy, GM pared back a lot on dealerships that weren't meeting sales targets, and that process was continuing. At the next board meeting, I prompted, "You might say that you're going to shut down so many dealers because they're not performing, or something like that."

The board wasn't looking for a magic bullet—there was no quick fix for what ailed GM. "Board members just want to see that you have a plan," I told him.

Simplify, clarify. In other words: Keep it simple. This was the same advice I'd been giving Fritz all along. Now I was basically saying the same thing again, only more forcefully. I wasn't trying to jam anything down Fritz's throat—well, maybe I was, a little. I recognized that this was his call to make as CEO. But I was also trying to convey a sense of urgency, because Fritz's job, quite literally, was now on the line. And I knew that, even if he didn't.

Fritz didn't say much, except to point out that ninety days wasn't a lot of time. It was a fair point—three months was like yesterday. But it was what it was. "We'll know in ninety days if you're on the right track," I responded, mostly because I didn't know what else to say. Fritz sort of nodded his head, and said okay.

CHAPTER 5

Ennis, Texas

The lessons of life that got handed my way when I was growing up were pretty straightforward: Use common sense. Treat people like you'd want to be treated. Never think you're better than anybody else—because you're not. Be courteous. Be on time. Don't be the kind of guy who's all hat and no cattle. (A phony, in other words.) Don't give up—hang in there. Be who you are. Be thankful.

Nobody sat around preaching all this stuff to me. I picked it up the way most kids do: by listening and observing. Family was a big part of that. So was my hometown, a little place just south of Dallas called Ennis. That's in Texas, of course.

Today you can jump on I-45 and be out of Ennis and in downtown Dallas in about thirty minutes. When I was growing up in the 1940s, the only thing connecting Ennis and Dallas was a long stretch of two-lane highway. So that forty-mile trip could take you an hour, or longer if you happened to get stuck behind a slow-moving truck or caught by weather. That's why we didn't go too often, I guess—just wasn't worth the hassle.

A bigger reason, though, was this: Dallas was *their* town— the people who lived there, I am referring to—and Ennis was *our* town. Nothing wrong with Dallas, mind you. It's a fine city.

But Ennis had everything we really needed or wanted. My family was there, my friends were there, my school, favorite fishing holes; everything that had meaning to me was there. And I had no interest in leaving. When I was growing up I always assumed I'd spend the rest of my life in Ennis. And I probably would have, but fate—and my mother—intervened.

Back then, there were basically two industries in Ennis: cotton tags—a local factory made the tags that went on cotton bales. And the railroad. Southern Pacific, one of the oldest railroads in the country, had a "roundhouse" on the edge of town—that's a circular track that trains use to get turned around in the opposite direction; the engineer can't exactly do a three-point turn, so that's how they do it. Ennis also had a mattress factory, an ice factory, a creamery, a couple of other local businesses. But the biggest employers, by far, were those two. So in Ennis, at that time, that's pretty much how it was: Your daddy worked for either the cotton tag factory or the railroad. Mine worked for the railroad.

My daddy—his name was Edward Earl Whitacre; that's whom I'm named after—was born in Milan, Missouri, but raised in Allen, Oklahoma. He was the oldest of four brothers, and all but one worked for the railroad, as did their daddy, Harry Earl. The one brother who did not work for the railroad was an officer with the US Air Force, based in Shreveport; he was a navigator on B-52 bombers. Daddy's mother was named Myrtle. She was a matronly, silver-headed, sweet woman. The family was not particularly close. Or talkative. Nice people, just not big talkers.

Working for the railroad was a real point of pride in the Whitacre family. So when Daddy got old enough, he quit school and started looking for a job. He was in the eleventh grade. The old Kansas, Oklahoma & Gulf Railroad (KO&G) ran through Allen—that's where his daddy worked. But it was not hiring. So he headed over to Ennis to see about Southern Pacific. They had one job to offer him: "fireman." That's the guy who shovels coal into the engine firebox, which is what kept the train moving. Firemen had other duties, but that's the main one. (Most trains ran on steam in those days, so if the fire died the train died.) It was hard work. Shifts could go eight to ten hours, and you had to wear heavy gloves and overalls to keep from getting burned. So that was Daddy's first job—railroad fireman.

Daddy had never really been out of Allen, except to visit his relatives in Milan. So even though Ennis was only a couple of hours away, it was still a pretty big deal. But Daddy was a quiet sort, so he didn't make a fuss. When he got the job he sent a penny postcard—written in pencil, I still have it—to let his family know: "I got a job. I'm three-times out"—meaning he was on the third train to leave Ennis that day—"would you please send my clothes to me. Signed, Earl." And that's it—no big good-bye, no nothing. He just hopped a train and away he went. Daddy sent the postcard to his mother c/o General Delivery, which was common back then because Allen was so small everybody knew where everybody else lived.

Mother—her name was Lola—was from Hearne, Texas. Mooney was her maiden name; she was one of seven children. Mother had one brother who was older, two brothers who were younger, and three sisters. Being the oldest girl, Mother helped raise the kids in her family. And that was fine by her, because she loved children and grew up dreaming of having her own family one day.

She also dreamed of going to college. Mother was the valedictorian in her high school class and won a scholarship to Baylor College, in Belton, Texas—today it's known as the University of Mary Hardin-Baylor; it's one of the oldest schools in the state. Her father and mother were good people, very hardworking. But neither had a formal education, so they were really proud when their little girl won that scholarship. And it was quite an accomplishment, because back then—this was around 1925—a lot of women didn't go to college. And that was particularly true of women from small towns in rural Texas.

Mother was a good student and loved college life. But she had to drop out after one semester. Her family could not afford to keep her in school. Her father, John, had a little grocery store in Hearne, but he extended credit to too many people who couldn't pay. He eventually went broke and lost the store. Mother had no money to pay for college, so she had no choice but to come back home and find a job.

Mother was one of the sweetest, kindest people I have ever known. But she also had inner steel. It wasn't so obvious when you first met her, but it was there—believe me. And that tenacity had a way of coming out when times got tough, or when she just got it in her head to do something. In this case, she needed a job, quickly. Not the easiest thing to do in 1925. The Great Depression was still a few years off but times were already turning hard, so jobs were scarce.

Mother hung in there. She started asking around and got a job offer in Henry Prairie, Texas—that's in Robertson County, about six miles from Hearne. It's a small spot of a town, more of an outpost, really—a few dozen families, at most, have ever lived there. But it did have a one-room schoolhouse, and they needed a teacher for elementary-aged kids. She took the job.

Mother's unexpected return home turned out to be a stroke of luck—or fate or whatever you want to call it. That twist owed a little something to basic geography: Hearne, as it happens, is midway between Dallas and Houston on the railroad line. So it was a major depot for Southern Pacific in terms of the track split—one fork took trains south to San Antonio, the other continued on to Houston. Regardless of which direction they were headed, all the trains stopped in Hearne—to pick up people, supplies, fuel, freight, whatever. And Daddy, as it turned out, was working that Hearne run pretty regularly.

So one day, don't you know, Mother happened to be in downtown Hearne and spotted this "good looking" guy walking down the street—those are Mother's words, not mine. She had no idea who the guy was; she'd never seen him before. And Hearne was small, as I mentioned, so she pretty much knew everybody who lived there. And she was intrigued, I guess, because Mother said she watched that guy walk down the street until he was clear out of sight. All the time wondering to herself just who that guy was, and what he was doing in Hearne.

That "guy," of course, was Daddy. He was on a layover with Southern Pacific, and happened to be downtown walking around that day. The fact that he caught her eye, in some ways, is not so surprising. Daddy was what Hollywood used to call the "strong, silent type." And he did look the part: He had jet-black hair, hazel eyes, and usually had a cigarette hanging off to one side of his mouth. He looked a lot like "Pretty Boy" Floyd, the notorious 1930s gangster—so much, in fact, that local law enforcement tried to arrest him one time, thinking he *was* Pretty Boy Floyd. Daddy did not take too kindly to the comparison, or the attempt to arrest him, as you might expect.

Daddy was not a tough guy by any stretch. But he wasn't overly friendly, either—just not a big talker, especially if he had no business with you. And Daddy had a way of making it clear which one it was without saying a word to you. He was not a big man: five-foot-ten, maybe 180 pounds. But he was lean and strong from working the railroad—shoveling coal ten hours a day will do that to you. So he had the quiet confidence of a man who could handle himself. That's the sort of thing other men notice; ladies, too, only in a different way. Mother said she liked Daddy's looks right away, and decided she might like to meet him. She kept an eye out for him after that.

Daddy never mentioned the first time he saw Mother—just not a big talker, like I said. But eventually, he did notice her. That was not too surprising, either. Mother was quite the Texas rose: five-foot-six, maybe 120 pounds, with fair skin, brown eyes, and a laugh that could light up a room. She mostly wore dresses—the prim and proper kind that you'd expect a school-teacher to wear—never shorts, and pants rarely. She had a Texas twang, but it was soft and easy on the ear, not hard.

But her most distinctive feature, by far, was her hair: flaming red. Not sort of red, or almost red—but *flaming* red. Two of her three sisters and younger brother had that same hair. They got it from their maternal grandmother—her last name was Lefevre, she was a little, bitty French lady and also lived in Hearne. I always thought the whole hair-color thing was pretty interest-ing, because her parents were both brunettes, as were the rest of her siblings. Mother was proud of her hair and often wore hats—the kind with feathers and netting in them. That had a way of drawing even more attention to her hair. Not that you could miss that five-alarm fire on her head, even if you tried.

I don't know if it was the hair, or a hat, or something else, but one day Daddy saw Mother in Hearne and thunder must have struck because he made a beeline over and started talking. Which is saying something, because Daddy didn't make small talk with people he knew, much less people he didn't know. Mother must've lit up like a firefly, because Daddy asked her out on a date that same day. They started seeing each other regu-larly after that, and got married a year later. Mother moved to Ennis after the wedding, and they started working on a family right away.

But ten years into their marriage, they were still childless, and losing hope. By the time their thirteenth wedding anni-versary rolled around, they *still* had no children—so they gave up. Mother, by then, had become convinced that having chil-dren just wasn't their fate. And you could hardly blame them for thinking that—at that point they'd been trying and hoping and praying for children for thirteen years. Mother prayed, anyway. She was Southern Baptist and went to church every Sunday.

Daddy didn't do that. All that church socializing, just not his thing.

Mother and Daddy were very disappointed by life's turn. Mother was beyond crushed. But they were also pragmatic. Since they weren't going to have any children to support, they decided they may as well spend the money they'd been saving for that purpose—around $3,000. That was a lot of money in 1941. Back then, the average income in America was around $1,700 a year. So this was major money, especially to a working-class railroad couple.

They spent every last dime. Daddy bought a brand-new car—their first—for $750. It was a 1941 Dodge, teal green, had those big rolled fenders—beautiful. They also bought a house in Ennis. Paid cash—$2,500, I still have the sales receipt. The house was right by the rail yards, so Daddy could walk to work without having to drive his new Dodge and worry about where to park it—man, he loved that car. And they still had enough left over to buy all-new furniture for the house.

The very next month, don't you know, Mother woke up one morning and felt just terrible. She was throwing up, sick as a dog. Mother thought she might be coming down with the flu, so she went over to see the doctor. Mother said the doctor examined her, then busted out laughing: "Lola, you are pregnant!" And, in fact, she was. I was born nine months later, on November 4, 1941, at Florence Nightingale Maternity Hospital in Dallas. Mother was thirty-four; Daddy was thirty-six.

Daddy drove Mother and me home from the hospital in that same green Dodge, to that house by the rail yards. They figured that was it for them, as far as kids were concerned. Turned out, they were wrong about that, too. Five years later my sister, Jeannine, came along. She was born in that same hospital, in Dallas. We still had that green Dodge, and we were still living in that same two-bedroom house. The place got a little crowded after my sister came along. But we were a family, and that's all that really mattered. I was only five years old, and not too crazy about having to share my room with a crying baby. But I got along just fine, I guess.

Ennis in the 1940s was a working-class town. Also a union town—the railroad, as I mentioned, was one of the biggest employers, so union people were everywhere. Most daddies, including mine, worked long days. So they were too busy working and trying to put food on the table to even think about sitting down with their kids to talk about "life." But valuable lessons got handed my way. One of the people who taught me the most, I'd have to say, was my grandfather on my mother's side, John Mooney. By the time I came along most people around Hearne had taken to calling him "Judge," and I'll tell you why a little later. But to me he'll always be "Papa."

Papa was not an educated man—he attended a small country school as a boy but never stayed long enough to learn how to read and write. Nor was he a man of wealth, at least not in the classic sense. But he was, without question, one of the most impressive people I've ever met, in terms of how he dealt with personal challenges and setbacks. That, in my view, tells you everything you need to know about a person's makeup and character. Papa didn't just tackle those tall mountains; he scaled them in supreme fashion, and against the highest odds imaginable. His sense of fair play came as naturally to him as breathing. I wouldn't call Papa a warm man; his life was too hard for that. But he was a compassionate man, and his diverse circle of friends and admirers was rich testament to it. By his own example, Papa taught me a lot about life. And about character: what it is and why it matters. Not by preaching, but by doing. Those lessons stuck.

Papa's life, to some degree, was a case study in human resiliency. After he lost the grocery store in Hearne—Mother was in college when that happened, as I mentioned—he went into a deep, black depression. Papa was in a tough spot: no income,

no savings, and no job, but with a wife and seven kids to support. The family scraped along like this for a year. Mother was
making a little money teaching, which helped. Then one day,
Mother said, he just snapped himself out of it: Papa decided to
become a blacksmith. Hearne was in cotton country, so farmers
were always having to get equipment fixed, horses shoed, fences
mended, things like that. So Papa figured it'd be steady money.

Just one problem: Papa didn't know the first thing about
blacksmithing. The only thing he'd ever done was run a grocery
and dry-goods store, and he went broke doing it. But Papa was
not deterred. By then he'd taught himself to read and write—he
wrote everything phonetically, but had a beautiful hand. (His
wife, Clara—I called her "Big Mama"—never did know how to
read and write that I know of.) I guess Papa figured if he could
teach himself to do that, he could teach himself to do anything.
So that's basically what he did: He taught himself. Before too
long he could bend hot metal, repair cotton gins, shoe plow
horses, and do all the other things that blacksmiths do. Papa
never talked about how he taught himself to do all this stuff,
and to tell you the truth I never asked. He just did it.

After a while Papa started getting some clients, so he set up
a little blacksmith shop on the far end of Hearne, on the corner
of Cedar and Third streets. As a kid, I used to love going to that
blacksmith shop. It was a dark, sooty place, full of coal, old
tools, fires—it was a boy's dream, really. Papa would show me
how to heat pieces of metal to red-hot, then white-hot, then let
me pound them with a hammer until they stuck to each other.
I could mess around doing that for hours, and often did. The
people part was also pretty interesting—they were coming and
going from that shop all day long. I was always sitting on the
sidelines, watching. I was only six or seven, so this was pretty
exciting stuff to me.

Papa didn't own a car—never did, as far as I can recall—or
even know how to drive. So every morning he'd get up and

walk that mile across town to his shop, work all day, then walk back home ten or twelve hours later when he was done. Papa must've been pretty good, because everybody came to see him. He was glad to finally have a steady income, so he never turned anybody down.

Back then—this was the late 1940s—racial segregation in America, and in Texas, certainly, was pretty pervasive. Some white-owned restaurants wouldn't serve blacks, or if they did people had to sit in a special section. Same for stores, movie theaters, water fountains, you name it. Papa was color-blind. In his eyes, people were just people; no man was better than another. He never said that outright—I don't ever recall the subject of race ever being brought up. But his actions said a lot. So long as people could pay, Papa didn't care what color they were—white, black, yellow, purple—he'd do work for them.

By the same token, if you *couldn't* pay—white, black, yellow, purple—he wouldn't do work for you. Papa got pretty tight with a dollar after he lost that grocery store. Mother and her sisters used to joke how he could just wear a dime completely thin. If Papa loaned his children money, for example, he expected them to pay him back. And he would not throw away food. If he burned a piece of toast, which he did every morning when he was making his breakfast—I watched him do this a thousand times—he'd scrape off the top and eat it, no matter how burned it was. But I could certainly understand why he felt that way, given what he'd gone through with that grocery store.

What Papa cared about a lot, though, was doing right by people. This got conveyed to me in a variety of ways, most of them nonverbal. I remember well the way Papa treated people, and the friendly back-and-forth he'd have with everybody— blacks, whites, those who had a little more than the rest of us, those who had nothing. I was just a boy but even then I could see, and feel, the mutual respect and affection. I absorbed that lesson like a sponge.

Another big lesson I learned had to do with your basic approach to the world—the importance of having a positive outlook, which is the first step to creating opportunities for yourself in life. Papa, for example, never seemed to look at his own life and see the limitations. He only saw the possibilities. Papa just fundamentally believed in himself, and in the power of focus and hard work to change the course of his life; that was his bible, and he read from the good book daily. Papa didn't express it like that—he was not prone to preaching, like I said. But that is how he lived his life: as a series of interesting possibilities just waiting to happen. And as a result he wound up having a pretty amazing life.

Which brings us to another watershed year: 1928. That year, out of the blue, Papa decided to run for justice of the peace for Precinct 2 in Robertson County, which is where Hearne is located. He was already putting in full workweeks as a blacksmith. But Papa figured a little extra pocket money wouldn't hurt, so he decided to go for it. The justice of the peace is a pretty serious job—you have to be able to perform civil marriages, officiate traffic tickets and other misdemeanors, things like that. There are lots of rules and regulations around this stuff, as you can imagine; you can't just wing it.

Papa didn't know the first thing about being a justice of the peace—zero. But he'd already taught himself to read and write and be a blacksmith, so I guess he figured if he could do all that he could teach himself to be a justice of the peace.

And that's exactly what he did.

Don't ask me how, he just bucked up and did it. And Papa was not the fastest reader—he spelled everything phonetically, as I mentioned. So it must've taken some doing to get through all the legal jargon in the state statutes to learn all this stuff. But I guess he did okay, because Papa ran for that justice of the peace job...and won. And he didn't just win by a little—he won by a landslide. Thanks to all his years of blacksmithing, Papa by then was a pretty popular guy around Robertson County—whites liked him, blacks liked him, rich people, poor people, all kinds. And *everybody* turned out to vote for him. Except the guy he was running against, I am assuming, who pretty much got creamed. The vote was like four hundred to one. I am exaggerating, but not by much. Papa ran for reelection every two years after that, and won—by a landslide—every single time. After a while nobody even bothered to run against him.

After he got elected, people took to calling Papa "Judge," and I think he liked it, because he didn't discourage it. Papa never stopped his blacksmithing. He kept on shoeing horses, fixing farm machinery, and all that other stuff. He'd stop long enough to carry out his official duties, right there in his blacksmith shop, then he'd go back to shoeing or welding or whatever it was he was working on. Locals used to joke about "justice before the anvil," and I guess Papa liked that, too, because he didn't discourage that, either. And Papa was not shy about stating his preferences. The anvil, in case you don't know, is a basic tool of the blacksmithing trade. You can pound a sledgehammer on it for hours and not put a dent in it. That's a pretty good analogy for Papa, now that I think about it. He was a tough son-of-a-gun, I will say.

Papa's duties as justice didn't stop with the end of his workday. He was basically on call twenty-four hours a day. That's how that job worked—when the law needed him to officiate something, they'd swing by his shop or, if it was after hours, go to his house. A few times—I remember this well—the Texas Highway Patrol came over late at night to Papa's house with somebody they'd caught drunk or doing something they shouldn't have been doing. Papa would listen to the charges and fine them on the spot. One time, a young couple came knocking on Papa's door about eleven o'clock at night, wanting to get married. Papa performed the ceremony right there in the living room. I never saw him get mad because of people knocking on his door like that. And Papa put in long days as a black-smith, so some nights he must've been pretty tired. But he never showed that. Papa's attitude was basically: *We're all in the world together, so treat people like you'd want to be treated if you were in their shoes.* He never said that, or even talked about it. He just did it.

Mother was the same way. One day we were driving back to Hearne, just the two of us; I might've been eight or nine. We were going to Papa's house, still had another fifteen miles or so to go. An old black man happened to be walking along the side of the road. He was maybe sixty or sixty-five, had a sack tossed over one shoulder. He was hitchhiking in our direction. As soon as we got past him, Mother looked in the rearview mirror and said, "Well, that's old So-and-so"—I can't recall the guy's name. She immediately slammed on the brakes and wheeled the car around to go pick him up.

I didn't say a word, but I was terrified. The guy looked scary to me; he had a grizzled face, shabby clothes. Not the sort you want sitting next to you in a car. I was just a kid, so I didn't say anything. But I was most uncomfortable with her doing this—did not like it at all. So Mother stopped, he climbed in, and we continued on our way to Hearne. Turned out he was a really nice guy. Mother had known him since she was a kid, and she was really glad to see him, I could tell. He was glad to see her, too. They laughed and joked all the way home. I remember that like it was yesterday. It's one of my favorite memories now, and it also taught me a lesson about making snap judgments about people based on looks alone.

Mother was always doing things like that. She used to buy her eggs from a lady in Ennis named Rose; she was really poor, had nothing. Every week, Rose would show up at our door with a basket full of eggs; Mother would take the eggs and pay her right there in the kitchen. So one day I asked Mother: "Why don't you just give Rose some money, if you want to help her, and buy our eggs the regular way—at the grocery store?" This lady coming by our house every week, it just seemed odd to me.

"Because that woman doesn't have anything, Edward," she said—that's what Mother always called me—"and this is my way of helping her."

I was just a kid, maybe ten, so I didn't get the meaning of what Mother was saying at the time. But as I got older I came to understand that this very simple gesture—buying eggs— was Mother's way of lending a helping hand, but in a way that allowed that lady to keep her dignity and self-respect. That's a very basic human need: to feel good about ourselves when we look in the mirror. I want that, you want that, we all want that. So did Rose. I never forgot that lesson, either.

Big Mama—Papa's wife, real name Clara—had the same attitude. She and Papa lived near the railroad tracks in Hearne, so hoboes were always coming around for a hot meal. I never saw her turn one down. No matter what the hour, or how ragged they looked, Big Mama would help. Most times, they'd take their food and sit under a tree by the back steps to eat. If it was cold or raining, Big Mama would ask them to come inside and sit at the table. Some of these people looked pretty rough—raggedy clothes, scruffy faces, everything they owned tied up in a sack. Big Mama never said a word. No mention of their hard situation or appearance. It was like she was inviting in the next-door neighbors.

One day I asked Big Mama why she was always giving our food away to people we didn't know like that. It wasn't like we were rich, or even close to being rich. She came right back, sweet but direct: "Because they're hungry, Edward. We have food and they don't." I was only eight or nine, I guess. But I sat and thought about that and decided Big Mama was right. These people were down on their luck and trying to get by the best way they could—just like our family, just like every family I knew. I never asked that question again.

Simplicity, to some degree, was the hallmark of my childhood. Life in Ennis was comfortable, familiar—and I loved it. My best friend, Tommy Snell, lived right across the street—we were born a month apart, and we're still friends to this day. Back then we were inseparable, rode our bikes together everywhere. Baseball was our game: I was addicted. I played first base and was an okay hitter—not great, but I got by. In the summers I played every day, sometimes twice a day. In the street, ballparks, sand lots, anywhere we could get a game up. I wasn't much of an athlete, but I kept trying. I played high school football, linebacker and center positions. I wasn't that good. I also wasn't that big—just five-foot-eight at sixteen. I broke my right knee in the eleventh grade, was in a cast for six weeks. That pretty much ended my football career.

One of my favorite pastimes, besides baseball, was fishing. I also liked to hunt—rabbits, duck, quail, anything I could get a bead on. Daddy wasn't an outdoorsy type, but his daddy—I called him "Dad"—loved all that stuff. I used to look forward to our family visits to Oklahoma because that meant I'd get to go fishing and hunting with Dad. He was left-handed, an accomplished outdoorsman—I learned a lot from him growing up. Dad had a little aluminum boat with a motor on it—it seemed gigantic to me at the time. Dad used to let me work the motor and drive the boat; I really liked that. Other times we'd hike back in the woods to go hunting—Dad had spots all over the place. I loved every minute. It was basically a boy's dream.

One fishing trip will always stick with me. We were at a local lake, in the boat. I was driving. I guess I wasn't paying attention, because I hit a tree in the water; that jarred loose a wasp's nest. That thing fell straight down on top of us. Those wasps swarmed all over the boat. I panicked and jumped into the lake. When I did, I pushed the boat farther into the black cloud of wasps—they were all over us, I mean to tell you. Dad picked up a paddle and started swatting; never got stung even once. I was in the water and got stung fifteen or twenty times. After things calmed down, I crawled back into the boat—I was very embarrassed. We went to shore and I lay down on the ground, put ice on my face. Man, I was a mess—both eyes swelled shut. And the worst part was, we didn't catch a single fish. Dad never said a word. After a while we got back in the car and went home. I was a lot more careful driving the boat after that.

In Ennis, Tommy and I were always messing around doing something. We'd go to the local butcher's shop and get a piece of liver, then walk down to the river and "tightline"—that's when you throw a fishing line out, no cork, just weight and bait, and let it sit on the bottom. We caught lots of catfish that way. We'd catch them and throw them back, did that for hours.

We also liked chasing after the DDT trucks; we played hide-and-seek in the fog they left behind. DDT is actually a powerful insecticide, and quite toxic. It got banned in this country years ago for health reasons, and Tommy and I were playing in it, you know? But I guess I survived. Another favorite spot was the oil pit on the edge of town—it was basically a dumping ground for oil, looked like a small lake, with the consistency of Jell-O. Tommy and I thought this stuff was pretty cool. We'd wade around the edges for hours, poking it with sticks. Boy stuff. We were always doing things like that.

Socially, I was pretty awkward growing up. I was introverted, withdrawn—just really shy. Any sort of public speaking terrified me. I didn't dance—*wouldn't dance*, is more like it. The jitterbug was popular, but I was too self-conscious—all that hopping around. So I wouldn't do it. Mother wanted me to be a well-adjusted kid, so she was always encouraging me to join things: I was a Boy Scout for a while. I also played basketball, did a little track and field, was a shotputter for a while. Wasn't very good at any of it. Mother tried to get me to try out for the school play, but I was too shy for that. Just the thought of talking in front of people made me so nervous, my throat would close up. Mother loved piano and made me take lessons for a while. I did it to make her happy, but I thought it made me look like a sissy. And I wasn't very good, so that didn't last long, either.

I was an average student scholastically. But my senior year my grades finally got good enough to get me nominated for the National Honor Society. Being in the National Honor Society was a big deal in my school—it gave you social acceptance, to some degree, made you part of the "in" crowd, or at least that's how I looked at it. My friend Don and I had the grades that year, so we were really excited about the prospect of joining.

But we didn't get in. Some of our friends got elected, but we weren't. I was really hurt. Also confused, because my grades were good enough. Things like that just crush you when you're in high school—everybody wants to be liked, and popular, or at least accepted. My class wasn't all that big, less than a hundred students. So that really hit me hard. Mother knew how much that meant to me, so when I didn't get in she sat me down and talked to me about it. Told me she was really proud of me, that she knew I had the grades and that I had nothing to feel bad about. That made me feel a little better. But I guess I went on to do okay, so maybe those failures inspire you in life. To this day I don't know why I didn't get in, but I still find myself thinking about it sometimes.

Mother was very loving and caring with me like that. She never talked to me about my shyness, but she must've noticed because she was always trying to boost me up. Not a day went by that she wouldn't kiss me, or hug me. She'd say, "You look handsome today," or "You look nice in those clothes," which she always ironed. She'd also whip me with a yardstick if I was taunting my sister, which I guess I sometimes did—just boy stuff, I was not a mean kid. But I did sometimes push it too far when I got to teasing my sister, and Mother would let me know about it. She never let me forget how much she loved me, though. Like I said, not a day went by.

Daddy wasn't around as much, mostly because he was always working. Railroad work is hard work, also demanding on your schedule. Southern Pacific used to call him at all hours of the night and day, and off he'd go. Daddy never seemed to mind. He never talked about his work too much, but one time I did ask him if he liked driving the train. By then Daddy was a senior engineer—that's the person who drives the train and makes sure the engine is in good working order. I will always remember what he said: "Yes, it's very satisfying, but it's not much fun trying to dodge gasoline trucks and people trying to beat you at the crossing." He did not elaborate. But I think he'd hit four or five people at railroad crossings over the years. That bothered him a lot, I could tell. I found out later that Daddy was a consummate engineer, had a reputation among his fellow trainmen for being able to get the most out of a train's performance. Other engineers tried to emulate him, and were always going to him for advice. Daddy never talked about that, either.

One thing Daddy did talk about was the union. He was very pro-union, and very proud of the association. Around the dinner table at night, Daddy and I would sometimes get to talking about the union—I was young and optimistic that managements would do the right thing by workers, so I was of the mind that we really didn't need unions. Daddy would get pretty riled up, in a friendly way, and argue right back: "Oh yes we do, and here's why...," he'd say, then tell me why I was wrong and why unions were fundamental to the railroad, and to America. And Daddy knew his facts, I will say. He was a union official for a while, and one of his jobs was taking the grievances of union members up to management. I always found that sort of ironic. At home, you couldn't get a word out of him—like trying to squeeze blood out of a turnip. But at work, apparently, he was a pretty good communicator. I guess everybody's got their public face and their private face.

Daddy was a very independent thinker. If one of the union's

members was trying to get one over on the railroad—by filing a bogus grievance, or something else that he considered shady—Daddy would do his job and represent them. But he knew they were not doing right, and he'd voice that to me. Another thing he was adamant about: his politics. Mother, too. They were both hard-line Democrats—didn't matter who was running, they'd always pull the Democratic levers in the voting booth. To his dying day, Daddy thought unions and Democrats are necessary. And to my dying day, I think I will always say they're okay, too, because I got that infused into me pretty early. As for my politics, I basically vote for who I think is the best person for the job, regardless of their political affiliation.

I truly expected to follow my father into the railroad business. That's how it worked back then: If you were in a railroad family, then the assumption was that you'd go to work for the railroad after you graduated from high school. You didn't think about it, or talk about it, or debate it—you just did it. My second assumption was that I'd spend the rest of my life in Ennis. Again, in my circle this wasn't something you even thought about—that's just how it was. And I was pretty happy about the idea of living in Ennis the rest of my life, because everybody I loved, and everything I knew or had meaning to me, was right there.

Then came the moment that changed my way of thinking, and my life.

I don't recall how or why this came up, exactly, but I do remember that our family was sitting around the dinner table one night when the subject of what I planned to do after high school came up. I was around sixteen, so I had another year or so to go before graduation.

I did not hesitate to answer.

"I guess I'll go to work for the railroad," I said pretty matter-of-factly.

Before I could take a breath to say another word—I will always remember this—Mother cut in: "Oh, no, Edward," she said, just as matter-of-factly. "You are *not* going to work for the railroad." She used that voice that mothers use when they're really serious, so I knew something was up.

I was confused by her statement—her declaration, was more like it. I had no career ambitions or plans beyond Southern Pacific.

"Well, what am I going to do, Mother?"

"You are going to go to college, Edward."

I was shocked. College, to me, was a foreign concept. I'd never even considered going to college. I had no social skills, no smarts. I considered myself to be very average. But hearing Mother say that, to my own surprise, made me pause and smile inside. Because it made me think, for the very first time, that maybe the predetermined nature of my life wasn't so predetermined after all. If I'd protested—like I did on piano lessons— I'm sure Mother wouldn't have forced the issue. But I didn't. Instead I just sat there, scared and excited, and silently chewed on the bigger implications of what she was saying—I savored them, actually. And I think I did that because maybe, somewhere deep inside, I was hoping, praying, for something more for myself. Until that moment, I never believed in myself enough to think that was a possibility, much less say it out loud.

I was speechless. Mother, however, was not. She told me, in a fast stream of warm but firm words, that she had higher aspirations for me, and that I might want to start thinking along those lines, as well. Nothing wrong with the railroad, of course—it's a fine institution. Mother just thought I had potential that went beyond Ennis, and beyond Southern Pacific. Why she thought that I had no idea; she just did.

One problem with Mother's plan: We had no money for college. Daddy made enough to pay the bills and keep food on the table. But our family had no rainy-day savings, no college fund. And college was expensive—$75 a semester at the local school; the closest one was an hour away. I had no car, so how would I get there? I'd also need money for books, living expenses, and food. We didn't have that kind of money. I knew it as soon as she brought up the college idea. Mother knew it, too.

But Mother, being Mother, and being a Mooney, was not deterred. She'd made up her mind that I was going to college, and that was that.

And so about a year later, right before graduation, Mother put her plan into action: She marched herself down to the local Citizen's Bank in downtown Ennis, me trailing behind. Mother had a checking account there. Every week, she'd get Daddy's paycheck, give him $40 for spending money, and put the rest in that checking account. She'd been doing this for years, so Mother knew everybody at Citizen's, including the bank president, Cecil Tolleson. Mother walked right up to him, me still trailing behind, and said she needed a word in private. I followed them in and sat down in a big leather chair in Mr. Tolleson's office.

"Cecil," she told him, "we want this boy to go to college." I was seated next to Mother as she was talking, staring at my shoes and feeling terrified.

Mr. Tolleson was direct but friendly: "How much you need, Lola?"

Mother said she wanted $750. She figured that would be enough to get me started. And one more thing: Mother wanted the money that day. College was starting soon, she said, so preparations had to be made. She couldn't wait.

He asked Mother how she planned to pay back the loan. "I don't know, Cecil," she said, looking him dead in the eye. "We'll pay it back as soon as we can."

Mr. Tolleson didn't question her—can't say I blame him. Mother was pretty fired up. He sort of nodded and said okay. Then he pulled out a piece of paper, good for $750, and gave it to Mother. She thanked him, then got up and went straight to the bank teller. She cashed the note and got her $750 that day.

So that's how it started—with a mother who believed in me and $750 from the local Ennis bank.

Walking out of the bank that day, I got the feeling that maybe, just *maybe*, there might be something out there for me—beyond Ennis, beyond the railroad business, beyond the safety and security of the only home I'd ever known. I was seventeen and scared to death. But I was also excited about the prospect of trying something new. My heart beat fast just thinking about it. Was there really a future out there for me? I didn't have any idea about that. But the fast swirl of thoughts running around my head told me I was finally ready to find out.

CHAPTER 6

Keeping It Between the Ditches

The prospect of going to college—and leaving Ennis—terrified me. I felt excited to be going, but I was racked by a lot of fears: Would I do okay in school? Would people like me? Would I fit in? One reason I was wrestling so hard with this, I think, was because I had no idea what to expect.

My college life started, but did not end, at Arlington State College. The school today is part of the University of Texas system—technically, it's called the University of Texas at Arlington. But back in my day it was just good old Arlington State. I majored in engineering. And I guess it's a good thing I did because that set me down a path to AT&T and General Motors. If I'd gone down some other road, life could have turned out a lot different.

My decision to go for an engineering degree, like so many other watershed moments in my life—and I guess this is true for most people—had a lot to do with luck and timing. My high school math teacher, Mr. Blair, was a big influence. He was also a football coach at Ennis High. Unlike a lot of football coaches, who are teachers in title only, Mr. Blair was a teacher first and foremost. He cared about academic achievement, always going the extra mile to help students learn and excel. And as a result, his students tried that much harder. At least I know I did.

I was a very average student in every other subject—history, chemistry, and English. But in Mr. Blair's math class I regularly scored ninety and above. My senior year something remarkable happened: Mr. Blair pulled me aside one day to let me know he thought I had a good head for math and should consider "doing something with that" in college. Maybe engineering, he said, because that was a field with a lot of numbers attached to it.

I'd never had a teacher tell me I was good at *anything*, so that got my attention. I blinked hard and mumbled something like, "Really?" Just to make sure he wasn't joking. Mr. Blair looked right at me and said, "Yeah, really," or something like that. So I knew he was serious. A simple exchange, I know, but it got me thinking.

Well, one thing led to another, and I decided to major in engineering. I didn't have any better ideas, to be honest—up to then I'd always figured I'd be working for the railroad. I also thought engineering would give me a good shot at finding a job after graduation—a steady paycheck was all I was after, really. And I sort of liked the idea of calling myself an "engineer," I will admit—thought it sounded sort of cool. I still thought about the railroad now and again; most of my friends planned to work for Southern Pacific after high school. But I'd promised Mother I'd give college my best shot, so engineering it was.

A friend of mine from Ennis—Billy Ranton, we went to high school together—was also going to Arlington State. So we decided to room together. I had no car; he had no car. And we had no money. So our weekly routine was this: Every Sunday, either his mother or my mother, or his daddy or my daddy, would drive us over to Arlington and drop us off—it's about an hour's drive from Ennis. Then somebody would come back Friday afternoon, after class let out, and pick us up. During the week we lived on campus—Billy and I were in Room 104 at Davis Hall, I will always remember that. As college life goes, there wasn't much to it. We were never on campus long enough to make many friends, so we had a commuter's existence, and that was pretty much it.

Billy had a girlfriend, at least. I didn't. I also had no social life in Ennis; most of my friends weren't around on weekends, because they were all working for the railroad. I don't know if it was half or a third, but a big portion of my high school class worked there. So I wasn't really enjoying my weekends in Ennis. And I wasn't enjoying college life in Arlington. I also didn't feel like I was learning very much. I didn't know what college life was supposed to be like, exactly, but I figured it wasn't this. So that got me to thinking.

Will Rogers, the great American humorist, had this famous quote: "If you find yourself in a hole, the first thing to do is stop digging." That was me—stuck in a hole that was getting bigger by the day. So I stopped digging. At the end of my first year at Arlington State, I decided to transfer to the state school in Lubbock. Today it's called Texas Tech University, and it's one of the finest state-supported schools in the country. Back when I was going it was called Texas Technological College, but everybody called it Texas Tech—still do. And it was, and still is, located on the south plains of West Texas. That's almost four hundred miles from Ennis. Even on a good day that drive can take you five and a half hours. Throw in rain and heavy traffic and it can take a lot longer than that.

The implications of my decision to transfer to this school were huge. Because of the distance, I'd have to move to Lubbock and live there full-time. So no more commuting home on weekends, and no more hanging on to what was left of my old life in Ennis. Daddy said it was okay by him if I wanted to transfer to Lubbock, but he was very clear about who would be paying the tuition: *me.*

"I'm not helping you," he told me point-blank. "I'm not buying you a car, not doing anything—you can do it on your own." Daddy didn't say this in a mean way, just matter-of-factly.

His firm line did not sit too well with Mother. They never fussed about this in front of me, but I learned later that they did have some words. Those exchanges, as I understand it, went something like this:

Mother: "Why don't you help him get a car?"
Daddy: "Well, he can get one on his own."
Mother: "Why don't you encourage him?"
Daddy: "Well, I told him he could go to Lubbock if he wanted to."

And so on.

Why Daddy had that reaction, I really don't know. I do know that he loved me—I never questioned that. But I also think, in his own way, that he was telling me something about life: *It's a tough world out there and you'd better figure it out.* And you know what? He was right. Life is tough; at times it can even be harsh. But it can also be pretty wonderful, and quite rewarding. The trick, I think, is being willing to push yourself outside your comfort zone once in a while, so you can see the sort of stuff you're made of. Otherwise you'll never know. In other words, give it a try. Things might not work out on the first try—or even the second or third. But if you hang in there, try to learn from your mistakes, and apply that to the next situation you run up against, you'll build knowledge, build confidence, and do a lot better picking your spots. There's an old saying in Texas: *Keep it between the ditches.* That's a shorthand way of telling you to take care of yourself out there—whether you're driving a car, figuring out the direction of your life, or running your business.

I was in the ditch right then, no question. And there's only one thing to do when you find yourself in a fix like that—figure out an exit strategy. My most immediate challenge was money. I got lucky. A friend of mine in Ennis happened to know somebody at the Rix funeral home in downtown Lubbock. In addition to the full range of funeral services, Rix also provided general transport services to local hospitals. Rix needed a driver. And I needed money, so I hustled up and got my chauffeur's license. I got the job.

My duties were pretty straightforward: I was responsible for driving Rix's emergency ambulance to accident scenes, homes, other places, picking up people and taking them to the local hospital or wherever they wanted to go. Occasionally I also had to retrieve victims at accident scenes and deliver them to the funeral home. But most of the time, thankfully, the people I picked up had plenty of life left in them. On the plus side, the job gave me a lot of time to study because I only got called when somebody had to go to the hospital or there was a bad wreck. On the downside, the money wasn't very steady. And waiting around for bad things to happen—car accidents, heart attacks, and so on—isn't the most inspiring way to spend your time. After a year or so I started looking for another job.

I got one pretty quick, at Gristy's Cleaners in downtown Lubbock. Tim Gristy, the owner, hired me. The thing I remember most was that dry-cleaning smell; it's from all the naphtha they used to dry-clean clothes. It's a petroleum-based cleaning solvent, has a really distinctive odor. Gristy's had huge washing machines. Instead of soap and water, they'd be full of naphtha. I'd stand there for hours and load clothes into those machines. Once they were done, the ladies who worked at Gristy's would iron all this stuff, then hang everything up in plastic bags. I'd load those bags into an old VW microbus—it belonged to Gristy's—and start delivering them to people all over town. That was my routine for a couple of years: I'd go to school from eight in the morning to noon, and work at Gristy's from two in the afternoon to about eight or nine at night.

During summer breaks I lived at home in Ennis and worked full-time. (Mother still had some of that $750 left over, but not

much.) My first two summers—that would have been my fresh-
man and sophomore years—I worked for Red Arrow Freight
Lines. It was a big trucking outfit that hauled in stuff for local
merchants. These eighteen-wheelers would roll in to the load-
ing docks and a bunch of us would scramble around to unload
whatever it was they happened to be carrying that day—
furniture, dresses, appliances, whatever. It was hard physical
labor, but it was also a steady paycheck.

My junior year, right after Christmas, I was headed home for
the winter break. A fraternity brother asked me if I'd give a ride
to a friend of his sister's. The friend lived in Fort Worth. I had to
go through there anyway to get home, so I said sure. So I went
over to pick up this girl at her dorm, and out came Linda Lawrence: five-foot-seven, dark hair, fair skin, big doe-brown eyes.
And she was wearing these wheat-colored jeans—man, did she
look good in those jeans. Linda just sort of looked at me and
smiled. And I thought to myself: *Well, this isn't going to be too
bad.* I was seeing another girl at the time, so I didn't ask Linda
out. But she definitely left an impression.

By the time the spring break rolled around, I was no longer
seeing that girl, but Linda was still very much on my mind. I was
headed home to Ennis, so I called up Linda to see if she might
need another ride. She said okay, so off I went to Linda's dorm
to pick her up. I had a 1957 Ford at the time; it was green and
white with a crack in the windshield and no air-conditioning.
Linda came out with all these duffel bags. She was taking an art
class, so she had sacks of paints with her. When I loaded the
car, I made sure to shove those paints as far up under the seat as
I could get them, where she'd never be able to reach. I was still
a little on the shy side, so I had not yet asked her out. I wanted
a reason to go see her again, and I figured the paints would do
the trick. And they did, I guess, because we started dating on a
regular basis not too long after that.

That summer—this was still my junior year—I planned to

work for Red Arrow again. But I happened to see a job posting on a bulletin board at school, and it caught my eye: Southwestern Bell was offering paid summer internships in Dallas. I was intrigued. I knew the company by name, of course; everybody did. Southwestern Bell was part of AT&T; that was one of the biggest corporations in the world—at the time AT&T had close to one million employees. Southwestern Bell was well known locally, because it provided phone service throughout Texas, including Ennis.

I didn't know the first thing about the phone business, but I liked the idea of working for a big, respected company like that. I had no idea what sort of work the job entailed. But I figured it couldn't be any worse than unloading freight all day long in the Texas sun. So I decided to give it a shot. That night I sat down and wrote a letter to the hiring manager—Frank Witten was the name on the ad—and told him I was interested. To my surprise, Mr. Witten agreed to see me. So I drove into Dallas to see him.

Mr. Witten was a crusty but gentle white-headed guy. Chain-smoked the whole time. He was friendly but also direct: "We don't have any jobs left," he told me point-blank.

I had just driven forty miles to see Mr. Witten. And I really wanted that job. So I was not in the mind to take no for an answer.

"You don't understand, Mr. Witten," I said, leaning forward to press my case. By then I'd shot up to six-foot-four, so my frame easily filled the chair. "I have *got* to have this job."

Mr. Witten seemed a little surprised, but he held his ground: "Well, we don't have any jobs," he repeated, stern but still friendly. By now, he'd stopped puffing on his cigarette long enough to sort of stare at me. And I could tell what he was thinking: Who *is* this kid?

I was like a dog with a bone at this point, and I wasn't letting go.

"But you don't understand, Mr. Witten," I said, coming back

for Round Two. "I have *got* to get a job. I don't have any money and I have one more year to go in Lubbock, so I really do need this job."

My argument was weak as water, but I delivered it with as much conviction as a Baptist preacher at one of Mother's Bible retreats. I was basically begging for a job. I knew it, but I didn't care. I wanted that job. I *needed* that job. Red Arrow was looking less and less interesting by the second. And the fact that Mr. Witten was telling me no just made me want it that much more.

We went one more round after that. Mr. Witten again insisted there were no jobs to be had—they'd all been assigned to other students. I again insisted that he clearly did not understand the gravity of my situation. I lost that round, too. But I could also tell that my gumption left an impression. Right before I left, I wrote down my phone number and asked Mr. Witten to call me if any jobs opened up. He sort of smiled at that, and said okay.

Mr. Witten called me back the very next day.

"Okay," he said, trying to sound gruff but not doing a very good job of it. "How'd you like to be a student engineer for the summer?"

Then I heard my salary: around $60 a week. Plus free telephone service and a credit for $5 a month in long-distance. I was thrilled.

"I won't disappoint you," I promised him. Mr. Witten didn't say a whole lot, but I could practically hear him smiling through the phone.

As a "student engineer" I mostly worked on smaller jobs: putting up telephone poles, staking and driving cables, digging ditches; I also got to climb a few telephone poles and learned the finer points of getting to the top without falling off. So nothing too big and important, as far as high-end telephone engineering goes. But I loved every minute of it. Loved the company, loved the people, loved the feeling it gave me to tell my friends and family that I was working for one of the most admired companies in America, just loved it—period.

The people of Southwestern Bell—that was the best part. My boss that summer was a fellow by the name of Lloyd Davis. He was the head engineer, big, robust guy. Mr. Davis was a pretty keen observer of people. He could figure out pretty quick if somebody was good, sincere, and accurate—or not. And he'd talk to me about that. I listened closely to everything Mr. Davis told me. Threw out some, but kept the rest in my head.

That summer I spent a lot of time with linemen, repairmen, cable splicers, other craftspeople. I could tell that they really cared a lot: about the company, the quality of their work, customers, and each other. Nobody preached that at me—you could just see it in their faces and hear it in their voices. Work, for them, wasn't just a job—it was a real point of pride. These workers were a part of something that mattered to them, something they were proud to talk about with their friends and neighbors; something that made them feel good inside. Just like the railroad was for my daddy. That was an eye-opener for me. All I'd been looking for was a steady paycheck. Instead I wound up finding my heartbeat and a brand-new direction in life.

I learned something else that summer: I really didn't want to be an engineer. It's fine and important work, no question. Without engineers, buildings don't get built, roads don't get laid, lots of things don't happen. But I also knew—and my experience that summer confirmed as much—that sitting in a cubicle working with numbers and blueprints just wasn't my calling. I wanted to be around people. My shyness was still there—and still is, to some degree. But by then it was no longer ruling my life. And the truth of the matter was, I enjoyed being around people. I liked talking to them, seeing what made them tick. I wanted to be part of a crew and a team that accomplished something. Didn't matter what it was, really, I just wanted to do something—anything—that had me working shoulder-to-shoulder

with people toward a common goal, be it putting up a telephone pole or changing the world.

By the time I headed back to Lubbock for my last year
of school, Southwestern Bell was fully on my mind. I got an
appointment with a local manager, Ward Wilkinson. He was a
former all-American football player, responsible for all of West
Texas. I told him I was interested in a part-time job while I was
still in school. Mr. Wilkinson was friendly enough but told me
he only had full-time, salaried positions. What I knew about the
phone business could fill a thimble, to be honest. But I'd also
gotten better at stating my case: "I'll do you a heck of a job for
half a day if you'll hire me," I told him. I probably sounded a
little desperate—and I was. But I also had a lot of enthusiasm,
and that probably came through, as well.

He hired me—as a lineman with some engineering responsibilities. That gave me my second exposure to the people and
culture of Southwestern Bell. And once again, I loved it. The
guys I worked with were pretty good-natured about it. They'd
say, "Okay, college boy, where you want us to put this?" No matter what I told them, somebody would usually start ribbing me
about something. I'd rib them right back. I'd say, "Okay, Joe"—or
whatever the guy's name was—"if you don't think that's where
the pole should go then you put it where you want it and I'll tell
you if I think it will fall down or not." I'd grown up in a union
environment, so I understood the humor and where they were
coming from. That felt pretty familiar to me. And I liked that
feeling, a lot.

As for Linda Lawrence, the gal with the paints (and the
wheat jeans), that turned out to be a lucky break, too. We dated
for a year and a half and got married—on August 8, 1964—at a
church wedding in Fort Worth. I still had that green Ford, and
it still had that crack in the window. We recently celebrated our
forty-seventh wedding anniversary, so I guess she didn't mind
too much.

CHAPTER 7

(Good) Vibrations

Management styles in America today are all over the map. Some of these approaches are pretty effective, or at least can be, in my view. Others are neutral at best, which ultimately defeats the point of good management: to *manage* your business. Some are downright harmful.

With some CEOs, it's all about the "numbers." I'm referring to the financial benchmarks that Wall Street analysts look at when they are evaluating your company as an investment opportunity. Things like revenue, net profit, share price, earnings per share, dividend history, and anything you're doing, or even contemplating doing, that might negatively affect any of that. Big acquisitions that have a lot of zeros attached to them—as in billions—*really* get their attention, because deals of that size can easily affect those other numbers. Sometimes it's a short-term hit—just a few days. Other times, depending on the size of the deal, the financial effects can last for years.

For this reason, some CEOs won't do a deal—any deal—if the numbers don't work out perfectly on paper. Their concern, basically, is that the negative effects of the transaction will outweigh the benefits over the long term. There's no way to know, with 100 percent certainty, how things will play out over the long term, of course, so at the end of the day you're always rolling the dice whenever you do a big, potentially dilutive deal. These CEOs just aren't willing to take that risk, and no amount of discussion will move them off the dime. And I can certainly understand why they feel that way, because it is not easy to sit there and watch your stock price get pounded because some analyst or reporter has decided that the deal you just announced and spent months pulling together is no good. Billions of stockholder value can get siphoned off in a single day—a single *hour* in some cases. That is rough stuff, let me tell you.

Other CEOs are all about productivity—Six Sigma comes to mind. If you're not familiar with that term, Six Sigma is a set of management principles that use a lot of statistics and employee productivity measurements to let you know how you're doing. Originally it was a set of quality-control practices designed by Motorola in the 1980s to reduce manufacturing defects. As time went by and more companies started using it, Six Sigma evolved into something with wider application. Today all sorts of companies use it.

Earnings per share, also known as your EPS, is a key measure with the Six Sigma crowd. Management sets the target, then does whatever it takes to hit that number. The approach varies a lot by company, but one thing is pretty consistent: Employees get measured against a series of performance benchmarks, and if they don't meet the bar they can get fired or reassigned. By continually whacking the poorest performers—this is an ongoing process—companies wind up with the cream-of-the-crop employees, or so the theory goes.

Some CEOs are always tweaking and tricking. They're all about the management theorem of the day; the goal is to make their companies look good on paper, and they'll try just about anything if they think it will attract investors. There's really no cohesive strategy or vision; that would require careful thought and an actual game plan. With this group, it's more about making a fast buck and seeing what they can get away with. I am not naming names here for obvious reasons, but believe me when I tell you—corporate America has plenty of these types.

Then there are the CEOs who try to outrun the market—they're always selling off underperforming assets and making new acquisitions to make their balance sheets look good. One sure sign of a company in this mode is constant deal churn; it just never stops. On the plus side, nonstop deal making allows these companies to show consistent growth. That's no small thing, because EPS is a very important performance measure in the investment community—this wraps back to the "numbers" I talked about a little earlier. These CEOs have a hard focus on the numbers. Everything they do, in fact, is geared to those numbers. Everything else tends to take a backseat.

So here's my take on all this, in order:

The numbers never work. When you're looking at numbers in the context of a big transaction, what you're looking at, really, is a financial snapshot at a *specific moment in time.* And that's it. What those numbers don't tell you is what that snapshot might look like after that asset—the one you are buying—is attached to your company. That's a big distinction. It's a vision of what's *going* to happen once this asset has good management, inspired people, and lots of capital, as opposed to "This thing is never going to amount to much because the numbers don't work *right now,* and there's not a thing we can do about that."

When I was at AT&T, I only asked myself two questions whenever we had a big deal on the table: One, *What can we make out of this asset we're about to buy?* And two, *Does it have the possibility to become more than what the current numbers are suggesting?* I never concerned myself with the numbers too much. And the truth is, never have I done a deal where the numbers worked—never. On paper, at least, the companies or assets we were looking at always had something wrong with them—they were too expensive or too compromised, had lackluster growth, or didn't fit our established business model. Every single deal. Including the deal we did with Apple for the iPhone—that one basically turned the traditional cell phone model upside down.

Don't get me wrong—we never ignored the numbers. We just didn't use them as our sole guidepost. We also didn't focus on the next quarter, or even the next year—we were always thinking about how things might look five years down the road, and well beyond. In other words, we never let the short-term numbers cloud our long-term view of where we thought the business was headed. And because of that, we were often willing to do things, and try things, that a lot of other companies wouldn't. And in the long term I do think that worked to our benefit, because we were able to turn the smallest of the seven Bells into the largest telecommunications company in the world. As for the iPhone, that turned out to be one of the smartest wireless deals we ever made. And I'll tell you why a little later.

Six Sigma puts the onus on employees—not the CEO or management. One of my core beliefs, as I have said before, is that management is 100 percent responsible for what happens to a business. With Six Sigma, senior management is responsible for setting the "vision," but it's up to employees, ultimately, to deliver. That's a very handy way to pass the buck, it seems to me. Because no matter how off-track the strategy or vision is, or how badly *management* performs, senior managers don't get the blame—employees do. Not fair. Employees aren't making the big calls about vision and the direction of the company. They're also not the ones who create the environment inside a company that allows people to be successful and perform well—that's management's responsibility.

My orientation: Make everything right with the people, and the numbers will show up at the end. You have to make your processes right and spend money to get all this stuff in order, of course. But taking care of your people is number one. As for using the threat of firing as a way to get people to deliver for you—give me a break. I can't think of a faster way to inspire fear and shatter confidence than to constantly dangle the threat of a pink slip in front of somebody's face. And it completely ignores the responsibility of management to cultivate a work environment that inspires people to be successful and do their best work. In my organization, if employees are consistently falling short I'm not going to look at the employees—I'm going to take a long, hard look at those managers.

Gimmicks—that's a loser's game. This, to me, is just common sense, but I'll say it anyway: If you're not treating your business as a serious, long-term proposition, then you've got bigger problems than trying to figure out which flavor of management strategy to use. Business is 99 percent about people; people are 99 percent about human interactions and relationships—and the strongest relationships, in life and in business, are built on a strong foundation of trust. You can't build trust by tricking and tweaking, and you can't build a business, either. Enough said.

Growth by acquisition has its place, but at some point you actually have to run your business. CEOs who buy, buy, buy with no real vision or strategy in mind can quickly end up with a big operational mess on their hands. It's also hard on your people, because they're the ones who have to make all this stuff work. But these CEOs really don't care about the people part of their business—all they care about is the numbers. Too often, though, they achieve their numbers at a great cost, it seems to me. Because what they wind up with, over time, is a disenfranchised workforce and a bunch of discombobulated assets that don't hang together very well. That's a financial snapshot nobody wants. Plus, it's just not sustainable. Nonstop deal making just wears people down.

When I was CEO of AT&T, I was sometimes accused of using

acquisitions to fuel our growth. And I really can't disagree with that top-line assessment, because we did, in fact, do a lot of big deals. But we never forgot about the people part; that was always at the front of our minds. Employees, I believe, felt pretty good about what we were doing because they were part of something they were proud of, something that had meaning to them. As we got bigger, that translated into a lot of opportunities for our employees—for new jobs, new challenges, new rewards. That's one reason we always promoted from within: It was a way to say thanks to people for all their hard work. Investors felt pretty good, too, because they wound up making a lot of money. And I was glad they did, because without their risk capital, we couldn't have executed on our long-term business strategy.

AT&T was not a Six Sigma company, and we never used gimmicks. We delivered results the old-fashioned way: by sticking to our vision and executing as best we could. AT&T's investor relations department was kind enough to run some numbers for me recently, and here's what they found: If you'd invested $10,000 in Southwestern Bell in January 1990, the year I was named CEO, it would have been worth $50,342 in June 2007—that's when I stepped down. (By then the company was called AT&T.) That's a 403 percent increase. This assumes that you reinvested dividends, and held on to all shares, which split multiple times during that seventeen-year period. There are lots of ways to slice and dice our numbers, but my basic point is this: we did okay.

I didn't do much of that on my own, of course—no CEO ever does. We got there thanks to a lot of hard work by a lot of dedicated people. Everybody contributed: telephone installers, people who worked in our wireless business, marketing folks, network experts, the crews who kept our phone lines in shape, the people who answered the phones when customers had problems, thousands of others. Senior management drove the vision and set the business strategy. And we did our best to create a good environment for people. But the actual execution of the strategy—that was all employees. *Management was 100 percent responsible*, to be clear. If things messed up, and occasionally that happened, that was our fault—not employees'.

Business, for me, has always been about the people. It goes back to a basic feeling I have that 99.99 percent of people want to feel successful and that they're making a contribution to something that has meaning to them. In the case of GM, I wanted those employees to feel that they had a big part in the company's turnaround—because they did. Same thing at AT&T. My point is this: Employees work hard to make good things happen in business; they will if you show respect and treat them right, at least—this has been my experience over the years. That's one reason I've always been a fan of paying people more, not less, when you can. I never wanted anybody to feel like we were beating them down just to save a dollar an hour, or they had to come to work in a prison every day. Deep down inside people just want to feel that they made something good happen in their lives, something that made them proud. That's just human nature.

The biggest mistake managers make, I think, is ignoring, or not recognizing this need in people—it just goes right over their heads. For whatever reason, they operate without the inputs of the people around them, like they just don't care what employees think or how they're feeling. I don't think these sorts of managers dislike workers, necessarily—well, some of them probably do, but that's another discussion. For the most part, I think they're just incapable of relating to people on a human-to-human basis. The best bosses and managers make an art of relating to people. It is most important to do this in business, because people aren't a commodity—they're a treasure to be cared for and looked after.

The importance of treating people right got rooted with me early, starting with my very first job at Southwestern Bell. Like anyone starting out, I had my share of mess-ups—had some doozies, in fact. But I also learned from my many mistakes, or tried to anyway. Those lessons stayed with me.

I graduated from Texas Tech in 1964, with a degree in engineering. By then, as you know, I'd already decided I really didn't want to be an engineer—I wanted a job that put me in contact with people. So Southwestern Bell put me on a management track, just to see how I'd do. But they put me on the "plant" side of the business—the part that deals with the phone network—so my job still had an engineering flavor to it. Back then, Southwestern Bell was part of the Bell Telephone System, known universally as "Ma Bell." AT&T was the corporate head of the family; it only sold long-distance service. The Bells sold local phone service, so that was my main focus: maintaining our local phone networks.

My very first job was installation foreman in Mesquite, Texas, a suburb of Dallas. "Foreman" was an entry-level management position, and it had me overseeing local installation crews—repairmen, linemen, cable splicers, other craftsmen. Some of these guys were pretty salty. They were also a lot older than me and had tons of experience—twenty years or more, in some cases. I was just shy of twenty-two, with a grand total of eighteen months' experience, most of that part-time. And I was their boss. So I had my work cut out for me.

Plant work is technical, also very physical. If you're in this line of work, you're going to wind up, at some point, with a shovel in your hand digging ditches. Or with a hard hat and safety gear on climbing some telephone pole—they're forty feet tall, on average, but some poles are double that. Utility poles have high-voltage lines attached to them, so climbing these things is a lot more involved than you might think. On the ground, linemen are always rooting around in the dirt trying to repair some busted phone line—that's a big part of the job, repairing busted lines. You come across all sorts of things—gas lines, water mains, historical artifacts. And dogs sometimes don't take it too kindly when you start digging up their bone-yards. So you're always dealing with something, it seems.

My big boss, two levels up, was Charles Isom. He was an older guy who'd been with Southwestern Bell for thirty years or so. Mr. Isom was highly knowledgeable about plant work, which impressed me. But he was a people person first and fore-most, which impressed me even more.

I got my first lesson in managing people shortly after I arrived. I had a crew working late trying to repair a cut cable. It was a difficult repair, so it was taking a long time to fix. By then it was close to dark, and the guys still weren't even close to being done. I was in the work center, back in Mesquite, monitoring the whole thing by phone. (No Internet or cell service in those days.)

Mr. Isom came by my office and asked me for an update on the situation. So I told him. He sort of leveled an eye at me—said okay, let's take a ride and go look. So we jumped in his car and drove out to the job site—it was way out in the country, fifteen or twenty miles. When we got there, we both hopped out of the car and started walking around. A couple of minutes later, I looked around—Mr. Isom was gone. His car was gone; he'd left me there. And I didn't have a ride back. I got the message instantly: *You might be the boss, but you're still part of a team.* Needless to say, I stayed out there until that job was done, then rode back to the office with the guys in the work truck. Didn't sleep for a whole week thinking about what I'd done—I felt awful, like I'd let down Mr. Isom, and let down my crew. I never forgot that les-son or leadership principle. And I never did that again.

Mr. Isom, like all good bosses, was a keen observer of people. One time, he happened to read a story in the newspaper about a guy in Fair Park—that's in east Dallas—who was starting an after-school program for kids from low-income families. Mr. Isom swung by my office to tell me this, and said he was going to drive over to Fair Park to meet this guy to "see if he's for real"—or words to that effect. I asked him why he didn't just call on the phone; it would have been a lot easier, and safer, it seemed to me. Fair Park was a pretty rough neighborhood at the time.

He had his reasons: Mr. Isom said he wanted to look the guy straight in the eyes when he was talking to him, because that's the only way he could know for sure if the man was sincere, or if he was just trying to pull a fast one. That made me stop and think, I will say. Mr. Isom told me later he wound up talking to that guy for an hour. He decided the guy was for real, so he contributed $100 to the program.

The lesson I learned? *Go see for yourself.* Make your own determinations by talking to people, face-to-face. Not by emailing, or by calling on the phone, or with a memo. Talking eyeball-to-eyeball sometimes takes a little more effort, or even a lot more effort, depending on the circumstances. But the payback is so much greater—you can pick up things you'd never get over the phone, or with an email.

That's one reason I was never a big email guy, to be honest. I always want to see what a person's eyes and body language are saying. With an email, you don't know what people's reaction is when they read it. But if I'm standing there looking them dead in the eye, I know instantly. I've always had computers, always had the latest wireless devices—I have an Apple iPhone now; I'm never without it, even when I'm out hunting. But when it comes to having meaningful interactions with people, I'm an eyeball-to-eyeball sort of guy. Simple, straightforward conversation, face-to-face—there is no replacement for that. I've had that reinforced to me a thousand times over the years. But Mr. Isom was the first one who drove that home for me.

Some years later, after I got a little higher up in the company, I had the privilege of promoting Mr. Isom's grandson to become our head network guy in Connecticut. He had the same qualities as his grandfather: strong work ethic, believed in getting things done. And great with people, just like Mr. Isom—I could never bring myself to call him Charlie, even after I got to be CEO.

Another great boss was Bob Pope. I was working in Arkansas as a division plant manager, overseeing local phone networks, and he was the chief engineer in Houston. A chain-smoker, Bob was about ten years older than me. We had never worked together directly; I only knew him by reputation at the time. But we wound up meeting—Bob asked me to give a presentation to a group of engineers about a work productivity measurement program called the E5400 that was a big deal in the Bell System. It was crazy complicated; lots and lots of numbers. Bob told me afterward I was the first person who'd ever been able to explain it in a way that he could understand—which always sort of amazed me, because Bob was one of the smartest guys I've ever met. I later went to work for him, and we eventually became lifelong friends.

Bob was not what you'd call a "people person," but he was a very astute *observer* of people, and particularly astute when it came to corporate politics. I was never very good at that stuff, myself—I always tried to avoid it as best I could. Bob was an engineer by training, but his real talent was problem solving: He could dissect a problem faster, and cleaner, than just about anybody I've ever met.

He eventually became the vice chairman of Southwestern Bell under Zane Barnes, who was the CEO at the time. Even then, Bob continued to keep an eye out for me. I had many mentors over the course of my career, but Bob was just special. We used to go fishing; we'd spend the entire day throwing lines and talking, mostly about work. I learned a lot from Bob over the years—about people, corporate dynamics, a lot of other intangibles that figure into management. And he learned a thing or two from me, too—I basically taught him how to fish. He turned out to be a pretty good fisherman.

Part of being a good boss means you have to be firm, but fair. Mr. Isom taught me that, too—like when he left me out at that job site. Being firm doesn't mean you bully people or treat them disrespectfully. Bob, same thing. He could be a very tough taskmaster—Bob had pretty high standards. But he was fair with his people. I always tried to do the same.

Part of my job as foreman was to make sure the daily workload got done on time. Because if it didn't get done on time, we'd run into overtime, which was a lot more expensive for the company, time and a half. Crews were aware of this, of course, and they liked overtime. I'd sometimes see an installation truck sitting outside some coffee shop; I'd ride around for a few minutes and come back, and if it was still there I'd walk inside and drag those guys out of there. I say "drag," but it was more like nudging them out the door in a firm but friendly way. These guys would moan and groan when I caught them, but nobody ever got mad or upset. And the reason, I think, was because we were all friends and trusted each other, so we could have those sorts of exchanges without tempers getting riled. That's just human nature: If somebody likes you, and respects you, you can have pretty honest exchanges. If they don't, you can sugarcoat things all day long and they still won't listen to you. That, also, is human nature.

With most employees, a little compassion goes a long way. I found that out firsthand, too, because I messed up so many times it was unbelievable. One time, I was pulling out of a company parking lot and hit my boss's car; caved in the entire side of it. I was mortified, as you might expect. As soon as I hit his car, I just sat there, sort of frozen, with my hands on the wheel. I was so embarrassed.

I didn't try to gloss it over. I went inside and found my boss, Mr. Lankford.

"Mr. Lankford," I said—by then beads of sweat had popped up on my forehead—"I just caved in the whole side of your car."

Those are the moments when seconds seem like hours, you know. Southwestern Bell was big on safety—that was a big part of my job, in fact. So I looked doubly stupid, and I knew it. Mr.

Lankford did, too, but he didn't say that outright. He just shook his head, said, "Don't worry, I'll get it fixed." I was so appreciative of that, and relieved. I never forgot that feeling.

Then there was the time my boss called and asked me to meet him at seven o'clock the next morning for breakfast. Well, I must've been really tired, because I slept straight through my alarm the next day, didn't wake up until seven thirty—missed the whole meeting. When I finally reached him later that morning, I was most apologetic. He was really nice about it—said, "Aw, forget it; it was kind of nice to have breakfast by myself. So let's just meet for lunch." In other words, he didn't beat me over the head with it. I always remembered that as well.

My work ethic got formed early, when I was growing up in Ennis. Mother used to tell me: If you're going to work for somebody, *work*. And as I got into my career, the wisdom of what she'd been telling me all along was pretty obvious: If you want to get ahead, you come in early, stay late, and work hard. That shows you are ambitious, shows you want to get ahead. That means you don't come in an hour late, and leave an hour early, and try to convince your boss that you can do the job by working less. If you do that, you're viewed as a slacker: lazy and not too concerned about your job.

I always had the view that you should do what your boss asks you, so long as it isn't unethical or illegal, of course. Even if you don't think what he's asking you to do is important. Once, I had a boss ask me to give him a tally, by the hour, of dispatchable reports that came in—phone service complaints that required us to dispatch a crew to fix. I thought it was a dumb request—what difference did it make? But I did it. A week or so later, he told me the reason: He was trying to figure out the optimum number of repairmen he needed, by dispatch area, during regular business hours so he could cut overtime.

Ed's lightbulb on that? *Don't make assumptions.* People

sometimes have very solid reasons for the things they do, even though they might not seem so obvious to you at first. That's not to say that you shouldn't ask questions. But if your boss has been around for a long time, chances are good that he or she knows a thing or two, so have some respect, you know? Otherwise you can end up with your foot in your mouth real quick, and I should know because I've done that plenty of times, too.

During the early part of my career, I had the good fortune to have one of the best mentors ever: Austin McKinsey. He was a district-level plant manager in Dallas. I was a local foreman in that same facility; Austin was my boss. He'd started out as a lineman and worked his way up to management. I was twenty-four or so; Austin was in his early forties. I knew we were on the same wavelength as soon as we met.

Austin had a big job. He was responsible for all of South Dallas, including a district "test center"—that's where trouble reports for network outages, cut cables, and the like come in. Running a test center is very demanding, because people are calling twenty-four hours a day with problems that need fixing right away. It just never stops. As a test center foreman, it was my job to help analyze trouble reports and dispatch repair crews. Austin had overall responsibility for the test center, along with the rest of South Dallas.

Austin was quite a character: red hair, full of energy, could be quite emotional at times, particularly if he got riled up about something. And Austin was always riled up about something, mostly because he cared so much about the company and the people who worked for him. He was not universally liked—some people thought he was *too* enthusiastic. And he did not always follow the rules, which rubbed some people the wrong way.

And the Bell System had rules for just about everything you can imagine, from how big executive offices were supposed to be, in terms of square footage (the higher up the ladder you went, the bigger the office), to how far apart you space tacks when phone wires are being installed inside a residence (sixteen inches). There was a handbook for all this stuff; that was the Bell bible, and most people followed it to the letter. Not Austin. He was respectful of the company, but he also had his own way of looking at things, and doing things. I admired him for that.

As a boss and motivator, none was better: Austin had that rare combination of ambition, ability, passion, and people sense. With a big emphasis on people—Austin was a good observer of humanity. He understood people better than just about any manager I have ever met, before or since. But he also had a lot of humility as a boss. Austin didn't hold himself up high and mighty above everybody else. He thought of himself as a common man, and that came across. People responded to that and worked hard for him.

Austin and I used to spend hours talking about management theory—how important it is to have the right people in the right jobs, and how you figure that out. *Can this person learn and succeed?* That was always the number one thing Austin considered when he was looking at a job candidate—never the technical skills. Those things can be taught—that was his view. What Austin cared about most were the things that *can't* be taught, like character, attitude, willingness and ability to learn, ambition, and so forth. According to Austin, those were the things that separate high achievers from basic "plodders"—people who are happy doing their jobs, with no real interest in moving up the ladder.

Austin asked a lot of other questions before he made a hiring decision; none of it had to do with the person's credentials. Stuff like: *Is this a good guy?* (I'm using *guy* as a generic term here—this applies to men and women equally.) *Does he like people? Does he have a burning desire to get ahead? Can he walk up to you and have a conversation with you and not tick you off?* Some people can't do that, you know. *Does he think beyond the box—meaning, is he an independent thinker?* If Austin spotted something in you—enthusiasm, leadership ability, whatever it was he put together in his mind—he'd see to it that you got promoted into management. And it was not unusual for Austin to promote somebody who was a craftsman—blue collar—into management. Most Southwestern Bell managers had college degrees; Austin didn't, and he didn't really care if you did, either. But he understood the internal need most of us have to rise and do well in business. So if he thought you were good and deserved a shot, he'd find a way to make sure you got promoted, college degree or not.

Good bosses like Austin, Bob, and Mr. Isom lift you up; they push you in a good way and make you want to do your best. Bad bosses do just the opposite.

Bad bosses are not hard to spot, but you have to pay attention to the signs, or "vibrations," that people give you. And by "vibrations," I'm referring to the emotions and feelings that people throw off when they're talking about their jobs, their bosses, their ambitions, things that have meaning to them. Those vibrations come through not just in their words but also the tone of their voices, the amount of eye contact they're making, basic body language. When you talk with somebody who's got a bad boss and ask them how things are going, they'll usually lower their voice and come back with something pretty neutral—"It's okay," something like that. And meantime they're looking everywhere but right at you. That's the first sign that you've got a bad-boss problem on your hands.

And when I say "bad boss," I'm not referring to bad people. Some people are just not cut out to be managers; they don't have the bearing or people sense. Or they just have no desire to become a manager, which has a lot of inherent responsibility. That's a basic ambition issue. What I'm talking about is basically an office bully. He (or she) is just sitting on people, squeezing the life out of them. Nothing's ever good enough, nothing's ever done on time; there are no words of encouragement, no talking about life. No talk about where you want to go, or what you want to accomplish. No talk about "Is this exciting to you?" or giving people the authority and responsibility to get things done so they can get excited and enthused. That's what really turns most people on in business—to feel like they belong, that they can contribute and make something happen on their own. With bad bosses, nobody ever gets promoted or succeeds. After a while people lose faith and stop wanting to come to work in the morning. Bad bosses destroy people's confidence, destroy workplace productivity. I will not tolerate a bad boss. I am very attuned to things like this, always have been. I think I was just born that way. When I was at AT&T, and later at GM, I worried constantly—mostly about employees. I actually hurt if things weren't going right for them. Being so sensitive is a blessing and a curse. A blessing because when you care a lot you can spot things; you naturally detect things in people and situations that others might overlook. But it's also a curse, because you can lose a lot of sleep. When I was at GM, I spent so many nights staring at the ceiling. I just could not sleep a lot of nights, what with all those jobs on the line, the impact of our decisions on the families of people who worked at GM. I thought about that stuff nonstop.

That brings me to another core management belief: People will sometimes surprise you in wonderful ways if you let them. But for that to happen you have to be willing, as a manager, to step out of the way and let people show what they can really do. Talent doesn't always come in a nice, neat package with wing-tip shoes and a fancy college degree. Sometimes the roughest diamonds are the ones that shine the brightest. You just have to dig around a little more to find them.

I used to move people around all the time at AT&T, and later at GM, to see who could swim and who had lead weights on their ankles. I'd take a person from marketing and put her into an operational job, or swap out a person in communications and put him in a technical job. Or pluck somebody out of the management line three or four levels down and put her into a senior position. Sometimes they'd fall flatter than a pancake. But sometimes they'd do okay. And man, do people feel good about themselves when they do that. And that makes me feel good, as a manager, because part of my job—part of *every* manager's job—is to help people succeed and feel good about themselves.

Sometimes, if you're *really* lucky, you find a Stan Sigman.

Like me, Stan was an old telephone guy from Texas—West Texas, in Stan's case. He started out at Southwestern Bell as a stockman: loaded trucks by day, and cleaned the buildings and bathrooms at night. I never worked directly with Stan early on, but we were both on the plant side of the business, so I knew him by reputation. In 1985 I pulled Stan out of the network group in Odessa, Texas—that's out in the panhandle—and put him in charge of wireless. Back then the business was pretty small, around thirty-five thousand customers. Southwestern Bell Mobile—our wireless division—had a grand total of 236 employees.

Stan didn't know the first thing about wireless. But he was a fast learner, good with people, and full of enthusiasm. Stan knocked it out of the park. He eventually became the CEO of AT&T's wireless business, and was instrumental in getting us the iPhone deal—that was all Stan. And the iPhone turned out to be one of the smartest wireless deals we ever made.

CHAPTER 8

Buenos Días, San Antonio

Ann Richards, the late, great governor of Texas, was a friend of mine. She was a woman of strong opinions and strong character. And she was not shy about shaking things up. "I feel very strongly that change is good because it stirs up the system," she once said.

I'm with Ann on that. I am not a status quo guy. I don't know why that is in me, but if it ain't happening, I'm going to make it happen. That's not to say I go against the grain just to do it. I always have my reasons.

I became the chairman and CEO of Southwestern Bell in 1990. My appointment was announced in 1988, and it came as a big surprise to a lot of people—including me. I don't say that to be modest, it's just a fact—I really never saw it coming. At the time I was the chief financial officer of Southwestern Bell, which was then based in St. Louis—it had been there forever. The long-standing chairman and CEO, Zane Barnes, was getting ready to retire, and there was no debate as to who would succeed him: John E. Hayes.

John was the president of Southwestern Bell; good guy, smart, very capable. He was a good talker, polished. John had made his mark on the non-technical side of the business and

was widely admired for his ability to deal with politicians—
state governors knew him by name. He'd been born and
raised in Kansas City, so he had a solid Midwest sensibility
that meshed well with the locals. Around St. Louis, John was
hugely popular—everybody knew him and liked him. Inside
Southwestern Bell, same thing—John was a star. And *everybody*
expected him to become the next chairman and CEO of Southwestern Bell.

Then there was me.

I was a Texan from the plant side of the business, so I knew
a lot about running phone networks and telephone poles. But
not so much about politics or St. Louis society, just not my bag.
I was also a little rough around the edges; still am. Had a pretty
hard Texas twang; still do. Didn't particularly like talking with
reporters and politicians; didn't particularly like talking, period.
John was a few years older, so he had more experience than
me. And he had boatloads of personality, for sure. So the question of me versus John wasn't even on the table—it was a done
deal. Or so everybody thought, me included.

Twenty-four hours before the board vote on Zane's successor, I got a call. It was Zane. He asked me to come to his office,
because he had something important he wanted to discuss.

I was astounded by what he told me.

"I know this is going to upset some people," Zane started,
looking me dead in the eye, "and it may be hard for a while, but
you're the right choice to lead this company. So I've decided to
recommend to the board tomorrow that you be named my successor" as chairman and CEO of Southwestern Bell. Words to
that effect, I am paraphrasing from memory.

But I do remember this comment like it was yesterday:
You're the right choice to lead this company.

I couldn't believe what I was hearing. I probably had that
look dogs get when they're watching TV—you know that look?
They sort of cock their head to one side, like what they're see-

ing and hearing just isn't computing. That was me at that exact moment. After a few seconds, reality sank in: I felt elated, also grateful and incredibly honored.

"I will do my best to prove that what you did was the right decision," I said, fixing a stare straight back. "I want you to know that."

Zane, who was an old plant guy himself, seemed pleased by my response. And that was pretty much that. The next day, right after the board vote, my appointment as chairman and CEO was formally announced. Under the succession plan approved by the board, I'd be elevated to president and chief operating officer for a one-year transition period, and become chairman and CEO when Zane retired in 1990.

People were very surprised. And some of them were not too happy by my selection. *They picked the wrong guy* was pretty much the feeling. One senior executive told a good friend of mine, flat out, that Zane made a bad call. Not exactly the vote of confidence you'd hoped for in that circumstance, you know? All the second-guessing didn't make me feel too good inside, I will admit. But it didn't buckle my knees, either. I saw Zane a few days later and told him: "You picked the right guy." Zane didn't miss a beat: "I know it."

We never spoke of it again.

For his part, John was an absolute gentleman. Right after the board vote he came to my office to offer his personal congratulations. The irony of this situation wasn't lost on either of us: Just a few hours earlier, before the vote, he'd asked me to stay on after he became CEO, to help run Southwestern Bell. Now the vote was over, and I was the CEO—not John. I felt bad for him; I'm sure he was crushed. But it was what it was. So I asked John the same thing he'd asked me: to stay on after I became CEO and help run the company. John said he'd think about it, then turned on his heel and walked out. He resigned a few days later. I never saw or talked to him again. That was more than twenty years ago. That still makes me sad, I have to say. I always liked John, and admired him greatly.

So why did I get the job? The honest answer is: I don't know. I never really asked Zane directly, or anybody else for that matter—that would not have been proper, or respectful of the board's nomination process. Picking a CEO is a lot more subjective than you might think, and I know this because I've sat in on two CEO nominations, at AT&T and later at General Motors. But the bottom line is this: Boards, in general, tend to go with candidates they feel the most comfortable with at a given point in time; personal relationships also come into play. Business, as I have said, is 99 percent about people, and it's no different in the boardroom.

All that said, I do think—I know—a few people went to bat for me, like Bob Pope, my longtime friend and mentor, and the former vice chairman of Southwestern Bell. So did Zane, obviously. In addition to being a true gentleman, Zane was never shy about stirring things up. (Even though he grew up in Ohio, Zane had a lot of Texas in him.) And the Southwestern Bell board, of course, which made the final decision.

All these years later, I am still amazed, and humbled, by that turn in my life. I wasn't some Ivy League grad on the fast track to becoming CEO; I was Edward from Ennis. I grew up in a union family, liked to fish and hunt, and had a degree from a state school in Texas. I was married with two young daughters, and like everybody else I just wanted to do right by my family and my company. Deep down inside, I'm not so sure I even considered myself CEO material. Just the sound of that—"chief executive officer"—is a little rich for my blood, to be honest. Which is why I've never introduced myself as CEO, I guess. I've just never got comfortable saying that.

But the thing that stood out the most was this: If Zane and the board were willing to give me a chance, then I was going to do my best to stand and deliver. Not just for Zane and the board, but for the people of Southwestern Bell—all the thousands of faithful employees who were the heart, soul, and backbone of that company. I was one of them. By then I'd been chipping away at it for twenty-four years—twenty-five if you include my turn as a student engineer in Dallas. And I will never forget what that feels like, to be a salaried employee who's just trying to do a good job and earn a fair day's pay. That's a part of me I hold close, and always will.

As the chairman and CEO, things would be different. I'd have ultimate responsibility for the interests and welfare of South-western Bell and all the people who worked there—linemen, installers, middle management; the people who made decisions in the boardroom, the lunchroom, and the mailroom. Each was important in his or her own way; each deserved respect and consideration. I took that responsibility very seriously.

I was forty-eight when I got named Zane's successor, old enough to have a perspective on life and business. I'd also had my share of jobs—facility engineer, assistant vice president of engineering, president of Kansas, group president over wire-less and directory services, to name just a few. I had a short stint with AT&T—then called American Telephone & Telegraph Co.—in New York. My job with AT&T was not that exciting—I was basically responsible for making sure modular phones got introduced by Bells across the country in a standardized fash-ion. But it was a great learning experience. And on a human level, the AT&T job, and a number of others, helped confirm what I already knew inside: that I liked working with people, not processes. And I was not a status quo guy. I was naturally drawn to independent thinkers—people like Austin McKinsey, Mr. Isom, Bob Pope, Zane Barnes. I just related better to those types.

New York itself was quite an adventure, so I'll mention it here briefly. Linda and I bought a little house across the river in Millington, New Jersey. (No air-conditioning—big mistake.)

So every day I was on the subway, dodging people, messenger bikes, you name it. But over the year or so our family lived there we also made some good friends, went to our first clambake, and learned about calzones and other foods I'd never come across before. I'm a Texas guy at heart, though—so is Linda, she's from Fort Worth. So when I got a job offer from Southwestern Bell—in Arkansas—we packed up the girls and headed out.

My run as chairman and CEO began, as scheduled, in 1990. At the time, Southwestern Bell really didn't have a well-developed strategic vision. This owed more to history than anything else. Until 1984, the assets of Southwestern Bell and the other Bell operating companies—there were twenty-two of them originally—were owned by AT&T. Under that structure, AT&T set the strategic vision, decided revenue targets, everything. So Bell managers weren't expected to do much strategizing, and didn't have authority to implement any plans even if they did.

In 1984 all that changed: AT&T got broken up by a federal court decree, and those twenty-two Bell operating companies were assembled into seven "Baby Bells" and spun off as separate companies. (Southwestern was one of the seven, and the smallest by far.) AT&T kept long-distance and became a stand-alone business. Those seven Bells also became independent companies. The net result: Each of the seven Bells finally had its own stock, investors, directors, and CEO. And the freedom, for the first time ever, to set its own strategic vision and management style.

One thing didn't change: Bell culture. It was just as firmly entrenched after divestiture as it had been before. Status quo ruled.

I'd spent most of my adult life at Southwestern Bell, so I certainly understood the mind-set. But that doesn't mean it all agreed with me. To be honest, some of the Bell ways just rubbed me wrong, and had for years, particularly the parts that had to do with how regular employees got treated versus senior management.

In the Bell culture, higher-ups in the corporate food chain had always been treated like royalty. They had private dining rooms, cars and drivers, and liberal use of the corporate jets. At Southwestern Bell senior people also had designated elevators; regular employees were not allowed in them. And the elevators that employees used were programmed to give higher-ups special treatment. So if a telephone installer got in and punched 10, and a senior executive got in and punched 42, the elevator would bypass the tenth floor and go directly to the forty-second. In addition, employees were not allowed to visit the upper floors, where senior officers were, unless expressly invited.

This stuff had never set too well with me; it just wasn't the right message to be sending our employee body. It was also inconsistent with what we were telling people: to be mindful of budget and do things in a cost-efficient manner, because we now had investors to answer to. How did that square with us having a line of cars and drivers waiting out front to take Joe Blow over to some appointment? It didn't. I could drive myself, and always had. They could do the same thing.

And why did executives need a private dining room? Or separate elevators—that's just ridiculous. Another thing: Why can't senior executives answer their own phones? I'd been doing that for years, and I had no plans to change now that I was CEO. So that's what I told everybody: "If you're in the office and your phone rings, pick it up!" Not so hard, right? We're all salaried workers at the end of the day, so don't forget that—that's basically what I was telling everybody. I wanted our managers to be *closer* to employees, and that sort of stuff—special elevators, private dining rooms, special this, special that—just drives people apart. It creates "haves" and "have-nots," and the gulf between those two is wide, especially if you're on the other side of the big glass window looking in. And I'd been on that side most of my life, so I knew what that felt like.

When I was a kid in Ennis, there was a local country club in town where all the well-to-do types belonged—doctors, lawyers, local business types. None of the daddies of my friends belonged. The people who did belong were good folks, I am sure, but they also had this air about them. I never forgot that. Special perks for senior executives was, to me, just another version of that: a way of telling people that they weren't as important. And that simply wasn't true. Southwestern Bell was one company, with one goal. And we all got our paycheck from the same place.

So I did away with all that stuff. I shut down the private dining room, cut way back on use of cars and drivers, had elevators reprogrammed, revoked flight privileges, and sold off most of our jets. You never heard such howling. You'd have thought I'd sawed somebody's arm off. And I was sorry that some of our senior managers felt that way, but I was far more concerned with making sure we sent the right message to employees. And getting rid of all that silly stuff was the first step.

I did keep one tradition, sort of: the annual holiday gift from the CEO. The custom, which started with AT&T and got passed along to the Bells, was for the CEO to give an expensive gift to senior officers every Christmas. Past gifts at Southwestern Bell had included some pretty pricey things: Waterford crystal, Gucci handbags for the ladies, TV sets. I thought a charitable donation made more sense. So the year I became CEO we gave to a local children's charity. I did give a gift to officers that first Christmas—a brown wooden box, made in the Philippines somebody told me, that held a double deck of playing cards. But that was the last time. I figured we were paying people enough that they could go out and buy their own gifts.

Honoring traditions that are a part of your corporate culture: That's important, don't get me wrong. I just don't think it's a

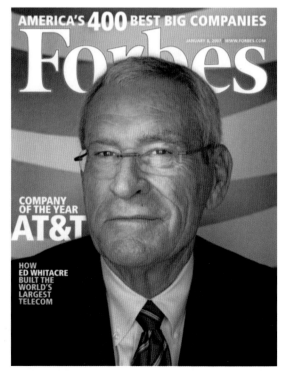

Ed and his team used deal making to expand SBC's footprint significantly in the 1990s. The buildup got a lot of attention and also created some controversy, as this *BusinessWeek* cover noted.

Entitled "Whitacre's Way," this cover story described how Ed and his team managed to turn the smallest of the "Baby Bells" into the largest telecom in the world. (By then the company was known as AT&T.) The piece appeared a few months before Ed announced his retirement, marking the end of his seventeen-year run as chairman and CEO.

Ed at three months old, being held by his mother, Lola (Courtesy of the Whitacre family)

Ed at age three (Courtesy of the Whitacre family)

Ed's father, Edward Earl Whitacre (Courtesy of the Whitacre family)

Ed's mother, Lola Whitacre (Courtesy of the Whitacre family)

John "Papa" Mooney, holding Ed (Courtesy of the Whitacre family)

Ed at age six (Courtesy of the Whitacre family)

Graduating from Texas Tech, 1964 (Courtesy of the Whitacre family)

Ed and Linda Whitacre on their wedding day, August 8, 1964 (Courtesy of the Whitacre family)

A portrait of Ed, then chairman and CEO of AT&T (Courtesy of Mark Katzman)

Ed (right) with (left to right) Jerry Blatherwick, Bob Pope, and Zane Barnes in a promotional shot for Southwestern Bell (© G. Robert Bishop, 1987)

Ed and Linda with
their daughters,
Jennifer (left) and
Jessica (Courtesy of
the Whitacre family)

A 1990 portrait of
Ed, then CEO of
Southwestern Bell
(Courtesy of Hank
Young/Young
Company)

With President
George H. W. Bush
(Courtesy of the
White House)

With President
Bill Clinton, First
Lady Hillary
Rodham Clinton,
and Linda at the
White House
(Courtesy of the
White House)

With President
George W. Bush,
First Lady Laura
Bush, and Linda
at the White
House (Courtesy
of the White
House)

As the new CEO
of General Motors
(Courtesy of GM)

Standing in front of
the Cadillac SRX
(Courtesy of GM)

With workers at McKinley Drilling, Ed's water-well company, in Pearsall, Texas (Courtesy of Alison Wright)

Ed with his dog, Lucille (Courtesy of Alison Wright)

Ed fishing with his grandson, Aaron (Courtesy of the Whitacre family)

At the dedication of the Edward E. Whitacre Jr. College of Engineering at Texas Tech (Courtesy of Texas Tech University)

TEXAS TECH UNIVERSITY

Edward E. Whitacre Jr.
College *of* Engineering™

good idea to go there with blinders on. You have to make sure the actions you're taking, and messages you're sending, are in sync with your current mind-set and business model. Holding steady with the status quo just because you don't know what else to do or you're afraid of rattling too many cages is never the answer. You can't grow a company if you treat it like some museum, and you're just hanging around as house curator trying to protect the historical assets. Legacy is important, yes. But it really has no place in the context of a business decision.

Which brings me to one of the most visible, and controversial, decisions I made early on as CEO: We pulled up stakes and left St. Louis. This was no small thing, because Southwestern Bell had been based in St. Louis for as long as there'd been a Southwestern Bell, and for a long time before that if you include the whole arc of development of the company, which traced its beginnings back to the old Missouri Bell Telephone Company and a couple of others. And that entity, then known as Southwestern Bell, had been in St. Louis for more than seventy years. The general expectation, by pretty much everybody, was that those roots were so deep that we'd be staying there forever. In other words, legacy was our destiny. I didn't see it that way. Our basic business problem was this: Thanks to the breakup of AT&T, we finally had the freedom to set our own strategic vision and follow wherever that took us. But to execute successfully we needed a fully engaged and energized workforce. And that was not going to happen so long as we stayed in St. Louis, I sadly determined.

How do I shake things up?

The answer, we concluded, was to move the company— guts, feathers, and all—a thousand miles away to San Antonio, Texas.

Why Texas?

For starters, about 60 percent of our revenue and customers were in Texas. It also had a growing Hispanic population and shared a border with Mexico. By then we were part owners of a majority stake in Mexico's national phone company, Teléfonos de México, or Telmex, so we had a big business interest in that community. In 1990 we partnered with a major financier in Mexico City, Carlos Slim—he's one of the most successful businessmen in the world—and France Telecom to buy the stake. So proximity to Mexico, going forward, was not insignificant.

But the biggest driver, by far, was the status quo: Things needed stirring up. *Dull, plodding*: That was the general vibe in our St. Louis headquarters. People routinely showed up late for work, and left early—I'd been watching this for years. A sense of entitlement permeated the upper ranks. That flowed down to the employee body, which didn't help morale or the general sense of excitement about the business. The bureaucracy was thick as mud, and it was *everywhere*. But people were firmly entrenched in their jobs. So there was no way to change that, or even beat it back all that much. You can't just walk out and fire people, and you wouldn't even if you could. But maintaining the status quo wasn't an option, either, because if we did that we'd never grow, never get to where we wanted to be as a company.

We briefly considered Dallas, but ultimately settled on San Antonio. It was a growing city of nine hundred thousand, offered plenty of affordable housing, had a nice airport just ten minutes from downtown. San Antonio also had a distinctly Southwestern air and attitude—the town is Texas tough, but welcoming of everybody. And the large Hispanic population— it's even larger today—gives it a warm, international flavor. That seemed like the perfect mix for our messaging and business strategy. Another plus: Only a few major corporations were based in San Antonio, so I figured we'd be special there. In Dallas, we'd just be one of many. Dallas was also a lot more expensive, had horrific traffic—a consideration for employees who commuted in—and the airport is a long haul, forty-five minutes from downtown on a good day.

We announced plans to leave St. Louis in September 1992, with the intention of being fully relocated by March 1993. Employees in our St. Louis headquarters were all invited to keep their jobs, but with the caveat that they'd have to move to San Antonio. I knew it would be a tough sell. But I also figured we'd find out, pretty fast, who was really committed to Southwestern Bell and who wasn't.

I did the first employee meeting, to talk about the move. It was held in the company auditorium. The place was packed, around five hundred people. Tension was thick in the air, you could just feel it. I got up on stage and began my remarks. I figured there was no use in being glum, so I tried to sound cheery: *"¡Buenos días!"*

Dead silence.

You could have heard a pin drop, I'm telling you. I thought: *Oh, boy, this is going to be tough.* And it was. People were particularly upset about having to pull their kids out of school, which I could fully appreciate. By then, I'd moved my family eighteen times for work. Our girls, Jessica and Jennifer, took the brunt of that, because they were always stopping and starting with new schools. As a parent, that sort of thing just makes you feel awful. But this wasn't about my family—and we were going to have to move again, too—or anybody else's family. This was about the future of Southwestern Bell.

The employee meeting got a little heated, at points. But I muddled through. Meantime the word was spreading. Calls, many of them quite angry, started streaming into my office and piling up. I also got a few calls of congratulations. One of those calls came from Ann Richards, the then-governor of Texas. She could not have been more gracious. Within hours of the announcement, Ann was standing in my office in St. Louis, offering a heartfelt welcome.

"If there's anything we can do to help, please let me know," she said—Ann had a trademark head of silver hair and a smile that was about as big as Texas. "And I want you to know that we are most glad to have you."

The other extreme was John Ashcroft, the then-governor of Missouri. (He later became the US attorney general.) He went to pieces. As soon as he heard we were leaving town, John flew to St. Louis to confront me. I didn't know he was coming, so I wasn't even there—I was in San Antonio that day. Jim Ellis, our general counsel, happened to bump into him in the elevator.

The sight of an angry, upset state governor is never a good sign, but Jim said he did his best. "Good morning, Governor."

John was in no mood: "Nothing good about it."

The two of them rode up the elevator—forty-two floors— without saying another word. (Jim told me later it was the longest elevator ride of his life.) They made their way over to Jim's office, which was right next to mine. Jim found me on my cell, then handed the phone over to John so we could talk about our relocation. "Talk" is a stretch—John basically barked at me, and I barked right back. John was incensed that we'd even consider leaving St. Louis.

I gave no ground. I told John exactly how I felt: that Missouri regulators had treated us poorly for years. They were always hounding us, making fun of us, had never given us proper respect. We were constantly being dragged into court for what amounted to a bunch of nonsense, which was expensive, time consuming, and morale draining. That sort of stuff had been going on for years, and we'd had enough.

After I ran through our litany of reasons for leaving, I put it right back to him: "Why would we stay here when we get treated like this? Give me one good reason."

John allowed that I might have a point.

"So there's nothing I can do about it?"

"Nothing," I told him. "We're gone."

Overnight, I pretty much became persona non grata around St. Louis. I got called a traitor. Some of my St. Louis friends wouldn't speak to me. Some people said we were going to San Antonio just because I wanted to get back home. Other people said we were leaving because I couldn't get into one of the local country clubs. None of it was true. San Antonio was a four-hour drive from Ennis; I'd only visited a couple of times in my life at that point. As for the country club theory, that was just nuts— but that didn't stop people from talking about it, or believing it. Other things got said as well. It was all a bunch of nonsense. We moved for one reason, primarily: to shake up the culture of Southwestern Bell. We got other residual benefits—like close proximity to Mexico, a better regulatory environment, and a more favorable tax structure—but culture change was the main driver.

In the end around 80 percent of the people in our St. Louis headquarters made the move. I don't know if it was the weather, the Mexican food, the prospect of something different, or maybe some combination of all that, but the energy level shot up immediately. People who made the jump—thousands eventually moved—really wanted to be there, you could tell. Almost instantly the vibration inside Southwestern Bell ramped up—it was almost electric. It was like we suddenly had a brand-new company and outlook. And in many ways I guess we did.

The status quo, with that one move, got broken to pieces. I made a solemn vow to myself that we would never let the bureaucracy build back up again. We'd run a lean and mean operation, one that gave people big jobs and held them accountable, but also gave them the authority to go out and get things done. That became our basic management model—clearly defined jobs and areas of responsibility, plus accountability, plus authority. That model would continue to anchor and define my management style for the next fifteen years, until I retired. And I would use the same management model, tweaked for the special character of Detroit and informed by my forty-four years in telecom, at General Motors.

As soon as we landed in San Antonio, things started happening—good things that profoundly changed the company, as well as the landscape of the US telecommunications industry.

But in hindsight, it all got kick-started by that move to San Antonio. Things could have turned out much differently, and probably would have, if we hadn't had the guts to pull up stakes and go west. But we did, and in the process we stirred a lot of things up, as Ann Richards might say. Boy, did we.

CHAPTER 9

Keep Going, Keep Growing

If you never score a touchdown in a football game because you're only worried about defense, you're never going to win. And you could wind up on the wrong end of an ugly rout if you're not careful.

It's the same in business.

My point: If you play defense all the time you will lose. None of us like it—we'd all like to be able to make progress by not taking risks, or making any changes. But that's impossible. The *only* way to make progress in business is through change. And change, by definition, has a certain amount of risk attached to it. But if you pick your shots, use your head, and apply good management, those rolls of the dice can turn out pretty good.

Sometimes they don't, of course—then it's time for Plan B. And if you don't have a Plan B, that's about the time you find yourself scrambling around to get one—I've been there, too.

But when things do work out, man, does that make people feel good. And it's in those moments, when beliefs, ideals, and actions come together, that the real magic happens: Companies start to grow and become stronger and more relevant versions of themselves. Management gets a boost because they see that they actually can pull this stuff off; employees feel good to be

121

working for a company that's successful and growing. All of a sudden the question people start asking isn't: *Can we do this?* It's: *So what are we doing next?* Your entire organization gets energized. You can see it on people's faces, and hear it in their voices. That's when you know you hit it right.

When you get right down to it, really, the only constant in business *is* change. That's progress for you. And that's business for you. So if you expect things to stay the same, it's already over for you—you're going to lose. If you're unwilling to change— and by that I mean take the risks that are sometimes necessary to make sure your company keeps going and growing—you're going to lose. You'll also lose if you're unwilling to do things that inspire and motivate your employees. Change is part of that, too. It has a way of energizing people in ways you can never anticipate, and that can open a lot of doors.

Management can't just contemplate—they *have* to act, that's the hard part. A lot of managers study things to death but never actually make a decision, because that causes accountability and responsibility to kick in. That sort of defensive posturing gets you nowhere. To force change, and allow change, you *must* pull the trigger. And you have to do it in a timely manner— otherwise, what's the point? History is littered with those that pondered too long:

AOL: "The King of Dial-Up" seemed unstoppable in the 1990s. The company failed to see the value of broadband until it was too late, and by the time it made the switch nobody cared. AOL today is a free service, and still losing customers.

Kodak: In its heyday in the 1970s Eastman Kodak controlled 90 percent of the US photographic film market. Digital film started showing promise in the 1990s, but Kodak paid little attention. Big mistake. Kodak, whose roots go back to the 1880s, filed for Chapter 11 bankruptcy protection in January 2012, and is in the process of reorganizing as this is being written.

Motorola: One of the grand names in wireless, Motorola literally invented the cell phone. It also came up with iconic hits like the Razr, a cutting-edge cell phone when it was introduced in 2004. But Motorola didn't keep innovating, and other handset makers passed it by.

Blockbuster: Slow response to technology advances cost Blockbuster dearly. Some customers also objected to its late fees on video rentals. One customer got so fed up he invented a streaming video service called Netflix, which helped drive Blockbuster into bankruptcy.

The old AT&T: Sat on its long-distance assets way too long. AT&T, in its final year as a stand-alone company, had the dubious distinction of posting twenty straight quarters of revenue decline.

Research in Motion: RIM—the maker of the BlackBerry— seemed unstoppable at one point. Its signature device was the smartphone of choice for business users worldwide. Then the Apple iPhone came along, proving, yet again, that just because you were everybody's favorite last year doesn't mean you will be this year, or the year after that. As of this writing, RIM's global market share is in a free fall, and its stock has lost more than 70 percent of its value in the last year alone.

The theme common to all these companies? Shortsighted management. In each case, steps were not taken to adequately prepare for the future. Instead, managers sat back and played defense. Maybe they thought about making moves but never did, or maybe they made some moves but it wasn't enough to move the ball. After all was said and done, a lot more got said than done. A few, like General Motors, did manage to pull it out at the last minute, and I'll be getting back to that miraculous recovery a little later. In the case of AT&T, we acquired it in 2005, so things also worked out okay there. But for AOL and the others, the clock basically ran out. Game over.

As a general rule I don't have a lot of rules—as far as I'm concerned, most rules are meant for bending or breaking. But I do have a few non-negotiables, and here's one: *Management has a duty to look out for the long-term health of the business it oversees.* The operative phrase there is *long-term*—I'm referring to years, not quarters.

This is one of the most important jobs management has, in my view; also one of the toughest, because it often involves making decisions that aren't very popular. Because what's popular today, most likely, won't be the thing that keeps your company going five or ten years out. So you always have to consider decisions through that long-term lens. AOL and Kodak got positioned well for the short term, but the long-term trend lines eventually caught up with them. And they suffered greatly as a result, as did investors and the thousands of people they employed.

Non-negotiable number two: *You have to pay back shareowners.* This might sound like common sense, and in a way it is, but it's always surprising to me how many companies don't do this. Or they do it so inconsistently that investors wind up feeling like an expendable commodity. It's a grievous mistake. Investors put risk capital into your business, and they expect a return, rightly so. They also expect you to do well over the long term. So any decisions you make—about next quarter or next year, or the year after that—have to be weighed with investors in mind. Will this deal/move work for shareowners? Will it work for employees? And those two are more closely linked than you might think, because how well your people perform largely determines how fast, and how much, you can pay back investors. People are the number one asset of any business. Don't ever forget that.

And that's how we ran AT&T when I was there: We made

our big moves based on our long-term view of the business. Never the short-term. We noted the short-term fluctuations, certainly. But the strategy was driven, almost exclusively, by our long-term vision and plan. And I guess we did okay, because our investors made a lot of money during the seventeen years that I was chairman and CEO. And they deserved to, because they stuck with us through some pretty unpopular decisions, starting with our first big deal in Mexico (see below). That was our first major transaction, so for me that one will always be a little special. Also instructive, because it drives home the larger point I've been making here about the need for management to be open to change, and willing to take the necessary risks to help make that happen in a way that is good for employees, and good for investors.

This was the situation: The year was 1990. I was the new CEO, and quite focused on the fact that Southwestern Bell was not in a growth mode. We had annual revenues of around $9 billion and operated in just five states. Local phone service accounted for nearly 100 percent of our profits. And those profits were capped by the states under "rate of return regulation," which was popular at the time. So we had no way to improve returns to investors, no way to energize employees, no way to extend our footprint beyond the Southwest. In short, we were basically stuck.

I figured it was time to throw the football.

Mexico's national phone company, Teléfonos de México— Telmex for short—was about to be privatized, and the government was looking for investors. The winning bidder would have to wire up Mexico for basic phone service, also construct a national wireless network. (You got wireless licenses as part of the deal.) Jim Kahan, our top business development person, flagged us on the opportunity—Jim had a nose for deals the way hound dogs do for squirrels. Jim's boss, Royce Caldwell, also helped lead the way. I was instantly interested.

The math, for me, was pretty simple: The wait time to get a telephone installed in Mexico, at that point, was three to five *years*—tens of thousands of people were waiting. Meantime, the population of Mexico was growing pretty fast. And the smart money was expecting that trend line to continue upward for the foreseeable future. I figured all those people were going to want phone service. So the deal, to me, was as good as money in the bank.

The problem? Southwestern Bell had never ventured outside its five-state operating area. And US regulators might not take too kindly to us expending time, energy, and resources south of the border. And because the project was 100 percent south of the US border, we'd be subject to the whims and rules of the Mexican government. The contract required us to bid with Mexico-based business partners. That was also a major consideration, because we'd be joined at the hip with those people if we won. The risks were obvious and numerous: Cultural barriers might crater the deal, growth might not materialize, the government could prove difficult, our local bidding partners might not deliver or could be difficult to work with. The "What Might Go Wrong" list was endless.

But that was the Chicken Little view—not my view. Things crossed my mind, sure. But I was looking ahead, not over my shoulder. And what I saw was this: the chance to diversify our asset base and start the process of moving Southwestern Bell in the direction of becoming bigger, more stable, and global. The growth potential in Mexico was huge. You didn't have to do a study to know that; common sense alone told you that much. And all that other stuff—the cultural divide, local bidding partners, and so on—I was not overly concerned, because I believed in my people. No matter what came our way, we'd work it out—that was my basic view.

We had the good fortune to wind up as partners with Grupo Carso, led by Carlos Slim. He's a very down-to-earth guy. No pretenses, doesn't wear fancy watches; what you see is what you get with Carlos. He couldn't speak much English, and I couldn't speak any Spanish, but we liked each other right away. I flew down to Mexico City to talk over the deal. We got a handshake agreement pretty quick, and agreed on final terms while he was driving me back to the airport—Carlos was behind the wheel, navigating and scribbling on a piece of paper the whole way there. Our wives were in a car right behind us. By the time we all got to the airport, we had a deal.

All in, it was a $1.76 billion investment for our bidding team. For that, we got a 20.4 percent stake in Telmex, but majority voting rights—so we had control of the asset. Southwestern Bell contributed $486 million; Grupo Carso kicked in $860 million; France Telecom, the third partner, contributed the rest. I felt great about working with Carlos. It was just a gut feeling on my part, but I could tell that he was a man of his word. With Carlos as our lead partner, I figured we couldn't miss.

We won the bid. And so, brimming with excitement and pride, Southwestern Bell formally announced its first-ever investment outside the United States. Then we sat back and waited for Wall Street's reaction.

It wasn't exactly a Bronx cheer, but it was close enough: Investors *hated* our deal. Reporters made fun of it. Nobody seemed to understand it. People thought it was crazy that we'd want to be mucking around the Mexican countryside installing phone service for people who lived pretty modestly; crazy that we'd sign on for a project where most people didn't speak our language, literally and figuratively. As for the long-term promise, nobody really saw that. Our stock didn't tank, but it didn't get any lift, either. Since I was the one who'd championed the deal, directors sort of looked to me for a grander explanation of why investors were so underwhelmed.

These are the moments as a senior manager when you either stand your ground or start looking for an excuse. We stood our ground. I was 100 percent convinced of the long-term value of the deal, as was our entire management team. So instead of trying to publicly explain or justify, we did something that became our signature move over the years: We just bucked up and carried on.

And I was glad we did, because Telmex turned out to be a wonderful deal, just like we thought—so good that we doubled down on our investment within a year. We worked well with our local partners to deploy phone and wireless services throughout Mexico. John Atterbury oversaw the entire project for Southwestern Bell, and did a tremendous job. And Carlos turned out to be every inch the gentleman and businessman I thought. We later got to be good friends, and we're still friends to this day. He's the best.

Telmex was my first big deal as CEO. But many others followed. After a while some people took to calling me a "serial acquirer." It hurts to read something like that, I'll be honest— I always worried about how employees felt, and what they thought when they saw things like that. Because it sounds like we're acquiring just to be acquiring. And that was not the case— we always had a definite strategy in mind.

Anytime you do a big deal, you're taking a calculated risk. And in the heat of a deal battle, things can happen that sort of light your hair on fire. But we were not a management team driven by fear; we were driven by the opportunity to push our company forward. That, to us, trumped everything. We also were not afraid to try things—our view was that we'll never know unless we try, so let's give it a shot. That was always our attitude. And if the deal works out like we think, and hope, then it's going to be real good, and if it doesn't, then it won't be so good and they'll throw us out, right? But we were always willing to take that risk because we just fundamentally believed in our people. That, for me, is what it always came down to: people. If they're with you, you can accomplish truly amazing things. And our people were with us, 100 percent. Management worked hard to create that sort of environment, mind you. But the point is that we had an employee body that was inspired and enthused, and as a result we were able to accomplish a lot of things that some people said were impossible.

We did a lot of deals in succession, yes. But we always had a plan, and this was the plan: to get a lot more customers and grow the company into something that had the assets, revenue, and cash flow to stay strong and keep growing. And a global reach—that was important to us, too. That sort of security makes employees feel good, makes management feel good; it also allows you to create opportunities for people, to promote them into interesting jobs that challenge and inspire them. That, ultimately, is what builds enthusiasm and momentum within a company—the feeling that *By God, we're actually doing something here; this company is on the move; I can be proud of where I work.* That's the main reason we kept changing our corporate name: to better reflect those changes. In 1995 we changed Southwestern Bell's name to SBC Communications. People thought the *SBC* was short for "Southwestern Bell Corp.," but it wasn't—it was just SBC. Not the most elegant or clever, I know—we basically made it up on the spot. But we felt it was important to get away from the "Southwest" reference, because we planned to become so much more. That might not have been so apparent in 1995, but I sure knew it.

Wireless was a big part of our growth strategy. And no deal was more important to the long-term plan than our acquisition of AT&T Wireless. That deal cemented our place in the US wireless industry. It also changed the landscape of the industry for all time. I knew that going in, which was why I pushed so hard. And man, I want to tell you, we pushed that one about as far as you could push.

It was a pretty interesting set of circumstances. And unusual. My recollections are as follows:

The year was 2004. AT&T Wireless was then a stand-alone enterprise, with its own publicly traded stock. And it was on the auction block. This caused a big commotion in the wireless industry, because AT&T Wireless held licenses for major markets across America. There are only so many national licenses in existence, and they rarely become available for purchase. So when the "For Sale" sign went up, *everybody* in the wireless world sat up and took notice.

We did, too. At the time, our wireless business was tied up in Cingular, a joint venture of SBC Communications and Bell-South, which was then based in Atlanta. Our two companies had contiguous service areas, so we'd decided to combine wireless some years earlier to help reduce costs and get the most out of our marketing dollars. We wanted to turn Cingular into a national player, but we needed national licenses to do that. So when AT&T Wireless became available, we jumped into the bidding.

It was a high-stakes poker game. We hung in there, and after multiple rounds just two players were left: Cingular and Vodafone, a big wireless outfit based in the UK. Unfortunately, we lost. Vodafone's winning bid was $38 billion. Ralph Larsen—he was on the AT&T Wireless board—called to give me the bad news. I was in my home office in San Antonio. Duane Ackerman, the CEO of BellSouth, also got a call. I immediately called Stan Sigman, the president of Cingular—he was in Atlanta, where Cingular was based—to let him know. (Duane was also in Atlanta.) We were all crushed.

I was very concerned as well. If Vodafone entered the US wireless market, Cingular could get trampled. Verizon and Sprint were coming on strong, and a number of regional carriers were building market share quickly. Cingular had the South and Southwest covered, but that wasn't good enough. For SBC to become a major player over the long term we needed a national footprint—a regional presence wasn't going to carry us. With the assets of AT&T Wireless in our back pocket, we'd instantly gain national standing and recognition. Without it, we'd always be a second-string player.

In my mind, this was not acceptable. Wireless was the way of the future. Millions of new wireless customers were piling on by the quarter, with no signs of slowing. The mobile web was also showing a lot of promise. We simply could not afford to permanently relegate ourselves to second-tier status. But I also recognized that we needed to make a move fast, otherwise that's exactly what we were looking at—a permanent number two spot. Right behind Verizon.

Time to throw the football downfield again.

By now it was 10 p.m. or so in New York, where our deal team was based. Around 3 a.m. in London, where Vodafone was based. Vodafone was the declared winner, but its board hadn't yet voted to finalize their win. That was expected to happen early the next morning, London time.

That turned out to be the break we needed.

Vodafone was paying the equivalent of $14 a share. To get AT&T's attention, we'd need to wow them. A few pennies' improvement, or even a quarter, wasn't enough. BellSouth had 50 percent management control over Cingular, so we both had to agree on big decisions. And this was a very big decision. By then Duane and I had been on the phone to each other, and to our respective boards, all day long.

Duane and I had a tough heart-to-heart.

"There's only one of these things," I told Duane. "This is beachfront property, and once it's gone, it's gone. We've got one shot here—let's top 'em." He fully agreed. Within a few minutes, we hatched our counterattack plan. We brought in our deal team in New York, which was standing by, to hash things over. On the fly, on the phone—not the smoothest way to plan a merger, but we were out of time and out of options. Meantime the clock was ticking. Minutes mattered.

We agreed on a bid of $15 a share, which was a full $1 more than what Vodafone had offered. The kicker: We'd make it an all-cash deal. The financial implications for SBC and BellSouth were not insignificant. But the downside to *not* winning AT&T Wireless could be devastating over the long term, we both agreed.

Technically, AT&T Wireless didn't have a signed deal—all they had was a verbal commitment from Vodafone. That was the slender thread we were hanging on to. If AT&T Wireless stood on principle and refused to engage, we'd be out of the running for good. As in *forever.* But fortunately for us, that didn't happen. To our delight and surprise, the AT&T Wireless board agreed to consider our sweetened offer. We wasted no time: $41 billion—all cash. With one caveat: AT&T Wireless had to accept upon receipt, and they couldn't shop it to any other bidder, otherwise we'd withdraw the offer. In other words, they couldn't tell Vodafone.

We submitted the offer and held our breath. Legally, there was nothing to stop AT&T Wireless from telling Vodafone. And we knew it; we just hoped they'd bite. Like I said, we were desperate.

AT&T Wireless accepted on the spot.

We were too shocked to do any high-fives, to be honest. Duane and I weren't about to make the same mistake as Vodafone, so we had our boards standing by to vote, so we could close the deal immediately. By now it was pushing toward 4 a.m. The Vodafone board was probably assembling to vote on the deal they thought they still had. That was in the back of my mind the whole time. So for us, right then, seconds counted.

Once our boards voted—it was unanimous—I called Stan at home to tell him the good news.

"You got yourself a new wireless company," I told him.

I woke him up out of a dead sleep. Stan was a little con-

fused, understandably. When he'd gone to bed a few hours earlier, we'd lost. Now I was telling him the exact opposite. Stan's
first reaction was total disbelief.

"You're kidding, right?" Two beats. "You been drinking?"

I assured him I was on the level. I asked Stan to get into the
office as quickly as possible so he could sign all the deal papers.
He was out the door within minutes.

By the time Vodafone found out, there was nothing they
could do—our deal was signed, sealed, and delivered. The
acquisition made Cingular the biggest wireless company in
America: forty-six million customers, with a reach from Maine to
California. Verizon, which had thirty-seven million customers,
got kicked down to the number two spot. Our employees *loved*
that. We all did. With that one deal, we were basically driving
our stake in the ground and telling the world *We're going to be
the biggest and the best.* Around our San Antonio headquarters
that morning, you could feel the sense of pride in the air. That
alone told me we'd done the right thing.

The $41 billion we paid set a corporate record as the larg-
est all-cash transaction in history. (Total acquisition cost:
$47.4 billion, including debt.) On the day we wired the payment
Stan said his hands were shaking—he'd never seen that many
zeros on a check. And it was a lot of money. But you know
what? We would have paid more if we'd had to. Because there
was only one AT&T Wireless, and we had exactly one shot to
get it right.

Telmex and AT&T Wireless were obvious, in terms of their
long-term appeal. In other situations, you have to dig a little
deeper, take a leap of faith. In these cases, it basically comes
down to what you believe, in your heart and in your gut.

That was pretty much the case with our acquisition of AT&T
in 2005. At the time, AT&T was a stripped-down long-distance
company with twenty straight quarters of declining revenue. It
was bleeding customers by the thousands, with no way to bring

them back. So it was basically dying, one quarter at a time. And that's all people saw when they looked at AT&T—a shell of a company with no future, a crummy balance sheet, and a tarnished brand name. The stock sank so low it eventually got dropped from the Dow Jones Industrial Average. That was Wall Street's way of saying AT&T no longer mattered.

You know what I saw?

Great assets. Great networks nobody could duplicate, a global presence in 127 countries, and lots of smart, talented people—AT&T always had great employees. The brand name was taking a beating in America, but it was still good world-wide. I knew in my gut we could bring it back; I never had any doubt. *Plus*, I thought, *this is a great name—people know "AT&T" instantly when you mention it*. Very few brand names have instant recognition like that, but AT&T did, even in that broken-down state.

I will also tell you that my entire management team opposed me on the AT&T deal—nobody but me, in the beginning, thought we should do that acquisition. At the time we were con-sidering whether to go after AT&T or BellSouth. I was interested in both, so I went around the table and asked—What do you think we should do? Every single person in the room said we should *not* buy AT&T first; that we should go after BellSouth.

I said, "Well, that might be your thought, but that's not mine—we're going to buy AT&T first" and then try BellSouth. And that's exactly what we did. To the credit of my team—a great group—once we made a decision everybody got behind it. So there was never any second-guessing or backbiting. There's no room for that sort of thing on a senior management team. Everybody has to be pulling in the same direction, and if they're not then you have to address the situation. And in the few cases that happened I did address it. But for the most part we were all on the same page when it came to our big strategic moves and deals.

So we bought AT&T for $16 billion in stock. (Total cost: $21.5 billion, including debt.) It was a great bargain for us; the network assets alone were worth more than that. There was a lot of debate at the time as to whether we should use the name—people said we'd be crazy to do that, given all the problems AT&T was having. But I never had any doubt.

Truth be told, I'd had my eye on AT&T since 1995, at least. I had made a few runs at it, too. I actually had a handshake deal with the former CEO, Bob Allen, but it fell apart after regulators got wind of it and went crazy. Reed Hundt, who was chairman of the Federal Communications Commission at the time, said an SBC-AT&T merger was "unthinkable." That was in 1997.

By 2005 it *was* thinkable, I guess, because we closed that deal in just ten months. And as soon as it closed we changed SBC's name to AT&T. We had some marketing types studying the question of whether we should use the AT&T name or come up with a new one. But I knew the day we bought the company it was going to be AT&T. (And I made sure of that because I had final say on the name we used.) We also adopted AT&T's famed trading symbol—a T, short for "telephone." Made me feel good to see AT&T's name back out there; it was like we'd restored a piece of American history. And in some ways I guess we did.

As soon as the AT&T deal closed we bought BellSouth. CEO Duane Ackerman and I agreed that a merger was the best thing for both companies over the long term. The deal gave us 100 percent control over Cingular—that was the major driver of the transaction. By then it was clear to us that wireless was the future of telecom, and we had big plans and hopes for the long-term development of that business. That turned out to be the last major acquisition I made as the CEO of AT&T.

So what did we get, in the final analysis, for all those years of deal making?

We got big, real big, that's what. By the time I retired in 2007, AT&T was the largest communications company in the world, with annual revenue of around $120 billion. Our assets were varied and deep: We owned the number one wireless business in America, four Bells—the original Southwestern Bell, plus BellSouth, Ameritech, and Pacific Telesis—a growing video business, broadband and Internet assets, and a vast collection of advanced long-distance networks that circled the globe. We also had a respectable portfolio of investments in foreign countries— Mexico, Israel, and South Africa, to name a few.

This assemblage of assets was no accident. And it certainly was not a "serial" occurrence. Our get-big strategy was based on a very simple but focused idea: that we needed to pull together a powerful mix of assets that would carry our stockholders and employees for a very long time. John Wayne had this great line: "Courage is being scared to death, and saddling up anyway." I can't say we were ever "scared to death," though we certainly had our moments. But we were always willing to saddle up and give it a try, and the things we accomplished—as a company and management team—are testament to that, I think.

One of my biggest regrets, to be perfectly honest, is that we didn't get more done. But I guess we did enough. Here's a partial list of our biggest mergers and acquisitions (including debt):

1. Pacific Telesis (1996/$23 billion)
2. Southern New England Telephone (1998/$5.7 billion)
3. Ameritech (1998/$84.9 billion)
4. Comcast Cellular (1999/$2.1 billion)
5. AT&T Wireless (2004/$47.4 billion)
6. AT&T (2005/$21.5 billion)
7. BellSouth (2006/$96.8 billion)

We closed every big deal we ever attempted—not a single one cratered or went off the rails. Part of that was luck; a lot of it was management focus. Ours was no democracy—I was in charge. Only one person can have final authority before going to the board. And in the final analysis I was the guy making those decisions, because that was my responsibility. CEOs don't get paid to be team players; they get paid to be team *leaders*. At least that's how I saw it, and that's how I played it for the seventeen years I had the honor and privilege of serving as the chairman and CEO of the company formerly known as Southwestern Bell—now known to the world as AT&T. If things had gone wrong, that would have been on my head, too. And rightly so. But they went right a lot more often than they went wrong, I'm happy to report, so I guess we did okay.

CHAPTER 10

Betting on People, Not Products

The Apple iPhone

Wireless isn't just a technology; it's a cultural touchstone. And no device has done more to fuel the imagination and push along that revolution, I think, than the Apple iPhone. Currently there are nearly two hundred million iPhones in use around the world, and the number keeps rising with each new release. Apple keeps innovating and adding new markets, so that trend will probably continue for a long, long time.

AT&T had a small role there, and we're very proud of that. In June 2007 AT&T, in partnership with Apple, launched the device in the United States—that was the first time the world got a look at the iPhone. It was an instant hit for us. And five years later it's still setting sales records.

Everybody's really happy about how things turned out, of course. But back in 2005 when we were negotiating that deal with Apple, we had no idea about any of this. To be honest, it was a total flier: We had no prototype to look at, no performance specs to consider, and no company track record to examine, because Apple had never designed a wireless device before. The financial terms were awful—Apple got a bunch of money up front. All we had to go on, really, was Steve Jobs's commitment to us that he could, and would, design a wireless device like no other.

And that was good enough for us.

The Apple iPhone, for us, was a bet on people—not a product. And the person we were betting on the most was Steve Jobs. Steve, as the world knows, was the chairman, CEO, and co-founder of Apple. He had many distinctions; one of the most admirable, in my mind, is that he lived the credo he preached: "People who are crazy enough to think they can change the world are the ones who do." That's a famous line from an Apple ad campaign, and it pretty much sums up the genius of Steve Jobs. He was fearless, both as a human being and as a CEO. And the world benefited greatly because of that.

AT&T also got swept up in Steve's special brand of magic. As a result of our iPhone experience, we learned a lot—about the wireless industry; about consumer marketing; about the importance of being open to new concepts and ideas, even if those ideas take direct aim at some of your closest-held beliefs and business practices. Some of those lessons were tough to take, to be honest—Apple's financial requirements turned our wireless business model upside down. But we figured it out, and I guess we did okay because AT&T wound up doing pretty well, financially speaking—more than 50 million iPhones have been sold to new and existing customers since the device made its US debut. The Apple halo also gave our hundred-year-old AT&T brand a lift, particularly with younger people. All due to the fact that Steve was "crazy" enough to push the status quo until the business reality matched his creative vision. And I'm glad he did. I think we all are.

In AT&T, I'd also say, Steve found a partner that was willing to take a leap with him, to see where his unique ideas about wireless took him. How our partnership came together is a pretty interesting story, also instructive, I think. A lot of what

I'm about to tell you comes directly from Stan Sigman, who was the CEO of our wireless business and negotiated the original Apple deal. And the story goes like this...

It was the spring of 2005. Stan was the CEO of Cingular—we were still operating under that brand name at the time. We were rocking along pretty good in wireless: We had around fifty million customers and were adding new ones at a good clip every quarter.

One evening around nine thirty or so, Stan got a call on his cell phone. It was Steve Jobs. Stan didn't know Steve, had never met him or ever had a conversation with the guy. But he recognized the voice immediately.

Steve was friendly but direct.

"Hi, I'm Steve Jobs," he said, "I want to do a phone. Can you meet with me?" Or words to that effect—Stan relayed all this to me from memory.

Stan had no idea what Steve had in mind, but he did make one assumption right away: that the head of Verizon Wireless was getting the exact same call. AT&T and Verizon had been archrivals for years. (And still are.) Stan's very competitive, so anything he can do to get a leg up on Verizon, he's going to do. And I'm with him on that—I always felt it was important for AT&T to be the number one wireless company in America.

Steve was going to New York the following week, and asked Stan to meet him there. So off Stan went. Steve was staying at a hotel near Times Square. Stan said it was a big, nice suite. But the thing he remembered most was that it had a big picture window with a clear view of an Apple store down on the street. Steve, as usual, was in a black turtleneck and jeans. Had one guy with him, but Steve did all the talking. Stan also had somebody with him, Ralph de la Vega—he was the number two guy at Cingular behind Stan.

So everybody sat down at the table in this hotel suite—and Steve immediately jumped up and started talking about Motorola. Apple had an iTunes deal with them to put songs into a cell phone. Steve didn't care for the device Motorola came up with; he thought it was a joke, in fact. Then he went on to say that he thought most big handset makers didn't understand consumers, didn't understand the interface—didn't understand how important it is to make a wireless device simple and easy to use, particularly as it relates to the mobile web.

He didn't like the way Cingular operated, or other wireless carriers, for that matter. He also thought our distribution system was all wrong. And he really didn't like the industry practice of using third-party vendors to sign up customers and sell devices. Steve thought that was misdirected, because you're basically giving the customer relationship to people you don't know and have no control over—that, to Steve, was just dumb. Stan said Steve had a lot of other things to say about traditional wireless—all of them bad.

Jobs, at that point, had no interest in partnering with Cingular. He just wanted access to our wireless networks so he could do his own thing as a "reseller"—meaning he wanted to buy wholesale minutes from Cingular and resell them under the Apple brand name. Apple didn't have a wireless device in hand at the time, or even on the drawing board—that was all in his head, basically. But Steve did have financial terms worked out: He wanted to pay Cingular $45 a month for every customer Apple managed to sign up, and for that flat fee he wanted unlimited monthly access to our wireless networks.

Stan had no interest in a reseller deal with Apple—zero. There was no money in that for Cingular. Or for Apple, either; the profit margins are razor-thin in the reseller business. But Stan had a *ton* of interest in Steve Jobs. The two of them couldn't have been more different: Steve's a California-cool sort of guy, an icon in the technology world. Stan's a slow-talking cowboy type from Hereford, Texas. Not showy; drives pickup trucks and likes to ride horses. But Stan instinctually felt that Steve was somebody he could work with. Not on a reseller deal, but on *something*. Apple had great technology and an incredible brand name. And you'd never want to bet against Apple designers; they're some of the best in the world. So Stan was pretty intrigued.

In that first meeting, Stan didn't say he thought Steve was wrong about the reseller idea. Stan wisely decided that would not be the thing to say to a guy like Jobs, especially if he wanted a second meeting. So he just sat there and listened, mostly. By the time that meeting ended three hours later, Stan said he felt like they'd had a good exchange of ideas. And I guess Steve did, too, because he asked Stan for another meeting.

For the next six months or so, Steve and Stan continued to meet and discuss the wireless business. They usually met at Apple, which is based in Cupertino, California—that's in the heart of Silicon Valley. The first few times they met, Stan said they sort of circled each other like two junkyard dogs, trying to get comfortable. But after a couple of meetings, they did get comfortable, and that's when their talks started to turn substantive. By then, Steve had largely abandoned the reseller idea, mostly for financial reasons—Stan convinced him that this business model, for Apple, would not be worth the time or trouble. But Steve still wanted to design a smartphone, because he thought the ones that were out there weren't very good, or user-friendly. So that's what they talked about mostly. Stan continued to listen. He knew a lot about wireless networks, but not a thing about phone design. But that worked out, too, because Steve, as it turned out, didn't know a whole lot about wireless networks: how they are designed, the impact of high-volume data usage on capacity, the capital requirements to maintain them, things like that. So they wound up having some pretty spirited conversations around all this stuff.

Steve had no prototype or even artist's sketch to offer of the device he had in mind. But he had a very clear idea about the performance: It would make the mobile web easy and fun to use. At the time—this was in 2005, keep in mind—there was no shortage of web-enabled smartphones on the market. But the navigation functions were pretty clumsy and complex, requiring people to go through multiple steps to get to where they wanted to go. Steve was convinced that Apple engineers could do a whole lot better with the "interface"—he was sure of it, in fact. But he wanted a lot of money, along with hard control—over pricing, marketing, advertising, a bunch of other things—to do it.

Jobs also wanted something else: long-term exclusivity, as in *ten years* long. Steve said he planned to build one phone, for one carrier, using one technology platform. And that was it, at least for a while. Stan got the message: If Cingular didn't do the deal with Apple, he'd find a way to work it out with Verizon. That had major competitive implications, because Cingular was on the global "GSM" standard and Verizon used "CDMA" technology. The two technologies were not compatible. So if Verizon got the phone and we didn't, that meant it could be a long time before we got our hands on it.

The biggest bone of contention, by far, was revenue sharing. Steve initially wanted a 50-50 split of all revenue generated by iPhone customers. Stan's biggest concern was existing customers: If half of Cingular's fifty million customers migrated over, we'd be looking at billions in lost revenue. And the pain would be strung out...for ten long years.

Stan swallowed hard on that one. Up to then, big carriers like Cingular controlled everything: advertising, marketing, distribution, pricing, you name it. As for the idea of "revenue sharing," that just wasn't done. Handset makers, traditionally, had no vote in that stuff. That's because wireless had always been a carrier-ruled world, and it had been that way for as long as wireless had been around. What Steve was asking, essentially, was for us to *abandon* our business model and use Apple's. And Apple's model broke every rule in the wireless handbook.

Stan never blinked. He and Steve, and a few support people, kept talking this thing through into the winter of 2005. That's when we got to the Go–No Go stage: Steve was ready to move forward; if we weren't with him, he was going to walk. So we had to either pull the trigger or let it go. Stan didn't know, for sure, if Verizon and Apple were even close. But he did know this: If we passed and Verizon got it, and the device became a big hit, we'd be kicking ourselves in the butt for years. Stan still had a lot of concerns about the financial terms, but he also had his eye on the long-term prospects of wireless, and the mobile web was clearly where it was at.

Because of the unusual nature of the deal, Stan thought it would be prudent to talk it over before he pulled the trigger. That's when he came to me. By then, Stan had backed Steve off the ten-year exclusive idea, but the commitment was still substantial—five years. Apple also got 8 percent of all revenue generated by the new device. That was a lot better than the 50 percent Steve had demanded initially, but still significant in terms of monthly dollars out of our pocket. If half of our existing customers made the switch, we'd wind up owing Apple hundreds of millions of dollars. Or more, depending how many people jumped.

Normally, you'd at least have a prototype to look at before you made a big decision like this. We had nothing. Not even an artist's rendering or product name. But the potential, if Steve delivered, was most intriguing: a web-enabled device that was super-easy to use. No such animal existed for the consumer market at that time.

Stan's not the sort to be overly dramatic, about anything. But I could tell that his antenna was all the way up on this one: "If this thing works," he said, "it could be good. *Real* good.

"Should we go for it?" he asked.

I put it right back to him: "Sigman, you're responsible for this thing," I said—I had a habit of calling Stan by his last name whenever we got into a serious business discussion. "You're the one shoving the chips out on the table. What do you think we should do?"

Stan did not hesitate.

"I think we ought to give it a shot."

"I think we should, too," I said. "Let's do it."

And that was it. The entire conversation lasted all of twenty minutes. It was a rich deal, no question. And the risks were undeniable. Apple wanted more up front than any other handset maker we'd ever dealt with—Motorola, Nokia, all the big names. And these companies had decades of wireless experience. But so what? If this thing worked, it could be a magnitude leap for our wireless business. Plus, we just fundamentally believed in Steve Jobs. He said he could do this, and we believed him. It was that simple.

Nobody on our senior management team, with the exception of Stan, liked the deal. Everybody thought the financial terms were much too steep. And the revenue-sharing idea really grated. People also didn't like the fact that Apple would wind up with so much control. I didn't like all that stuff, either, to be honest. But I overruled everybody and approved the deal anyway. I thought the overarching positive—the potential to drive market share—was just too attractive to pass up. Plus, I didn't want Verizon to get it.

So we did the deal. The contract got signed in early 2006. Because so much was unknown about the unknown (and still unnamed) Apple device, the contract had some pretty general language in it. Most times, you wouldn't do that; you'd cross every *t* and dot every *i*. But we weren't too worried; we figured we'd just work those things out as they came along. Stan pegged Steve as a straight shooter from the start, and figured he'd be fair with us. (And, in fact, that's how things worked out.)

Stan did not see the first iPhone prototype until that December. Stan was attending the National Finals Rodeo in Las Vegas—it's the Super Bowl of rodeos; bull riders, ropers, and steer wrestlers come in from all over the place. Stan loves that stuff. Anyway, Stan was taking a few days off to attend this thing when Steve called. Said he wanted to come out to Las Vegas because he had something to show him.

So Steve flew out, made his way up to Stan's room. He walked in and didn't even bother to sit down: he immediately reached into his pocket, pulled out the iPhone, and held it out in the palm of his hand. Like he was displaying a rare jewel or something, and in a way I guess he was.

Stan was completely blown away. He'd never seen anything like that, and Stan's not a guy who's easily impressed; he's been in the wireless business since 1985. Touch screens on smartphones are pretty common today, but back in 2006 nobody had ever done a version quite like the iPhone. It was sleek, elegant, almost sculptural looking; it was wireless art, really. Stan said Steve was grinning from ear to ear, like a father with a new baby.

As soon as he saw it, Stan said, he got chills down his spine—because he knew we had a winner.

Stan said these words just came tumbling out of his mouth:

"This is a game changer, Steve. This is going to change the industry."

Stan said Steve seemed really happy to hear that, but he still wouldn't part with it so Stan could bring it back to Texas and show me, at least. He wouldn't even let Stan hold it for too long; every time Stan tried to play around with it Steve would grab it out of his hands to show him something else—all the bells and whistles. Stan said they visited for an hour or so like that, then Steve slipped the iPhone back into his pocket and left.

The rest of the AT&T management team didn't get to see the iPhone for another few months—right before we announced the deal, in fact. We made the formal announcement in January 2007 at Macworld in San Francisco. That's the annual event, hosted by Apple, where new products are introduced. Steve was always the host and star of the show. When I finally saw the iPhone for the first time—I still remember that moment—I, too, was stunned. So was everybody on the senior management team. Steve's vision and Apple's technology just somehow meshed—and there it was, all wrapped up in this sleek, black glass case. Any lingering doubt anybody had about that deal melted away on the spot.

America had the same reaction.

By the time we finally started selling the iPhone—in June 2007—we knew we had a major hit on our hands. We had lines of people wrapped around our stores waiting to buy it. Some people camped out the night before. The same thing happened at Apple stores—people basically went nuts. I'd never seen anything like it. We had a few hitches here and there, but for the most part the launch went pretty smoothly.

People forget about this, but we changed Cingular's name to AT&T simultaneously with the iPhone launch—that was Stan's idea, too. We'd planned to make the switch earlier, but Stan thought—rightly—that it would be a better brand association if we did everything at the same time.

One little piece of trivia you might find interesting: The plan, all along, was to drop Cingular's signature color—orange—and adopt blue, which was AT&T's trademark color. Our original thinking was to bring wireless completely under the AT&T umbrella, and blue had been our color forever, and still is. And we would have proceeded with that plan had it not been for Steve Jobs. The day before Macworld, Stan happened to mention our plans to Steve. If you mentioned a color change to most people, it would probably slide right past them, hardly registering. Not Steve. Stan said Steve got a serious look on his face and said, pretty emphatically, that dropping orange would be a "big mistake."

Stan did a double take at that, and asked him why.

Steve didn't miss a beat: "Orange is new and fresh, and you own it," he said. "Not many companies own a color, but you do."

Stan listened. He figured nobody was better than Steve Jobs at figuring out what works for consumers, so after a lot of thinking—Stan said he spent the entire day rolling Steve's comment around in his head—he decided to take Steve's advice. So at the last minute, right before our announcement, Stan dumped the blue idea and stuck with orange—and that's the color associated with AT&T's wireless business to this day.

Stan later said he wished he'd taken Steve's cue on another thing: that ten-year exclusive. As noted above, Stan got Apple to agree to a five-year arrangement: an initial three-year exclusive, with the right to renew for an additional two years so long as both sides agreed. But on a positive note, AT&T got millions of new customers and a pretty good lift in its brand image, so we weren't exactly complaining. The original deal Stan cut also gave AT&T a percentage of revenues from iTunes, now called the App Store. There were a number of conditions around revenue-sharing— music and movies were exempt, for example—but the overarching positive was that AT&T was well positioned to take advantage of the applications boom that later developed. (The contract has undergone a number of changes since then, as I understand it.)

Looking back, I guess we were lucky. But sometimes you really do create your own luck. The most important thing in all of this, though, and the thought I'd like to leave you with, is that we used common sense. It's often lacking in business these days, but it really is the most important ingredient. Common sense, of course, is a function of the people you have, so once again we're back to one of my core beliefs about business: that it's 99 percent about people.

Keep it simple and use common sense—if you can just do those two things, you'll do okay in business, and sometimes you might even do a whole lot better than that.

CHAPTER 11

Personal Business

"It's just business—nothing personal."

How many times have you heard people say that? The inference, of course, is that whatever just got said, or done, or transacted that just made you feel lower than dirt is perfectly all right, because it wasn't directed at you personally—it's "only business."

Let me tell you something: It's *always* personal.

I don't care if you're talking about a multibillion-dollar corporate merger, a corporate relocation, or plant rotation schedules for assembly-line workers—it's all highly personal to the people who are directly affected. And that tracks because business is 99 percent about people, and people have feelings—strong feelings, in some cases. Those emotions don't magically shut off when you show up for work in the morning or head home at night. Anything that affects your business life, almost by definition, is going to ricochet out to your home and family life, and nothing is more personal than family.

The ripple effect doesn't stop there. Work life, to some degree, is a mirror we hold up to ourselves every day; it's a way of defining ourselves, more or less. I'm not saying that's how it ought to be, but I do think that's human nature. If you think otherwise, try asking some guy who just got laid off from his job how he feels about that. That person isn't less smart or less capable than before he got that pink slip—"It's just business, nothing personal," right? But it can sure feel that way if you're the one who has to go home and tell your family and friends that you just landed in the unemployment line.

On the flip side, the person who just sealed a big deal that makes her company look good to her boss, her peers, and the outside world is walking on air. She's not necessarily better at her job than the guy who just got laid off. But the perception issue has a way of overhanging all that. My point: *Never underestimate the personal impact that business decisions have on people's lives, their families, and their sense of self-worth.*

And the longer you hang around a place, the more closely tied those two worlds—personal and business—get mixed up with each other. AT&T was my business, certainly. But it was also highly personal.

And I knew the day would come when it would finally be time for me to go. That moment arrived in 2007. After forty-four years with the company, I knew, deep in my gut and my heart, that it was time to go. My growing impatience—with just about everything—was the first sign that maybe the end of my career was near. I never was very patient to begin with, I will admit: Doing a deep dive on the details is not my favorite thing, but if you want to take the hill, I'm your guy, you know? But what patience I did have left, by 2007, was pretty much shot. And that was not a good thing, because patience is something you need to get things done in business. Long-term planning, to some degree, is an exercise in management patience. Other things, too, but patience plays a part.

Our acquisition of AT&T is a good example.

As I've noted, we made our first run at AT&T in 1997. We arrived at a handshake deal with the then-CEO, Bob Allen, to buy the company. But regulators got wind of it and complained.

I was more than willing to plow ahead, but Bob lost interest and the deal died. His successor, Mike Armstrong, had little interest in selling AT&T—we checked periodically. But *his* successor, Dave Dorman, was very interested. So that's when we finally hit pay dirt—in 2005. By then AT&T was bleeding customers and revenue by the quarter, and Dave was most anxious to sell. And that was fine by me, because I was most anxious to buy.

That took a lot of patience to pull off, and I was glad that we waited it out. But after seventeen years of blocking and tackling, I just didn't have it in me anymore. Things I used to enjoy—like starting new projects, figuring out our next acquisition, developing up-and-coming talent—didn't give me the same inner spark they once did. I also had a *been there, done that* attitude creeping in that I just couldn't shake. In meetings, I would button my lip and try to not let anybody know. But inside I felt restless. I initially wrote it off as temporary fatigue—we'd been pushing things pretty hard for years. But those feelings only got stronger.

There was no defining moment for me that flipped the switch. But I did have a moment of clarity that caused me to take a hard look in the mirror: One afternoon, I happened to find myself in conversation with somebody who was struggling with a very specific issue, and the more he talked, the more agitated I felt inside. I didn't show that to him—I basically sat there, my cards held in close, and listened. But I couldn't understand why he was laboring so hard, because he was a smart guy and we'd been over this exact same ground a number of times already. That's when it hit me: I was actually remembering his *predecessor* in the job—not the fellow who was sitting in front of me. The guy I was talking to right then was brand new to the job, so he was still on a steep learning curve. The problem was, I didn't have patience for that, either.

That's when my second revelation hit: *I don't have enough energy left to help people learn anymore.* That was the moment I knew it was time. I was sixty-six years old; sixty-seven was just around the corner. Not young anymore, but not ready for the old folks' home, either. Was there a life for me beyond AT&T? I didn't have a clue, to be honest. And I wasn't so sure I wanted to find out. But this much I did know: A CEO with no patience is not a CEO I'd wish for any organization, much less an organization I loved, respected, and admired like AT&T.

But one thing gave me a lot of comfort: Randall Stephenson. He was our chief operating officer, and the individual I planned to recommend to the AT&T board as my successor. I'd been watching Randall for a number of years at that point, and I liked how he handled himself. During board presentations, Randall always seemed well versed in anything you asked him. He was also assertive. Not in a preachy, arrogant way, but in a way that suggested an inner confidence. I liked that, too. Employees constantly look to the CEO for signals that things are okay. It's important to be able to communicate confidence without beating people over the head with it, or talking down to them.

Randall was also his own man, and I respected that. He had opposed me on a couple of big deals over the years, but I liked the way he did it—friendly and respectful, but firm in his views. Randall wasn't the sort to pop off about things he didn't know about or try to buffalo you if he didn't know something; he's a very straight shooter. We still did all those deals, but the fact that Randall felt confident enough to speak his mind impressed me. And once we decided to move ahead, he was always most supportive. Other senior managers were the same—once we decided to go for something, there was no second-guessing or complaining. We were one company, one team, with one goal: doing the best job we could for our employees and our investors. Randall got that.

Randall also struck me as a people person—that, of course, was a huge consideration for me. I wanted to make sure the next CEO treated our people right. Layoffs, for us, had always been a last resort. We reduced our payroll by attrition, certainly. And we moved people around and retrained them for other jobs, sometimes in other cities, when we had to. But we really didn't do layoffs. Every once in a while our finance people would propose that kind of move to help cut costs, but I'd always tell them to go find another way. I just felt like employees were our most important asset, and if these people were going to be committed to us, then we needed to be committed to them. I felt a huge sense of obligation on this point, and I made sure Randall and the rest of the management team knew that. Randall seemed to be on the same page with me on this.

That combination—having a successor lined up and my increasing sense of impatience—convinced me that it was time to go. As a final gut check, I had a conversation with myself, and it went something like this:

"Ed, you're going to go from chairman and CEO to essentially nothing.

"You can only play so much golf, so you're going to have to figure out something else to do that doesn't involve AT&T.

"You won't have to wear a suit and tie or get up at 6 a.m. if you don't feel like it. And nobody's going to care, even if you do.

"Randall will be the CEO, you won't.

"Can you handle that?"

I didn't debate it in my head for too long: Yes, I could handle that. I looked forward to it, in fact. I had no idea what the future held, but I figured I could do a lot of hunting and fishing while I thought about life, which was all right by me.

That April (2007), I informed the AT&T board: I'd retire in June, at which time Randall could assume full operational control of AT&T as chairman and CEO. My decision caught some people by surprise. But the board also respected it, and that was pretty much that.

I left right around the time the iPhone launched. That was a nice send-off—long lines of people were wrapped around AT&T wireless stores across the country. Everything went pretty smoothly, and our employees felt great about all the attention.

But it was a bittersweet time for me, I will admit. I wasn't just leaving AT&T, I was also leaving the AT&T family I loved so dearly—all those employees who had worked so hard, for so many years, to make us successful. I didn't know every person by name; we had more than 250,000 employees, so that would have been a little tough. But I sure knew a lot of them, and I had friends all over the place—former bosses, guys in the network group, installers, linemen, people in the company cafeteria, lots of other people across the country, and around the world.

I gave Randall a few words of advice on my way out; not that he needed it—just a few things to think about. But I meant every word of it: "You are not here as a keeper of these assets," I told him. "There's a lot to be done yet—so make sure you keep going and keep growing." I told him that face-to-face, not by text or email. Just to make sure he heard me loud and clear.

And with that, I left. In June 2007 I formally resigned the CEO and chairman's titles, and also resigned from the board. And Randall took over. When the appointed day came, I basically packed up my boxes and my forty-four years' worth of memories and walked out the door—and on to the next chapter of my life, whatever it might hold.

I figured the real measure of Randall's management skill and style wouldn't show itself until after I was gone, which is the natural order of things when the baton gets passed from one CEO to the next. I made it a point to stay out of AT&T's head-quarters building—it was downtown on Houston Street, not too far from the Alamo. I will admit to having the urge to go back in, just to see a few friends, but I always resisted because I didn't want to be a distraction to anybody—Randall, especially. But I did keep a close eye on AT&T from afar—it's the sort of thing most former CEOs do, an occupational hazard, you might say. My hope, all along, was that Randall would not lose the momentum we'd built up, that he'd keep AT&T active and on the move, just as I'd asked him to do.

However, I didn't mean that literally.

One year later—on June 27, 2008—I got quite a surprise: AT&T announced plans to pull up stakes and leave San Antonio, and relocate 250 miles north in downtown Dallas. In a press release, AT&T said the move would give it "better access to customers and operations throughout the world," and to big partners and suppliers. AT&T made a point of saying the move was being done purely for business reasons, so nothing personal, San Antonio. With customers now in fifty states and 160 countries, AT&T said it had simply outgrown the city.

My reaction?

Saddest day of my life.

I don't say that lightly, but I do mean that sincerely: Aside from the deaths of my mother and father, AT&T's decision to move to Dallas was, hands down, the saddest day of my entire life. And it still makes me sad—I can hardly talk about it even now. That was a hard period for me. Friends, government people, civic leaders, and a lot of others called me when they heard the news—and I heard about it right before they did—and all I could say was: "You'll have to ask Mr. Stephenson, because I don't really know." I felt so inadequate, and so sad. I still do.

I do believe CEOs should have the leeway to make the decisions they deem necessary to run the business they're overseeing—let me say that up front. I'd moved the company from St. Louis to San Antonio, to refresh you. But that was a thousand-mile move that had everything to do with pumping up productivity and changing the corporate culture. In contrast, Dallas is a four-hour drive from San Antonio, and in the same state. What was that going to buy AT&T? I really had no idea.

And I'd now like to offer my two cents on the subject because this is important to me, and because I do think there are some larger lessons to be drawn.

If you're going to uproot a corporate headquarters and move it, I personally think you should have clear and convincing reasons for putting people through that kind of ordeal. Because whenever you do something like this, you disrupt the lives of a lot of employees, as well as their families, and extended families, so there needs to be a very clear payback. Dallas is basically a big-city version of San Antonio that sits straight north, only with higher prices, worse traffic, and less attractive housing options for employees. As for attracting talent, AT&T is one of the biggest and most respected companies in the world. We never had any trouble attracting people to San Antonio. Suppliers, same thing: We could have relocated to Timbuktu and they'd still be crawling all over us trying to get our business— my view. AT&T said the move to Dallas would give it access to a big airport—Dallas/Fort Worth, which has a lot more direct flights than the one in San Antonio. Fair point. The trade-off is that the Dallas airport takes you about forty-five minutes to get to; the one in San Antonio is a ten-minute drive from downtown. I've flown to cities all over the world from San Antonio, I would add, and still do.

But even if you throw all this stuff out, this one core fact is undeniable: AT&T was good for San Antonio, and San Antonio was good for AT&T. Bottom line. We were the biggest company there, so we were special, and viewed that way. In Dallas, AT&T is just one of many—not so special. San Antonio's Southwest character and charm was part of our culture and corporate personality. Sort of like Bentonville, Arkansas, is for Walmart, and Moline, Illinois, is for John Deere—that company's roots go back 175 years, to a one-man blacksmith shop. And that Americana identity is still very much a part of John Deere today, even though it's a $32 billion global enterprise. If you relocated John Deere to an office building in Midtown Manhattan, or Walmart to the Magnificent Mile in Chicago—where all the expensive stores are—it just wouldn't be the same. And Walmart is almost four times the size of AT&T.

But life goes on.

After I left AT&T, I wound up doing a lot of hunting and fishing. I stopped getting up at six o'clock every morning, and I shucked the suit and tie for jeans and work boots. I played less golf than I thought, and spent a lot more time at my ranch. Mostly, though, I just kept thinking about the next phase of my life. And the question I asked myself was basically this: *Okay, Ed, now what?*

The answer landed on my doorstep like a sack of cinder blocks when I got that call from the White House asking if I'd sign on as the chairman of General Motors, to see if I could help. As with many pivotal moments in life, this one arrived without much fanfare or notice, and in a fashion I could never have anticipated. It was a business opportunity, certainly. But nothing was ever more personal.

CHAPTER 12

GM

Rising to the Challenge

Cream rises to the top. A leader doing one thing is still a leader doing something else—those qualities just show up. And if he doesn't rise to the challenge, well, he's not going to be your man anyway.

That was the basic approach of the General Motors board with respect to Fritz Henderson. To recap, Fritz was the CEO—the White House appointed him in March 2009 after Rick Wagoner left. I was new as chairman, also at the request of the White House. Fritz didn't report to me directly—technically, he reported to the board. I was chairman of the board.

The board kept hoping that Fritz and his team would come in and clean house. But after five months on the job, not much had happened. A tweak here, a tweak there—that was pretty much it. That's why the board lost faith, essentially—because GM wasn't changing fast enough.

Fritz's commitment to GM was admirable. He got hired straight out of college and worked his way up from there. Over the course of his career he'd held every sort of job you can imagine: chief operating officer, chief financial officer, group vice president, managing director of operations in South America—the list went on and on. So Fritz knew the inner workings of GM's operations down to the nuts and bolts—and I mean that literally. He could tell you how to build a car from the ground up, and quote numbers backward and forward. It was impressive, I will say. The guy was like a machine.

But the CEO's job isn't about facts and figures. It's about being able to step into the top leadership position, and *lead*. It's an elusive quality, quite subjective when you get right down to it. But at the core of it, I think, is a strong sense of purpose: As CEO you have to be able to articulate a higher vision, and communicate that to people in a way they can relate to and believe in. Then you have to get your entire organization, from top managers to the most entry-level employees, focused and moving in that direction. You're never going to get 100 percent buy-in; you're always going to have holdouts. That's just human nature. But you can get 100 percent buy-in from top managers, and that's where the CEO comes in: *This is the direction we're going.* You'll notice that's a statement, not a request for a show of hands. It's up to the CEO to set the tempo, in terms of urgency; to establish long- and short-term business objectives; and to articulate performance expectations.

The implicit message to managers is that if you are not on board, then you will be leaving. I had to do that a few times when I was at AT&T, I'm sorry to say—move people out because they couldn't or wouldn't get behind something we were doing. But not too often, because when people understand what's expected of them, they tend to get on the same page with you pretty fast. That, too, is human nature.

Fritz had a personal sense of urgency, no question. But the tempo of the senior management team had changed very little. It was almost like, *Ho-hum, do we really have to do this?* So it was still business as usual, for the most part. With some seasoning, some board members thought Fritz could grow into the job—Wagoner had been grooming him for CEO when GM hit the wall. But we didn't have the luxury of time. GM had a morale problem, an image problem, and $50 billion in taxpayer money that needed to be paid back. Every decision and non-decision the company made was being monitored and picked apart. You couldn't turn on the TV or pick up a newspaper without reading something about General Motors, and most of it was bad. Everybody was looking for signs of a rebirth, and the longer it took for those signs to surface, the grumpier everybody was getting. Everybody felt the heat.

Fritz, at that point, had been given three months, roughly, to prove himself. If he did not show promise as a change-agent within that ninety-day window, the implicit understanding was that we'd have to find a new CEO. Fritz thought ninety days wasn't much time, and it wasn't. But he also understood our time constraints and respected the board's decision. I wasn't too happy about the probation, either, to be perfectly honest. About the last thing employees needed was to watch another CEO walk out the door, and about the last thing the board needed was to try to recruit a new CEO under these difficult circumstances.

Was Fritz the guy to lead GM? My gut told me no, based on what I'd seen up to then. But the wild card is human nature. The will to survive is a powerful thing. In fight circles it's called *heart*—boxers can be down for the count and suddenly tap into something so pure and so electric that they come back swinging, and win. Could Fritz steel himself and rise to the challenge? I didn't have the answer right then, but I hoped so. Fritz was a fighter in the best sense of the word. John F. "Jack" Smith, GM's retired chairman, gave Fritz a string of foreign assignments—in Brazil, Argentina, Africa, Latin America, Asia Pacific, other oper-ationally challenged markets. John had a fast explanation for that: "When you see a guy with talent, you give him a difficult assignment," he told *Businessweek* in 2004. This was going to be Fritz's toughest assignment by far. And I was pulling for him.

I figured there was no need to hang around and watch the paint dry. Fritz knew what the board expected; now it was time for him to stand and deliver. I told Fritz I was leaving, but would be back in two weeks. Fritz would have to give a progress report at the October board meeting; that was less than a month away. Right before I left, I told Fritz to call me if he needed anything. Then I headed for the airport and went home to San Antonio.

After a week or so I had not heard from Fritz, so I called him to check in. I was trying to give him enough room to make his own calls as CEO, but I was also mindful of the upcoming board meeting. I got right to the point.

"So how's it going with the reorganization?"

It was an open-ended question, but specific enough. Simplifying and streamlining GM's operational structure was Fritz's biggest challenge. This was also a top priority of the board.

"Things are going great!" Fritz said.

I let two beats go by, waiting for details to follow. They did not come. Instead, Fritz started talking about something else that had no bearing on the reorganization. Fritz had nothing specific he wanted to discuss, so it wound up being a very short conversation.

I showed up at GM a week or so later, just like I said. I made a beeline to see Fritz. He was holed up in his office, working. I was most interested to hear about the status of the reorganization. This time, though, I asked in a more detailed fashion:

Are you simplifying and streamlining?

What's your long-term strategic plan?

And the dealership shutdown—what's the progress on that? GM was in the process of shutting down more than two thousand dealerships across the country, around 40 percent of the total. The details got worked out in bankruptcy. Some dealerships were pushing back, so the slogging was pretty tough in some states.

"Everything is going great," Fritz said, friendly and optimistic as usual.

"Well, that's really good to hear," I said—I was not 100 percent convinced, to be honest, but I was hopeful. "So tell me about that."

But Fritz had no game-changing specifics to offer. He started in with some facts and figures, but none of it had any relevancy to the reorganization, GM's strategic plan, or the dealership shutdowns. And the more I tried to redirect the conversation to specifics, the more it became clear to me that no specifics would be forthcoming. My fast assessment: Fritz hadn't made much progress on the reorganization; he hadn't figured out a way to simplify and streamline; he had not rated his senior management team, in terms of their abilities. These were all things directors expected to hear Fritz talk about at the October board meeting, which was now less than two weeks away.

Fritz's management strategy, as best I could tell, was to stick with the same "matrix" approach that GM had used for years—decades, really. "Matrix" management, in case you are not familiar with the term, is when people have dual reporting lines. So instead of having just one boss in one area or group, you might report to several. Theoretically, matrix management is supposed to foster collaboration, because people are always interacting with different parts of the business. But in practice not much gets done, because nobody's really in charge, nobody's really responsible, and nobody has authority to make decisions—the "matrix" basically decides what gets done, and at what pace. As a result, not much gets decided, so not much gets done.

I have made a few runs at matrix management over the years—I was always trying things, just to see what might work. These were short-lived experiments, for the most part. And the main reason for that, I determined, is because people can't have two or three bosses. Human nature just won't allow it. In theory it seems smart, but in practice people tend to favor the boss who has control over their salaries and/or performance ratings. So you wind up wasting a lot of time, because people have to go through this matrix mash-up every time they want to do anything.

This style of management also doesn't lend itself to building confidence in senior managers. I'd argue it does the opposite, because they're always running around with training wheels on, more or less. The only way a manager can get comfortable with making big decisions is to actually make those decisions, then live with the results and consequences. In heavily matrixed organizations, there's no penalty for non-performance, or under-performance—the matrix absorbs all that. As a result, it's easy to distance yourself if things go off the rails. At GM, that was pretty much a way of life.

Fritz had grown up in that matrix environment at GM, so you almost couldn't blame him for not rushing to change it, because that's all he really knew. But at the same time that ninety-day clock was winding down fast. I was respectful of Fritz's role as CEO, but I also wasn't going to stand by and do nothing while he dug himself deeper—this was my thinking. So I decided to give him a few things to consider. The short version of what I told him went something like this:

"I want you to prepare a simplified presentation on revenue, expenses, and dealer shutdowns.

"Also talk about your plan for streamlining and reorganizing the business. Keep it short and to the point.

"Don't get bogged down in detail: If board members have any questions, they'll let you know. And that's it."

In other words, get in, get out, and resist the urge to run down all sorts of rabbit trails that had nothing to do with the reorganization plan or GM's financial health. If he stuck to that road map, I figured Fritz would do okay.

Well, Fritz didn't do that. Instead he showed up with a long, detailed presentation that probably would have been interesting if you were a car guy, but had little relevancy to the state of the overall business, or the reorganization. And this was just making a bad situation worse, because half our board members were brand new and not from the car business, so they were not familiar with a lot of the car lingo that Fritz was throwing around.

After the meeting, we immediately went into executive session—this is for outside directors only (non-GM employees), so Fritz was not present. The general consensus was that Fritz wasn't showing himself to be the change agent the board had been hoping for. Everybody liked Fritz personally—he was a good guy, worked hard, and was clearly trying to pull this thing out. But this wasn't a popularity contest—this was about the future of General Motors.

Steve Girsky—he was the union's representative on the board—was also there. He pretty much summed up the feeling in the room: "This is the same old GM."

And that was the basic problem. This was supposed to be the *new, improved* GM—not the bogged-down-to-the-headlights-in-mud version that got forced into bankruptcy. And here we were, in October 2009, nowhere closer to turning GM around than we were on the day it filed for Chapter 11 in June.

Some of the directors who'd been on the board for a while were used to these long GM-style presentations. So some of them thought we were being a little hard on Fritz, I will say. But not much. Other people, mostly the newer directors who came on around the time of the bankruptcy, thought we weren't being hard enough. Some weren't sure what to think—they just wanted the management issue fixed. We all did.

"Well, this is our first data point, ladies and gentlemen," I finally said, or something like that. I was still hoping that Fritz could pull it out, and with two months left on the clock I figured he had plenty of time to do that.

After the meeting ended, I again made a beeline to go see Fritz. Executive sessions are confidential, so I couldn't give him verbatim feedback from board members. But I left no doubt as to how the board was feeling.

"Fritz, this matrix management stuff doesn't work," I told him—I did not try to sugarcoat anything. That wasn't going to do anybody any good, especially Fritz.

Then I just sort of laid it out:

"Nobody has accountability, nobody's responsible; in my opinion, you have to change the organizational structure. *You're* the CEO, you make the decision. But you need a new management structure, and you need new people in some of these jobs. And your span of control right now is so great that you couldn't possibly get all this stuff done—so you've got to start delegating."

I was hoping to get a conversation going, not unload a lecture. So I asked him: "Do you agree? Do you disagree? These are my observations. Now tell me yours."

Fritz didn't have much to say, about anything. But I could tell from his body language that not only did he not agree with me—he wasn't even sure what I was talking about. So I started talking about leadership, the need for clear lines of responsibility, authority, and accountability; his mission, as CEO, to come up with a plan that could help GM move forward. Fritz kept nodding in agreement, but I could tell that he really wasn't buying it. *You don't know how this place runs, Ed, and you don't know the car business, either. You basically don't get it.* Fritz didn't say this to me directly, of course. But that was my gut feeling.

There wasn't much more for me to say, or do. Fritz was the CEO. It was up to him to make his calls as he saw fit.

The November board meeting came and went. Fritz's presentation, once again, was long and not exactly to the point. It is not my intention to belabor or string this out, so let me just say: The ninety-day clock kept ticking.

The December board meeting, like all GM board meetings,

would play out over the course of two days. In keeping with board protocol, there would be a dinner with directors and senior officers the night before, followed by the actual meeting the next morning—on December 1, in this case. At that meeting, Fritz would have to make another presentation. He had ample time to prepare; the meeting was still a few weeks off, at this point. Once again, I decided to throw in my two cents for his consideration. My suggestions went something like this:

1. The board is expecting you to have a strategic plan—so figure that one out pretty soon.
2. The board wants to see the financials of GM's global business in a streamlined, simplified form.
3. We don't have PhDs all over that room; board members have a varying mix of expertise and backgrounds. Show us what's important, and talk about that in a clear, concise way. And try to cut down on the car lingo; this is a board meeting, not an auto convention.
4. Dealer closings: How are they going? Number closed, number pending, other relevant data.
5. Organizational structure: If you plan to make changes, be specific as to what those changes are.
6. Strategy: long term versus short term. Summarize the goals, how you intend to get there. Again, try to be short, concise, and to the point.
7. If it's not relevant to GM's financials, organizational structure, or dealer closings—don't go there. If the board has questions, they'll ask.

I might have had a few other things to say, but that was the general idea—I am paraphrasing from memory. Focus was the common thread.

"These are my observations, for what they're worth, based on my time in management," I said, in closing. And then I added, for emphasis, "And I think you should consider these *strongly*." Fritz sort of smiled at that, and said okay.

Throughout this period, and my entire run at General Motors, I was in regular contact with the White House task force—Team Auto, as Steve Rattner used to say. Most of those conversations were on the phone, but not all. During one face-to-face meeting in Warren, Michigan, the team shared a document with me and a handful of board members. The report was, and still is, confidential, so I am unable to be too specific in describing its contents. But the basic conclusion was this: *GM is unfixable.*

The report was compiled during the bankruptcy process— Steve and his team took a fine-tooth comb to GM's books. It was basically a series of detailed assessments of GM's operations and administrative parts. Management also got put under the microscope: People don't know what they're doing; nobody knows who their bosses are; nobody knows the management hierarchy, the mission, the strategy, or almost anything else, for that matter. As a result, the report concluded, GM was paying more for goods and services than anybody else. This included Chrysler, presumably, which also went bankrupt. (Team Auto also had access to Chrysler's books.)

I did not disagree with the overarching message about GM's management. But I did disagree, strongly, with one thing: To me, GM *was* fixable. It might not have been fixable with the management team that was in place at that time. But the company was 100 percent fixable—of this I felt quite certain.

By now, the practical reality of the board's situation was starting to kick in. If Fritz didn't make it, we needed to have a replacement ready to go, because GM could not afford to be without a CEO for even one day. Nobody had any concrete names to offer, so we batted around some ideas on the phone— directors were in pretty regular contact during this period.

That's when I got asked, for the first time, if I might be interested in becoming GM's CEO. I had a fast answer for that: "No."

I'd signed on as chairman at the express request of the White House, with the understanding I'd hang around long enough to help the company get back on a good track. But taking on the role of CEO and assuming responsibility for day-to-day operations and management was a different proposition entirely. I was then visiting Detroit pretty regularly—a few times a month. But I was not living there full-time, and had no interest in doing that. I had a wife, family, and life back in San Antonio, and I was interested in getting back there full-time as soon as reasonably possible. So my fast answer to that question was, "Thanks but no thanks—not interested."

By then Ray Young, GM's chief financial officer, was also on the hot seat. Like Fritz, Ray was a product of the matrix. So he also struggled with his presentations to the board—they were too long and largely disorganized. Some members who had financial backgrounds did not take that well, which made for some tense moments for Ray on a couple of occasions. Everybody liked Ray, personally—good guy, smart, and highly knowledgeable about global operations, in particular. But his weak performance as CFO was most concerning. GM needed to rebuild credibility with the financial community as quickly as possible, and the board thought Ray wasn't helping. So the decision was made that he had to go. I felt we could find a place for Ray at GM elsewhere—just not in the finance department.

When I told Fritz, he immediately offered to take on Ray's job as CFO, in *addition* to being the CEO. "Yeah, I can do that job," he said, almost casually. "I used to be the CFO, as you know, so I have all this stuff in my head..."

Fritz was already overloaded and overextended, and he wanted to take on more? I brushed aside his comment and kept on talking.

"That's not what we're after," I said. "We're trying to build a team of very competent upper management here, so let's look at the candidate list."

Well, there was no candidate list. Fritz said GM didn't keep track of that sort of thing officially, so he just tracked it all in his head. He also didn't have any ideas about who could step in to replace Ray—GM's finance department had been gutted, along with a lot of other areas, during the bankruptcy. That's partly why he volunteered to do the job himself, I guess. I appreciated his willingness to load up his plate even higher, but the idea of Fritz serving as CFO and CEO was a non-starter: not happening. So I asked him to come up with a list of possible replacements for Ray, and left it at that.

Then came the December board meeting—Fritz was now at the end of his ninety-day probation period. Once again, Fritz's presentation did not go well. It was obvious from his commentary that there had been very little progress on the reorganization, very little progress on anything. Talks with potential buyers of Saab—the nameplate was discontinued during bankruptcy— were also not going well. Fritz was leading those talks; every time he got close to sealing the deal something would happen and negotiations would collapse. Fair or not, the lack of progress on Saab probably didn't help the mood in the boardroom, with respect to Fritz's leadership skills. And now the ninety-day clock was up.

After the board meeting, we immediately went into executive session. Fritz was not present; it was just me and outside directors.

Does Fritz stay on as CEO, or does he go?

I immediately put the question on the table. Right away the consensus in the room was that Fritz was not the change agent that GM needed right then. Everybody liked Fritz, respected his deep knowledge, and greatly appreciated his many years of service. But the decision was unanimous: Fritz had to go.

Then the question became: *Okay, then who are we going to get to run this place?*

By then we'd already hired Spencer Stuart, the executive

search firm, to come up with a list of potential candidates. (I told the person leading the search that he had to buy a GM car if he was going to do work for us; he called back the next week to let me know he'd bought a Buick.) It was a really great candidate list, I will say—it had a number of heavy hitters from *Fortune* 100 companies. These were household names, in some cases. Really impressive, you know?

But here's the thing: GM had no money to pay these people. We were operating under TARP rules—short for "Troubled Asset Relief Program," that's where the auto bailout money came from—so we were severely limited as to what we could offer. One of the candidates on the list—he turned around a company nobody thought could be saved a few years ago—was pulling down $15 million a year or so. Other people on the list were making even more. The most we could pay was $2 million, maybe. That's a lot of money, no question. But it's not even close to being competitive in terms of what top CEOs earn nowadays. I'm not saying that's right, but that's just how it is.

So any CEO we hired from the outside was basically going to have to take a big pay cut, or come on board and work for free as a public service. Spencer Stuart talked to a few of these people confidentially, as I understand it, just to gauge interest. But the GM board itself never talked to anybody directly. We figured that was just a waste of everybody's time. As for the idea of somebody coming to GM and working for free, we had no expectation of that.

This was not one of the board's finest moments. In truth, we should have been better prepared for this worst-case outcome. But the fact of the matter is, we weren't: We had no internal candidates that made sense, no external candidates that we could afford, and no time for Spencer Stuart to conduct a proper global search. And even if we had the time for that—and we didn't—we didn't have the kind of money it was going to take to recruit a top CEO. So why put everybody through that, especially our employees—who were about to watch the second CEO in less than a year, one of their own and a guy who was very well liked, walk out the door?

That's about the time somebody asked me again if I'd consider stepping in as CEO. I don't even remember who asked the question—we were all sitting around the table batting around ideas, so there was a lot of cross-talk in the room. But I do remember that the question registered with me, and I immediately threw it back out on the table for discussion:

"Does anybody here want the job?"

I looked around the room for any flicker of interest, any whatsoever.

Dead silence.

There were no volunteers, let me tell you. Dan Akerson, one of GM's most consistent critics throughout this entire period, sat silent. So did every other director. The mood was dripping with tension. Nobody made a move; all eyes were on me.

Two or three other people chimed in at that point: "Ed, will you do it?"

There are moments in life when you fold your cards and push back from the table, and moments when you double down. That, for me, was one of those moments. I had little interest in taking over day-to-day responsibility for General Motors, to be quite candid. But I also knew we couldn't just leave GM hanging. Somebody had to step up to the plate.

"Well, I know we don't have anybody," I said, still rolling the CEO question around in my head as I spoke. "So if nobody else wants the job...then I will do it. For some short period, I will do it."

It wasn't the most elegant answer, but it was an honest one. GM could not be without a CEO for even a single hour, not in this delicate state. Employees were already shattered; so was the public's confidence in GM's ability to come back strong. If we announced that Fritz was leaving, but had no ready replacement, we'd only succeed in making a bad situation worse. I didn't have the stomach for that. A quick show of hands was all it took: I was now the new interim CEO.

All that was left to do was to tell Fritz. He was waiting for me in his office. I remember exactly where I sat: just to Fritz's left, at the conference table in his corner office. Fritz sat with his back to the large window—I could see straight down the Detroit River over his shoulder. There was no good way to say this, so I just said it:

"Fritz, we promised you ninety days. We're now at ninety days, and the board thinks you should go. It's just not going to work out."

Fritz seemed surprised: "Really?"

"Yes, really, that's what we think."

Fritz said okay—calm as he could be—then asked when his last day was.

"Now," I told him. "This is your last day."

Fritz, as always, was an absolute gentleman. He didn't scream, didn't pitch a fit, didn't bad-mouth anybody. He did ask about his severance package, which was perfectly understandable. Fritz, like other senior executives, had already taken several pay cuts, and the bankruptcy pretty much wiped out his retirement. I promised to be in touch as soon as I found out. He sort of nodded, said he'd like to come back in over the weekend to clean out his office. I said okay, whatever you need. With that, Fritz got up, squared his shoulders, and walked out.

I sat there for a few minutes just contemplating the weight of the moment. It was a brilliant blue-sky day, which seemed at odds with what had just happened. Then I did a version of what Fritz had just done: I got up, got my composure, and walked out. The first person I saw was Vivian Costello, Fritz's executive assistant—she was Rick Wagoner's assistant before that. She was sitting at her desk just outside the door. I reflexively stopped and told her that Fritz no longer worked for GM. Vivian looked stunned, and asked me who was taking over as CEO.

"You're looking at him," I said.

I didn't have an office to go to—I was still working out of my conference room, just down the hall. So I made my way back there, shut the door, and just sat there. I had mixed emotions. On one hand, I felt relieved that the CEO issue was now resolved. But the reality of what I'd just agreed to do—to attempt a turnaround of a company the government considered "unfixable"—was starting to sink in.

What in the hell did you just do, Ed—are you nuts? I just sat there, feeling a little shell-shocked. It was quite a moment.

Within an hour the head of human resources found me. She was almost in a panic: I wasn't on the payroll, she pointed out, so how was GM going to pay me? I almost had to laugh at myself. I never discussed salary with the board, or if I'd even get a salary. I told her I'd make it easy for everybody—"I don't want any pay for December," I told her. "I don't want anything—we'll deal with that later." That was not the answer she wanted to hear, I could tell. But I was now the CEO, so she could only argue with me so much.

I made another decision, almost on the spot: that I was going to stick around Detroit for two weeks to help calm people down. Then I was leaving town and would not return until after the winter break—GM shuts down all its operations between Christmas and New Year's, and reopens the first business day after the break. It was a very deliberate decision: I wanted the whole organization to think about what had just happened. And I wanted everybody to talk about it—at the water fountains, at coffee shops, over lunch with their friends, wherever they might find themselves—and let them think that maybe nothing was going to change, that maybe it was going to be the same old matrix stuff and that this new CEO was just some guy they'd never see or have to deal with. I just wanted people to think about that for a couple of weeks.

And I, meantime, was going to be thinking about them every second. I would also be writing copious amounts of notes to myself about what I thought: about GM's organization, the senior management team, the morale issue, the culture issue, the focus issue, and lots of other things that I'd been thinking about since the day I'd stepped in the door as chairman.

I didn't have all the details of GM's reorganization worked out. But I did know this much: As soon as I got back to town, we were going to start making a lot of progress.

CHAPTER 13

January 2010

I walked in the door with a business plan. And I was ready to go.

One of the first things I did was to call a mandatory meeting with all the top managers of General Motors. I had two primary goals: simplification and a clear, concise management chart. Those were the two main components of my reorganization plan. I drafted it out over the Christmas break—took me two weeks, start to finish. Wasn't much to look at—I wrote the whole thing out by hand on a yellow legal pad, had a bunch of notes to myself scribbled all over it. But I hoped it would get the job done. That's all I cared about.

General Motors was way too complex—that was obvious to me from the day I became chairman. Matrix management was the main problem. I personally don't think a matrix approach works for most companies, for the reasons I have already talked about. But it *really* doesn't work for a company that's the size of a small country like GM—just too many places for people to hide and shuck responsibility. Liberal use of high-priced consultants—hundreds of these people were on the GM payroll—didn't help. That's just another way to avoid responsibility and accountability.

I decided to un-matrix GM. I was going to understand who was responsible for what at the top level before the end of my first week as CEO, and they were, too. Getting the matrix unraveled at the lower levels would probably take a while—years, most likely. GM had more than two hundred thousand employees spread around the world, and thousands of people in middle management. Getting people to adopt new ways of thinking, and acting, isn't something you can just decree—human nature will not allow that, especially when you're talking about human nature in the context of big, bureaucratic organizations. And GM's was so big and so deep and so wide that it even had its own nickname: the "frozen middle." The thaw would take a while, I knew. But once senior management was out of the matrix box, I figured the message would start to trickle down. So it wasn't a fast fix, but you have to start somewhere.

I approached my duties as the new CEO with a great sense of purpose. And I did that because, one, that's my wiring; and two, I have a strong personal philosophy about the job.

It's up to the CEO to set the tone in a company. By that I mean—to set expectations and to set the tempo, which is the sense of urgency that your people need to have regarding business objectives. The CEO has to communicate this to people in a way that makes sense. And with intent—people have to understand that there are consequences for non-performance. Publicly traded companies aren't social clubs, you know; they exist to make money for stockholders, and the only way you do that is by managing your business in a productive, efficient manner.

People are at the heart of this. I'm a big believer in giving managers a lot of support and encouragement, but if somebody isn't producing within a reasonable period of time, or consistently misses targets, the CEO is obliged to move that person out and find somebody else. It's never an easy thing to do that, but it is sometimes necessary. The people part of the CEO's job

is one of the most difficult. But it's also one of the most rewarding, because when people step up to challenges, man, does that
make them feel good. And that makes you feel good as a manager, to help people grow and stretch like that, so everybody
wins in the end.

So I called a meeting that first week and everybody showed
up—it was at the RenCen, GM's global headquarters. We all
settled into a conference room, around this big table. The paint
was still pretty wet on the change of command; Fritz had only
been gone a few weeks. So there was a certain amount of ner-
vousness in the air. And all eyes were on me.

That's when I told everybody, in a very direct fashion, that we
were going to start meeting every Monday—in that conference
room—to talk about what was going on with General Motors.
We'd discuss our problems, management strategies, what was
happening, what wasn't happening, anything else they wanted
to talk about. And the reason we were going to do this, I said,
was because I wanted to fully understand what was happening
inside GM, and I wanted every other person around that table
to know, too, because we now were a team, with one goal, and
one objective: to get General Motors turned around and healthy
again. That was my basic message to everybody: One company,
one team, one goal.

And as I was talking, I could see this was making some
people uneasy, because what I'd just told everybody, in effect,
was that life at GM as they knew it was about to change in a
pretty big way. From a management standpoint, every person
in that room was used to doing his or her own thing, with very
little oversight or obligation to engage in cross-discussion with
other senior managers. So now, with this simple declaration,
I'd just told them that that was over; that there was going to be
management transparency, open lines of communication, and
clear accountability. In other words: no more hiding behind the
matrix. People were sort of shifting in their seats and making

side glances with each other, and I knew what they were thinking: *Is he serious?*

Well, one guy piped up right away and said he couldn't
come to the next meeting because he was going to be in California. And I looked straight at him and said: "No, you're not.
You're going to be at the Monday meeting." Implying: *You'll be
here. And if you're not here, don't come back.* And that's exactly
what I meant, because I was dead serious about de-matrixing
General Motors, and that Monday-morning meeting was the first
step.

This was no democracy. I wasn't asking for a show of hands
as to who thought this was a good idea, or whether this was
convenient for them—this was how it was going to be. And I
guess everybody got the message, because they all showed up,
every single week, after that.

I had one more message to deliver—to the GM board. Just
to make sure we were all on the same page. At the first board
meeting after I got named CEO, we had a conversation: "I'm
going to do my best to turn GM around, and turn it around
quick," I said. "I need your full support, and I assume I have it.
But if I don't, speak now."

I had no idea how long it would take to get GM turned
around, but I knew I'd be moving a lot faster than what GM was
used to. I didn't want anybody on the board to be surprised or
upset by that, but I also didn't want any interference—too much
was riding on the outcome. The board was very supportive, I
would add. And I was most appreciative, because there was a
lot to do, and I was eager to get going.

I started in very quickly with moving people around, or
out, at the top level. I had some restrictions. Because of TARP,
salaries of senior executives were capped, as noted, and we
couldn't really compete for top talent outside of GM. On the
plus side, GM had some younger executives two or three levels
down who showed promise. GM had no formal system in place

for tracking these people. I was amazed that GM would treat executive development so casually—young talent is essential to the continuation of any business; that's where your future leaders come from. At AT&T, we used to talk about up-and-coming talent frequently. We did that for a couple of reasons: One, it helped me and other senior managers learn about people who were farther on down the management chain, and two, it was a way of making sure our top executives kept in touch with all parts of the organization, not just the upper tiers. I had a board tacked up on a wall in an office—only myself and my executive assistant had the key—with the names and bios of promising young managers all over it. I spent a lot of time studying that board, and referred to it often whenever I considered people for promotions, or needed to fill a big job. But GM didn't spend much time on talent development, so I basically had to wing it.

My most pressing need, by far, was for a new head of North America—this person basically oversees business in the United States, Canada, and Mexico. One focus is the dealership network, which is the customer interface for GM. If the car dealership relationship isn't right, GM won't sell as many cars, which means the company won't make as much money. There are lots of state laws around dealerships, so the job is a lot more involved than you might think. During the bankruptcy, GM shut down 40 percent of its dealer franchises—some of that precipitated by the suspension of the Saab, Saturn, and Hummer nameplates. A bunch of lawsuits got filed as a result, and many of those were still in progress around this time. So whoever got the North America job was going to have to have a high IQ for cars, people, and politics.

GM didn't have a list of internal candidates, as I mentioned, so I started nosing around on my own. One name kept coming up: Mark Reuss. He was then the vice president of the Vehicle Engineering Center—VEC for short—in Warren, Michigan.

That's a half hour's drive from the RenCen. The VEC is the nerve center of GM's engineering operation. More than eight thousand engineers work there on every sort of thing you can imagine. They're the ones who figure out how to make engines more gas-efficient, braking systems safer, and a thousand other things that impact a car's performance, safety, and marketability. So that's where Mark was—as the number two at the VEC.

I decided I wanted to meet Mark, so I called him up and asked him to come to the RenCen to see me. He showed up—it was just me and Mark, sitting in my office—and the first thing I asked was what he thought about General Motors. It was a fishing-expedition question, to some degree. I wanted to see if he'd give me the company line or an honest answer. Mark did not hesitate or parse words.

"I think we're all messed up," he said. He used stronger language to make his point, but that was the basic idea. Then he proceeded to tell me, in a thoughtful, deliberate fashion, why he felt that way. That led to a bigger conversation about the bankruptcy, senior management, employee morale, and some other things. Mark was well versed in all of it, which impressed me. We talked for a solid hour.

Mark was a mechanical engineer by training, had a solid understanding of the auto industry. But GM, for him, was also a family business. His dad had worked at GM, and just like Mark spent his entire career there. Mark didn't have much experience as a senior manager—he'd spent some time running GM's operations in Australia and New Zealand. (He told me he'd managed to make money there. I checked; he did.) But what he lacked in management experience he more than made up for in passion for the business, and for General Motors, specifically. Mark had GM in his blood. And he badly wanted to see things get turned around. That got my attention: Management skills can be learned. But passion is something that either you have or you don't. Mark had it.

I talked to a couple of other people about the North America job, but the conversation I had with Mark stuck with me. I called Mark back a day later and told him he had the job.

Well, Mark got a *version* of the North America job, I should say—the un-matrixed version. Historically at GM, the head of North America oversaw the dealership network, but marketing (and advertising, which falls under marketing at GM) was under somebody else, and that person reported to the CEO, as did the head of North America. In theory, these two people were supposed to coordinate and collaborate. But in reality, because of the GM matrix, that rarely happened; the left hand in North America never really knew what the right hand in marketing was doing, and vice versa.

This, to me, made no sense. So I de-matrixed both jobs: I put everything that related to North America, including marketing, under North America, and gave Mark Reuss 100 percent responsibility and decision-making authority for the whole thing. But the quid pro quo on that was that Mark was also 100 percent *accountable* for the results of North America, including marketing. So if things did not go well, he was going to have to answer for it.

This represented a big change for marketing, which had traditionally reported directly to the CEO of General Motors, not the president of North America. The number one marketing person at the time was Susan Docherty; she'd only had the job a few months, got elevated following the exit of Mark LaNeve. Susan wasn't too crazy about having to report to Mark Reuss, and Mark wasn't too familiar with the ins and outs of marketing and advertising—he was an engineer at heart, like I said. But I wasn't asking for a show of hands—that was the new management arrangement.

I also did a de-matrix with respect to Bob Lutz, the vice chairman of GM. At the time, Bob had broad but poorly defined responsibilities over design, engineering, and marketing, but no real accountability for anything. This arrangement, once again, went back to the GM matrix. Bob's oversight of engineering never made much sense to me. Bob had a great eye on car designs, no question. And he certainly knew the car business. But GM had a lot of talented engineers who were in the trenches every day trying to rebuild our product lines and credibility. To me, it just made sense to give day-to-day responsibility to some-body who was in the trenches with them. So that's what I did: I handed the whole thing over to Tom Stephens, chief of global product operations.

Tom's a mechanical engineer by training; he began his career as an hourly worker at Chevrolet's engineering center, which is also in Warren. Over the years he worked his way up the ranks and through the brands—he had stints at Cadillac, Buick, and Chevy. He eventually landed in the powertrain division in Pon-tiac, Michigan—that's the group that makes engines, transmis-sions, castings, and other components that go under the hood. Tom had a bunch of other jobs all focused on engineering, which at General Motors is a pretty rarefied world—engineers are sort of the unsung heroes of the company; the things they do, and the engineering problems they solve, are simply amaz-ing. And Tom was at the front and center of all that. I figured he didn't need help from Bob Lutz, or from me, or anybody else for that matter. Plus, I'm not a fan of adding layers of management to things; it just mucks up the responsibility and accountability part of the job.

As part of the de-matrix, I also gave Tom responsibility for global purchasing—the GM group that buys all the screws, pre-fab parts, and other components that go into cars and trucks. This, again, just seemed logical: Tom's people were engineer-ing all of our vehicles, so they were familiar with the parts that go into them. Traditionally at GM, the head of this group reported to the CEO of General Motors—why, I have no idea, but that's how it was when I got there. Some people weren't too wild about this reporting arrangement, either. But like I said—I wasn't asking for a show of hands.

We made another tweak in procurement, subtle but important: GM started being a little nicer with suppliers. GM had a reputation for squeezing suppliers for every last nickel—I found this out by talking with some of our biggest suppliers. (I did spot checks regularly at GM; I used to do the same thing at AT&T.) GM, I learned, had a reputation for being pretty tough on suppliers. Part of that had to do with size: As the biggest automaker in the country, GM had a lot of weight to throw around. And it regularly used that to grind down the prices. But just because you can kick people in the shin and get away with it doesn't mean you *should*. A lot of bad combinations and permutations come out of that: A supplier could lose a shipment, shut down a plant for a week and give it to somebody else instead of you, all sorts of paybacks. Getting products out on time was one of GM's biggest problems.

I didn't know if a friendly demeanor would help us with suppliers, but I figured it couldn't hurt. That doesn't mean you let people take advantage of you. But it does mean you treat people fairly and with respect. As a general rule, you don't tick off the people who are giving you the stuff you have to have to build your product, you know? That, to me, is just common sense.

As for Bob Lutz, I made him a senior adviser, in anticipation of his retirement, with no direct reports. I had a lot of respect for Bob's experience and industry knowledge. At seventy-eight, his institutional knowledge ran deep—I figured that could come in handy as we moved forward with the reorganization. Bob agreed to stay on for a few months and help, which I appreciated.

I brought in a number of people from outside. At the top of my list was John Montford. I'd met John years earlier in Texas.

He was then a state senator—back then I called him "Senator Montford"—and I was the CEO of AT&T. I was also chairman of the board of regents at my alma mater, Texas Tech. Ann Richards, the late governor of Texas, named me to that position.

I thought we needed to ramp things up at Texas Tech significantly. So I called John—by then he was in private industry—and asked him to come on board as chancellor. He agreed, and off we went to the races. Let me tell you, we turned that place upside down: We built new dorms, built new buildings, brought the school into the modern world; we put that school on the map, big time. We simplified and streamlined wherever possible. Texas Tech board meetings used to go on for two or three days. We cut those down to two to three hours. John was a superb chancellor, and did a lot of other things that helped contribute to the school's success and national profile. I guess the school appreciated all that, because Texas Tech later did me the supreme honor of naming the engineering school after me. I thought that was really nice. I'm a big supporter of the school to this day.

When I became the CEO of General Motors, I again called John, to take over our Washington office. John was a little resistant at first. He was right on the verge of taking another job—as the head of a big foundation in Texas.

So I asked him: "You want to spend your time looking over proposals for money or doing something good for America?"

John sort of laughed, said he needed to think it over. I said sure, take all the time you need—I'll call you back in thirty minutes. I called back half an hour later—on the dot—and John said okay. So off we went to the races again. I immediately called our human resources department. I got the head person on the phone, told her I wanted John on the GM payroll within twenty-four hours. And I remember there was dead silence on the end of the line when I said that.

So I waited.

"We don't do things like that around here," she finally told me.

"You just started," I said. "We have got to have somebody here *now*, we cannot wait thirty days. John is going to be our head lobbyist tomorrow, at this salary, so make this happen." And she did.

I also called Bob Ferguson. Bob had also worked at AT&T—he was in our public policy and external affairs operation, which is based out of Washington. Bob was then working in Austin, at a strategic counseling firm. I told Bob I wanted him to become the number two person in Washington, under John. Bob immediately understood the importance of saving General Motors, so he only had one question for me: "When?"

"Tomorrow," I said.

Bob knew me well enough to know I was serious. General Motors was wrestling with some big issues in Washington, so hours mattered. So just like John, Bob agreed to basically drop everything he was doing and make a beeline for Washington. I again got on the phone to human resources to get Bob on the payroll that day. By then I guess the word was starting to get around on me, so I didn't get any pushback. I took that as a small but positive sign.

Within a very short time—this was still early January—I was starting to see other signs that we were building a little momentum. GM was still matrixed to the gills, so we had a lot of work ahead of us. But senior management was starting to act like a team, or at least not heading off in a thousand different directions—everybody knew what was expected of them, and the lines of communication at the top were starting to open up. These were small steps, no question. But at least we were moving in the right direction.

I had a lot of things on my mind during those first few weeks of January, so it really didn't register when somebody—I don't remember who—asked me if I was ready for the "big move." A week or so later, Vivian Costello, my executive assistant, asked me the same thing. That got my attention. I had no idea what she was talking about. That led to a very interesting exchange:

Me: "What move?"

Vivian: "To Warren. You didn't know that?"

"We're moving to Warren?"

"Yes, we start next weekend."

"Warren?"

"Yes, Warren—everybody's going. You really didn't know that?"

"No, I really didn't know that."

Turned out, this thing had been planned for months. GM's real estate people were running around trying to get everything ready, because the move was supposed to start the following weekend. People were leaving in waves, and that was going to continue until GM's office towers were empty. Everybody was relocating to Warren, out by the engineering center. Once the move was done, GM planned to put the RenCen up for sale or lease.

And here's the craziest part: The CEO and a couple of others *weren't* moving with the others. We were supposed to stay behind at the RenCen, all by ourselves, in this big, vacant office building. But everybody else—almost four thousand people, including my entire senior management team—would be a thirty-minute drive away in Warren. The plan had been in the works for months, but nobody ever bothered to mention it to me or the GM board. And this was the first I was hearing of it— a week before it was supposed to happen.

The whole thing was nuts. A move like that would have killed what little momentum we'd managed to build up—that would have disappeared overnight. Not to mention the cost— $100 million, at least. The ripple effect would have been awful. Detroit was already struggling; if we pulled up stakes and left town, the city would have taken a big economic hit—the

RenCen is *the* economic driver in the downtown area, and anything that disrupts that revenue stream has a direct impact on the city. Stores and restaurants inside the RenCen would have taken the worst of it—they depend on GM employees to survive. Some businesses, like the Food Court—that was the de facto GM cafeteria—probably wouldn't have made it. I couldn't find one positive thing about the move, and yet we were on the verge of doing it.

I immediately assessed the situation and came to this conclusion: *We're not moving.*

I had the GM real estate guy on the phone about five seconds later: "It's over," I told him. "Shut this move down *today.*"

He pushed back a little; said GM had already spent a lot of money, done all this planning, blah, blah, blah. I didn't care about any of that. Any cost savings from the move—and that was highly doubtful to begin with—would have been a pittance in comparison with the cost to GM in terms of lost momentum and overall disruption to the organization. Not to mention the economic hit to Detroit and the RenCen businesses—these people would have gotten creamed. So I shut it down. With one phone call, I basically wiped out months of planning.

A short time later a one-line notice got sent around to the entire building: "The RenCen move is canceled." And that was the end of the Big Move.

I guess word got around in a hurry, because a lot of people came up to me soon after that and thanked me. I got the feeling a lot of employees did not want to move to Warren, and the businesses in the RenCen were most relieved that we didn't pull out of there. I appreciated all the supportive comments, I will say. But I would have pulled the plug regardless. Because my sole concern, and sole focus, was getting GM turned around. Anything that didn't contribute to that, or had the potential to detract from that, was not something I was going to tolerate—not for a day, or even an hour, if I could help it.

I felt the same way about the senior management team. I was telegraphing my expectations in a very straightforward manner, every chance I got. And if results did not materialize within a reasonable period of time, then I'd be making more executive changes. And more changes after that, if I had to, because I was dead serious about getting rid of that matrix stuff, and getting the focus back on the employees and the real mission: making money. That was the ultimate responsibility of senior management, and my responsibility as CEO.

I guess the board liked what I was doing, because at the end of January I was asked to become the permanent CEO. (Up to then I'd been the "acting" or interim CEO.) News of the permanent appointment was announced on January 25, 2010. In my prepared statement, I gave no hard time line for my tenure, just said I planned to be CEO "for a while." I wasn't trying to be cute or evasive—I honestly didn't know how long I'd be there. My plan, all along, was to stick around until GM got on a good track, and then get myself back to San Antonio. That's what I'd promised the board, and promised myself.

Some people thought it was going to take us years to get back on track, but I never thought that. And I especially didn't think that based on the internal reports I was seeing around this time. By then I could see trend lines starting to develop, and all signs pointed to a financial recovery a lot sooner than everybody thought. I didn't want to get us out too far on a limb by making promises we couldn't deliver on. But by the same token, I didn't want us to sit on our hands and say nothing, given our growing momentum. Anything we could do to send a strong signal to America, and to our employee body, I was all for.

So we made a pretty bold prediction: that General Motors would repay its loans to the United States and Canada by June of that year, around $8 billion total. The US government had another $43 billion invested in General Motors—as noted, this got converted into a 61 percent equity stake in the company.

The only way to repay that $43 billion was to stage an initial public offering, or IPO. I had no idea when we might be able to stage an IPO—at this point I'd been in the CEO's seat for less than a month, and GM still had a long way to go. But I was thinking about that IPO a lot.

In January I also attended my first auto show—the North American International Auto Show. It's held every year in Detroit, the first of a series of big shows around the country. The first night, Ford walked off with the North American Car of the Year—the Fusion Hybrid got the top honor. The Fusion Hybrid is the gas-electric version of the Fusion, one of Ford's best-selling cars. It was getting a lot of praise from car magazines and auto critics. People liked the look and feel of the car, as well as the gas efficiency.

Nice little car, but not even close to what GM had in the hopper: the Chevy Volt. The Volt was an "extended range" electric vehicle, the only one of its kind at the time. Unlike the typical electric vehicle, which can travel only as far as its battery will take it before needing to be recharged, the Volt can go all day long. (According to GM, Volt owners typically drive about nine hundred miles before refilling their nine-gallon gas tank.) It's also got a lot of pickup—punch the pedal and you can get that thing up to a hundred miles per hour pretty quick. Most hybrids, which work off a combination of gas and electric power for regular driving, can't do that.

The magic of the Volt owed to a series of technology advances that our engineers came up with—special power splits, gear ratios, and lots of things around the battery pack had to get worked out. But the matrix mind-set of GM was also hard at work. Engineers, at that point, were already starting to say that our November launch date was far too ambitious. (The GM matrix always wanted more time…for everything.) And this was only January.

That wouldn't do. This wasn't so much about a car as it was

about sending a signal—to our employees, and to America: *GM as a creative force is back.* That's really what the Volt represented. And there was no way I was going to stand by and let that bottled lightning sit on a shelf forever.

So I put it out there, at the Detroit auto show, that the Volt might be in the market even *earlier* than November. That came as a big surprise to some of our engineers—some people got pretty upset; they had no idea I planned to say that. But I also felt like some of them needed upsetting, to get the message across that this was an urgent situation. Even if we didn't launch early, I figured it would light a fire under everybody. And you know what? It did.

I enjoyed the Detroit auto show, but it was a little awkward for me, I will admit. I kept getting stopped every ten feet or so—somebody would recognize me, ask me some question about some car. I was brand new on the job, had no idea, so I just kept saying: "Great car!" I basically bungled my way through it. But it worked out okay. When it was over, I remember thinking to myself: *Thank God that's over, now we can go back to trying to straighten out GM.*

And that's all I was thinking about right then: how to simplify GM and ignite the employee body; how to change this culture of General Motors, and make that happen as soon as possible. And knowing, in the back of my mind, that if we could just make a little money, and show that to the world, show that to our employees, that was going to do the most to help GM turn this corner.

CHAPTER 14

"Design, Build, and Sell the World's Best Vehicles"

What is our main purpose as a company?

At one of our Monday-morning management meetings, this was the question I asked. Seven or eight people in the room. Everybody started hemming and hawing. I was just sitting there, not saying a word, waiting for these guys to come up with an answer.

Tom Stephens—he's head of engineering—thought for a few minutes. Then he looked at me and said: "We design, build, and sell the world's best vehicles." Just like that.

I knew that was the statement the moment I heard it. One of GM's biggest problems was that it was all over the map—no clear-cut mission, no purpose. And here was a simple statement that cut through all that—direct, concise, easy to understand. It was perfect.

After that, I started repeating that idea every chance I got: *Remember, guys, all we do is design, build, and sell the world's best vehicles.* And I guess I said it so much that it just sort of took off. And before too long it got to be GM's mantra. And that was important, because we needed something for employees to orient themselves to and get behind. All we do at GM is design, build, and sell cars. Everything else is superfluous. That was the underlying message in Tom's statement. So that was truly a defining moment for us, because I always thought if we could find a way to energize the employee body and create focus, we'd start making money again. And once we did that, we'd start to regain market share, and start to compete again.

By then I was showing up pretty regularly in the Food Court. Anybody can go there—it's like any food court you'd find in any mall. Except this one was GM's de facto company cafeteria, as I have mentioned. I've always believed that management should do everything it can to be closer to employees, not farther apart. That's why I've always been a fan of walking around and talking to people—it's a friendly way of relating to people. Plus, you can learn an awful lot. Senior managers, they tend to get filtered versions of everything, because people are always on their best behavior around them. So these sorts of inputs, from employees, can be quite valuable.

My lunchtime routine was pretty much the same every day: I'd show up in the Food Court by myself—it's on the lower level, in this big atrium—get my tray, and get in line. Then I'd just sort of roll with it.

I had a lot of great lunchtime conversations. And that was very gratifying to me, because the fact that people were willing to talk to me like that said that maybe they didn't view me as a person who was unapproachable. That they were in this with me; that we were in this together. That meant a lot to me. The conversations were all over the map, but I heard one comment over and over again: "We've never seen a CEO down here before." I must've heard that a hundred times, probably more. I'd usually say something to take the focus off me, like: "Well, I'm here, so let's eat—what'd you get?" Most times, that was all it took.

But privately, that one hit me hard. I really didn't understand why no one from upper management ever showed up down there.

Was it because they didn't have time? Or maybe they didn't think it was appropriate? But my biggest thought was this: *How could this happen?* How could GM's management not take the time to meet and mingle with the employee body at every level—how could they not do that? Employees are the ones who allow your business to exist. Without them you can't make, produce, or sell a single thing. Yet nobody ever bothered. That still amazes me.

The Food Court was a regular thing for me, but I was always looking for ways to get out and meet people. Most days, my schedule was pretty packed. But sometimes I'd have a thirty-minute break in between, and when I did, I'd start walking. I'd randomly show up in somebody's office, unannounced, and just start talking to them. My goal was pretty simple: I wanted to get to know the people of GM—how they felt, and what their attitudes were about their jobs, senior management, anything else they might be thinking about. I met a lot of great people that way. I also got a lot of insights into GM's world, and its culture.

One time I walked into a cubicle and the guy was so taken aback he could hardly speak—he was just shocked I was standing there. Well, I sat down and started chatting with him, and pretty soon he loosened up. He talked about how it felt to go home at night and have his neighbors shun him, so to speak, because of the bankruptcy; other things that mattered to him. I just sat there and listened. This was a guy who'd spent most of his career at GM, and he really wanted to see things get turned around. GM, for him, wasn't just a place to work; it was a big part of his life. And I could certainly relate to that, because that's how I always felt about AT&T. I spent forty-four years there; it was family. Still is. And that's how this guy felt about GM—it really meant something to him, which is why he took it so hard when things went bad.

After a while—we must've talked for thirty minutes or so—this guy got pretty comfortable, I guess, because he asked if he could bring in some of his co-workers, and would I mind talking with them, too? I said sure, that's great—I knew I'd be taking these people away from their jobs, but this seemed to be important to him. So he rounded up all these people, and pretty soon we had thirty people, maybe more, jammed around this little cubicle. I told them *GM can be a great company again, here's our plans; here's our vision—We design, build, and sell the world's best vehicles*; that sort of thing. I was really trying to boost their confidence that we could come back. *I know we can do that, because you folks are smart and I know you're going to work hard so we can do this.* We talked for a solid hour.

I did the same thing out at the VEC—as you recall, that's the engineering center in Warren. I showed up unannounced and started popping my head into offices. I opened the door of one room and there was a bunch of guys standing around talking—they designed equipment for OnStar, GM's in-vehicle security, communications, and diagnostics system. So we started talking about OnStar. They were complaining about OnStar marketing, in particular; thought they didn't do a very good job selling our product. And I did not disagree. OnStar was not selling up to potential at that time, and it had been that way for years. (OnStar is a subscription service; it's free in some vehicles for a period of time, then you have to start paying monthly.)

This one guy, in particular, was really fired up. He was very critical of the OnStar marketing department, said even he could do a better job. And he kept beating on this point, over and over again—even though he was an engineer, not a marketing type. That got my attention.

So I asked him: "You think you can market this stuff better?"

And he said: "I know I can." He used saltier language than that, but that was the basic gist of what he was saying.

So I put it back to him: "Okay, then starting tomorrow morning your job is marketing OnStar."

And right there, on the spot, I pulled out my cell phone and called Mark Reuss—he's head of North America—and told him to put this fellow into OnStar marketing. The guy who'd been complaining was sitting there listening to all this, and you could see every emotion running through his face: *Oh my God, what have I done?* That's pretty much what he was thinking, you could just tell. But it just struck me at the time as: *Okay, you think you can do better? Well, let's give you a chance and see what you can do with this.* We transferred that employee to OnStar marketing the next day. (OnStar sales did not improve, so I guess marketing was a little bit tougher than what he thought.)

On occasion, my surprise visits had a little more purpose to them. One time, I cornered a guy in his office out at the engineering center to talk about a truck that was coming out soon. He was a vehicle line executive, or VLE—that's the top engineer on a production vehicle. Every vehicle GM comes out with has a number of people attached to it—in design, engineering, manufacturing, et cetera. The VLE has overall engineering responsibility. That's the guy I was talking to on this particular day—the guy who was the VLE on this pickup.

The truck was running behind schedule. I was not happy about this, so I asked him to explain. Well, he started giving me a bunch of excuses—can't get the right parts, not his fault, blah, blah, blah. I basically cut him off: "You're responsible; you have the authority to make this happen, so if it doesn't happen it's on *your* head." That's what I told him. He was trying to back me down by giving me all these excuses, you know. And I was having none of it. As the VLE, he was 100 percent responsible for that pickup. So if it didn't get out on time it was his fault. That was the bottom line.

Well, this guy turned white as a cotton ball—he looked shocked. He'd never heard this kind of talk before, I am sure. Because at GM engineering—and this goes back to the matrix—making excuses was a way of life: The design's not quite right, needs more testing, wrong part, wrong this, wrong that; the list was endless. And the net result is that GM regularly ran late on production schedules. That was the norm, so nobody thought twice about it—including this fine young engineer, whose immediate response to my question was to start making excuses.

Sometimes I'd drive around GM facilities—the company has sprawling campuses all over the place—and stop at buildings I didn't recognize, just to see who was inside. That's how I came across the advanced research laboratory, also out in Warren. I was by myself, as usual. The fact that I used to do this stuff used to drive GM security crazy—the CEO, I was told, never went anywhere without an escort. I basically said thanks but no thanks, because I wanted people to be at ease when I was around. Figured a bunch of security types following me around wasn't going to make anybody comfortable, especially me. I did the same thing at AT&T—no escort. AT&T security didn't like it, either. But that's how it was, so we worked things out.

So I walked into this GM lab and went up to the first person I saw—this lady in a white coat, holding a beaker or something. And I introduced myself: "Hi, I'm Ed Whitacre and I work here. I'd like to talk to you for a few minutes if you have the time." Or something like that. She knew who I was, I could tell. And she was very perplexed, because the CEO of General Motors had never showed up there, either, I guess—not without a formal escort and a security detail. But there I was, so we started talking. Out of the corner of my eye, I could see people whispering—*Is that him? Why is he here?* Before too long, a few people came over to join us. And a few more after that. Pretty soon there were fifteen or twenty people in this little group, all standing around in the hall of the research lab, talking.

And they were asking me questions:

Are we making progress, Mr. Whitacre?

Do you think we can be successful again?

Are we important to this company?

Does anybody know what we're doing?

Is our company going to make it?

In other words, what these PhDs and research scientists wanted to know was exactly what that guy in the cubicle and all his friends wanted to know, what the people in the Food Court wanted to know, what assembly-line workers wanted to know, what *everybody* wanted to know: Does anybody care? And does GM have a future?

And that sort of broke my heart, but also confirmed for me, once again, that GM management had not communicated to employees that they were important, that they mattered. Had not gotten the message across that, yes, we will be successful because we have the talent, we have the product, we have the willpower to succeed. That we're in this together, and together we're going to figure this thing out—and here's how we're going to do it. But nobody ever bothered to get that message across in a way that people could believe and relate to, just like they never bothered to make the five-minute walk to the Food Court once in a while to be friendly and show a little interest, and maybe offer a little assurance.

So I did my best. I told these scientists the same thing I'd been telling people elsewhere in the company: *There is no doubt in my mind that we're going to design, build, and sell the world's best vehicles. You play a major role in that; you are the reason we will be successful, because I know you're going to work hard to make this happen.* And that was all true, every last word. And the more I talked with employees at different levels of the company—in Detroit, out at the assembly plants, at facilities across the country—the more convinced I became that we could turn this thing around, and turn it around quickly.

I also did a drive-by at the global design center, the hub of GM's design organization, also in Warren. I somehow wound up in the truck design area—had no idea where I was going, just wandered around until I saw all these trucks. That, to me, is like light to a moth—I love pickups. I've been driving trucks for as long as I've been driving—more than fifty years. I own a couple of them right now, Chevy and GMC brands. Great trucks. A couple of designers were standing around, so I went over to talk to them.

I don't know the first thing about design; I'll be the first to admit that. But as a longtime truck guy, I do have some opinions. And here's my biggest beef with GM truck designs: not enough backseat legroom for passengers. This is based on my own personal experience. I'm six-foot-four, that's the main problem. But the other problem is that the backseats of GM trucks always come up short. I can push the seat all the way back and sort of make it work, but a couple of extra inches of legroom would sure help. So that's what I told these truck designers.

Well, they immediately did a matrix on me: They started giving me a bunch of excuses as to why that's not possible, can't be done, no how, no way, the usual sort of thing. I was arguing right back with them, 'cause I'm not taking no for an answer. Other trucks don't have this problem, just GM—so I told them that. This was sort of pouring salt in the wound, because GM has been chasing the number one truck spot for years—GM's top US competitor had taken that honor many years running, and they all knew this, of course. And so did I, which was why I threw it out there. Anyway, we were sitting there going at it pretty good over this legroom issue, and in walked one of the senior engineers, Mike Simcoe. He's Australian, sharp as a tack, I could tell. So he joined in.

Well, I couldn't stand there all day and talk trucks, so I gave them my best parting shots—this legroom thing had been bugging me for years—and off I went. I rambled around for a while more; the design center is huge, has long halls that go on forever. I stuck around another thirty minutes or so, then I had to get back to the RenCen for some meeting. Just as I was about to walk out the door, Mike caught up with me.

"We'll make more legroom," he said, and winked. Just like that.

And you know what? I went back two weeks later and sure enough, Mike and his team had figured out how to get a couple more inches of legroom in the backseat. So this guy was responsive and quick. That impressed me.

The rest of the design operation, from a timing standpoint, was not so impressive. Part of this has to do with auto industry tradition; part has to do with the GM matrix. The design process has multiple steps and levels of management sign-off, so designs typically take years to complete—this is how Detroit has always done it. Designers spend weeks or months carving detailed clay models—they're pretty incredible, look just like the real thing only they're 100 percent clay. But most of these designs never make it out the door. So at the end of the day, you wind up wasting a lot of time, money, and clay.

I was not okay with this. I wanted design to step it up significantly, and said that pretty directly to the head of global design, Ed Welburn. We wound up having a very candid conversation about the need to insert a little urgency into this process. Ed, a very talented designer in his own right, promised to kick it up a notch. I took that as a positive sign; at least it was a start.

I tried to tamp down the matrix whenever I could. It wasn't easy—the matrix was embedded at every level of GM, and the organization was most resistant to change. But I never stopped trying. If something wasn't getting done because of a matrix roadblock, I'd instantly try to knock it down. My hope was that if I knocked down enough hurdles, and people saw the good effects of that, they'd start doing more of it on their own. Progress on this front was slow. But glimmers of change were everywhere.

One time, a manufacturing executive came to see me: He said he couldn't get something done on time because of a holdup in procurement—that's the group that buys all the parts that go into GM cars and trucks. As a result, he said, the vehicle was stalled in production. Could I help?

I listened to what he had to say—then picked up the phone and called procurement.

I got the head person on the line.

"This fellow says your organization is keeping him from getting something done," I said—the guy who'd been complaining
was standing there listening, nodding in agreement. "He says it's
your fault, that he can't get this car out without that part. What
do you have to say about that?"

The procurement guy sort of stumbled around, said he didn't
know the answer and would have to get back to me.

"Well, find out," I told him. "We need this vehicle out on
time, so it depends on *you*." Translation: If it doesn't happen, it's
his fault.

He got the part. In a hurry.

Another time, we had a holdup with the Cadillac CTS
coupe—the car had already been delayed and was in the process of being held back again. Why? A small spot on the left rear
fender wouldn't paint right. Tom Stephens, the head of engineering, was working with his people trying to fix it. But no matter
what they did, he said, this one small spot wouldn't budge—it
had a small crease in it, Tom said, so the paint looked funny.

This was an urgent situation: The entire CTS production line
was stalled over this paint issue. The CTS was one of GM's pre-
mier vehicles. It also sold for a lot of money, and dealers were
waiting for it. Delaying the launch date—*again*—was not an
option. So I grabbed Tom and we drove over to the CTS assem-
bly plant in Lansing. When we walked in, a bunch of engineers
were standing around a big metal press, the one that makes the
left rear fender. They were all looking pretty unhappy. Not good.

Tom took me over and pointed to this one spot: "See, it won't
paint right."

Well, I was staring at this spot—and I didn't see a thing. It
looked perfect to me. Nobody was saying a word. Everybody
was looking at me. I didn't know a thing about making rear
fenders, or painting them. But I did know one thing: We were
not delaying this car.

So I said to Tom: "We've got all this talent here, and we've got these multimillion-dollar presses, and every other piece of metal on the car is perfect, right?"

Tom: "Right."

"And that's the only reason for the holdup on this car—that one little spot?"

"Right."

That's all I had to hear.

"I don't care what you have to do. You have the responsibility, you have the decision-making authority. Get this thing fixed, and get it fixed quick, because we are shipping this car *on time*."

Within a week, the problem was fixed.

I'm not sure *how* it got fixed. I never asked, to be honest. The point is that Tom and his team had responsibility and decision-making authority to solve that problem, and they did—they stepped up. That was the accountability part of the equation. And that's all I cared about, really.

The Volt was also on my radar. It was running behind schedule. This had to do with a number of things, and some of it was pretty understandable. The Volt was a new breed of car, and so was the technology. The algorithms, which tell the car how to react in certain situations, were giving the engineers fits. That, in turn, was affecting the Volt's performance and reliability. The salespeople also couldn't figure out what to charge for it; there was endless discussion around that. So the Volt was moving along at typical GM speed: slow, slow, slow.

The Volt's launch date was still set for November. I thought it was really important for us to start taking orders as soon as possible, so we could start generating excitement around the GM name. Dealers kept calling asking when they could have it. Car enthusiasts were calling, too. A couple of doctors in New Jersey called my office trying to place orders. Other GM executives were getting similar calls. The good news was that people really seemed fired up about this car. The bad news: Engineering really wasn't sure when the car would be ready.

Engineering was still nervous about the November launch, and even more nervous about the prospect of us taking orders early—anytime you involve customers, that adds heat and pressure to the mix…which was exactly what I was hoping for. I wanted GM to start taking orders by summer, at the latest. I kept sending word back through the engineering channels that delay was not an option. But I also figured a little eyeball-to-eyeball conversation wouldn't hurt. So I made a trip out to Hamtramck, Michigan—that's where the Volt was being test-driven—to reinforce the urgency of the situation.

One problem with our reputation was that people thought GM never had anything new coming out. You know, it was the staid old Chevy Impala, or some other plain-Jane car; that's what people thought about when they thought about GM. The Volt was GM's way of sending a message to America—the world, really—and the message was: GM is going to design, build, and sell the world's best vehicles. Including a world-class, all-new concept of an electric car; one that wasn't limited by "range anxiety"—that's when people start worrying they're going to get stranded because their electric car doesn't have enough juice (range) to get them to where they want to go. That's why it was so important to get the Volt out there as soon as possible, so we could start moving the dial on GM's reputation.

The Volt was a game changer. It worked, it was electric, and it would go on forever—more than 350 miles on a single tank of gas. (This assumes the car is fully charged.) It was a good-looking car; it was substantial; it was roomy. In other words, it was like no other electric car on the planet. A lot of these things are as small as tin cans, and you're lucky to go a hundred miles before they run out of electricity. They're not so good on hills, and have weak pickup. The Volt, in sharp contrast, drives and feels like a regular car, and can go like a shot—the pickup is amazing. So this was a whole new deal for electric cars, and a whole new deal for GM. This was our way of saying to the world, *By God, GM can do something.*

That's what I tried to get across to those engineers: The Volt is important to GM's future. So we had to have it done by X date so we could go into production, because a lot was riding on us getting this thing out the door. My message to them, to everybody, was clear and direct: *Delay is not an option.*

The pricing issue was tricky. Developing new car technology is very expensive, so you try to build that in to the cost as best you can, sort of like pharmaceutical companies do when they're developing a new drug. Because of all those upfront costs, we didn't expect to make money off the Volt anytime soon—that was going to take years. But we didn't want to give it away, either. The government was offering people who bought electric cars a tax credit—up to $7,500. We figured that would help push along sales, but not enough to have a financial impact on GM anytime soon. But like I said, the Volt wasn't about sales per se; it was about getting that positive message out there.

The Volt engineers seemed surprised, and pleased, that I'd make a special trip just to talk to them. Said they'd do their best, and I believed them: I had no doubt that they could get this thing turned around. But just to make sure, I kept up the pressure on Tom Stephens—he was head of engineering, so he had ultimate responsibility and accountability. Rarely would a day go by that I didn't ask Tom: Is the Volt on schedule? And Tom knew there was just one answer I wanted to hear.

By then, word was starting to get around on me—*He can show up anywhere, anytime, and he can ask hard questions, and he doesn't much like to take no for an answer.* I did that deliberately: *You're the key to this organization; you're a part of GM's potential success. If you don't get it done, we're not going to make it. But I know you can get it done—so go do it.* That was my basic message to the Volt engineers. That was my message to the design people. That was my message to everybody. And I kept beating on that like a drum.

I also started pushing for less use of outside consultants. The situation was just so ridiculous: GM was full of car experts, industry experts, marketing experts; people who had deep knowledge on every sort of thing you can possibly imagine when it came to designing, building, and selling cars. So why did we need all these consultants?

I got the answers you'd expect: *These people know something; they're providing verification for what we think*—things like that. And I'd say, well, that just tells me that you're paying somebody to tell you something you already know. And by the way, this wasn't just a GM problem; lots of companies do this.

I personally consider most consultants to be of limited value. Not all, but most. I've observed a lot of consultants over the years, and it's always the same: They come back to you with the long studies and the nice booklets, neatly bound, and you sit in a big room and go over their results. And in a high percentage of the cases there's nothing new—you already knew whatever it was they were telling you. But for some reason you were just afraid to act on it, or reluctant.

So one of the things I started preaching in our Monday-morning meetings was less use of consultants. We were paying our people to use their responsibility and decision-making authority. That was the only way they were going to build the confidence they needed to get comfortable with making the hard calls and stepping up to the results of those decisions— good or bad. Bringing in a bunch of consultants is never the answer; that's just a high-priced crutch, a way to stall, delay, and avoid taking responsibility—and I wanted that to stop.

Of course, I got a lot of flak from consultants for doing that. A few called me up directly to express their concern. These people were terrified that this very dependable revenue source—some of these firms had been living off GM for *years,* and I am talking big money—was being attacked. And in a way they were right, but that wasn't my focus. My sole focus, and sole concern, was making sure GM management got back on a good track. So I listened to what these consultants had to say, but meantime I kept turning the screws. I got our chief financial officer, Chris Liddell, to start giving me monthly reports on how much we were paying these consultants. Word got around GM pretty quick, and our use of consultants went down substantially not too long after that.

One consultant we did hire was Fritz Henderson, the former CEO. We got some flak over that. Which I could understand, to some degree, because he'd only been gone a few months, and we were cutting way back on our use of consultants, like I said.

But this was a special case. Fritz, as it turned out, was not going to get anything from GM in terms of an exit package. Not one red cent. This had to do with the bankruptcy and TARP rules around executive pay. But the bottom line was this: Everything Fritz had earned over the course of his twenty-five years with GM—pension, stock options, other compensation—was now gone. All his stock was worthless or underwater. And he had no salary, of course.

I thought the whole thing was crummy. Here was a guy who had devoted his life to GM, moved his family all over the world for GM, done his best to clean up the mess he inherited at GM—and for all that time and dedication he got *nothing*? I had empathy for that. Tim Lee—head of our international operations—put Fritz on as a consultant. Fritz got a one-year contract with international, which was an area he knew a lot about. It was a minimal amount of money in the larger scheme of things, so we didn't make a big deal out of it. I just felt it was the right thing to do. Some people disagreed with our decision, and I could certainly understand why they might feel that way. But I wasn't asking for a show of hands on that one, either.

CHAPTER 15

Management

Focus, Focus, Focus

Management mind-set is a powerful thing. It's basically what separates effective management teams from the not-so-effective.

And focus is a big part of that. This sounds so basic and simple, I know. But my experience at General Motors reminded me how completely out-of-touch some management teams are to that business fundamental. GM isn't the only one that violates this rule, of course—lots of managers at lots of companies out there are drifting.

In our case, GM was in a race with the clock—the competitive pace in the global car business is unrelenting, and internal financial pressures were significant. Yet some senior managers acted like they had all the time in the world to get things done. My answer to that was to give people direct responsibility and decision-making authority—if managers were fully accountable for results, I figured they'd be forced to focus on the task at hand. To help drive home that point—focus, focus, focus—I spent a lot of time in one-on-ones with people. During these sessions, I let management know exactly what I expected. I also

appealed to their basic logic. My main points were pretty consistent:

> Look, we're designing, building, and selling the world's best
> vehicles. We are not doing it next century; we are not
> doing it five years from now—we are doing it tomorrow.

I also talked a lot about our business fundamentals: Expenses
have to be less than revenues, otherwise you go broke. That's
why GM went broke the first time: It ran out of money. This was
an urgent situation, so I tried to convey that:

> Does it make sense to you that if we want to be successful
> we have to generate revenue?
> How do we generate revenue? We only sell cars.
> How do we sell cars? We have to produce something that
> is good and sell it for a fair price, then get out there and
> push the heck out of it like everybody else.
> What is so difficult to understand about that? Why are we
> so slow at this? Give me an answer, Joe Blow, because
> we have no time to waste here. We don't want this done
> eventually; we want this done before the sun goes down.

Making cars is a long process; it takes a long time. But that
doesn't mean you can take forever to get things done, because
you're dragging your feet over this or that, or stuck in an endless matrix decision-making web. The world is changing, and pro-
gressing. And so are your competitors. But people at GM didn't
think that way, for the most part, because they'd never really been
asked to think that way. And the matrix made that easy, because
the complexity of GM gave people instant access to a thousand
reasons as to why some car or some project was going to be late,
delayed, or just generally messed up. And that's how it had always
been at General Motors. My goal was to change that way of

thinking. So that became my management focus at GM: finding those roadblocks and taking them away as fast as I could. Then I could stand there and say, "Okay, now what's your excuse?"

Part of my push, as CEO, was to get senior managers to execute their duties in a manner that brought them closer to employees, not farther apart. But they also needed to give people room to learn and grow. Otherwise they'd never build the sort of inner confidence that makes for focused, goal-oriented teams and organizations.

Here's a small example: When we named Mark Reuss president of North America, he initially decided to put his office in Tower 400 at the RenCen. It's adjacent to the executive tower where I was located. I asked him why; Mark said he wanted to be close to his direct reports, and most of them worked in Tower 400.

A good impulse, certainly—but here are a couple of things to consider, I told him: One, if you're in the middle of everybody, they're going to look to you to make all their decisions—that's just human nature. Two, you might be viewed as micromanaging, and familiarity breeds contempt. Not good for team building or focus. And three, we're trying to drive authority and responsibility through the organization, so whatever you do don't micromanage, because that's the exact opposite of what we're trying to accomplish. Mark thought about it, said I still want to go to Tower 400—so off he went.

I went over to Mark's office a short while later to see how things were going. I walked in unannounced, and he was surrounded by paper and people. He was so socked in he could hardly move; people all around him. And I could tell, just by looking at him, that he had no room, no thinking time. He was sitting in the corner office, and everybody was just sort of hovering around him.

So I said to him: Mark, maybe you ought to think about moving over to another place. Mark said he'd like that, but there was no space on 39—that's where I was, the thirty-ninth floor of an adjacent tower. I said no problem, we'll build you an office.

The lesson? By putting a little physical space between him and his team, Mark could send a strong signal to his people that he was giving them more responsibility, more authority, and full accountability; in short, that he believed in them. That way they could focus on what they had to do; Mark could focus on what he had to do. The net is that focus ratchets up all around the place, and the entire organization benefits from that.

Mark was still just a short walk away if he wanted to go see somebody in person, or they could come see him. But when they did visit it would mean something to them, because they'd have to make a special trip to go see him. So they were going to think about it more, and as a result be a little more deliberate in their communications and interactions.

So we built Mark an office in the same tower as me. Other senior managers also have their offices there. If I'd made Mark do that at the beginning, he never would have learned. But I felt he'd get that pretty quick, which is why I already had his office space scoped out and a contractor waiting and ready to go as soon as he gave the word.

I also got Tom Stephens, our engineering head, to relocate to the RenCen. He was most reluctant to leave Warren—that's where the hub of engineering is located. But he did start showing up at the RenCen two or three times a week, and I felt that was important from a messaging standpoint. I wanted employees to see the senior management team walking around together—in the Food Court, around the building, other places, so they could see that the top people of GM were all together. One company. One team. That was the idea, and I wanted employees to see that, and feel that, as much as possible.

Small signals, if you string enough of them together, can add up to a big message. *Urgency* was my central theme. I conveyed that in big and small ways.

Another example: PowerPoints. At GM historically, meetings invariably included a PowerPoint presentation accompanied by a thick, neatly bound booklet. This was how it had always been done at GM, and that's how it still was when I got to be CEO.

I am not a fan of PowerPoints.

This was true when I was at AT&T, and it was still true by the time I got to General Motors. I consider PowerPoints to be a waste of time and money, for the most part, and I had neither of those to spare during this period. If somebody came in to see me and started in with those slides, I'd say, "Wait, stop," and make them shut it down and talk to me. I don't need all those charts. I just need to know the end conclusion or larger point—tell me that, and then let's talk about it. But *tell* me—don't point with some laser from the other end of the room and click, click, click through fifty slides.

Here's my bottom line on PowerPoints, and this goes back to the focus issue: *You're in charge. You're responsible. You have decision-making authority.* Tell me what you want to do, and I'll tell you what I think. But don't sit there and waste our time by clicking through all these slides. And if you're unable to talk to me in a focused, intelligent way about something without a bunch of slides and a clicker, then my assumption is that you don't know your subject very well—so come back when you do. I walked out of a few meetings at General Motors over this. I know it probably embarrassed some people, but it was my way of saying: *Hey, guys, we don't have time to waste here.* And I guess people got the message, because I saw a lot less Power-Points after that.

Because of all the built-up bureaucracy and complexity at GM, a lot of managers weren't sure exactly who they needed to get approval from when they wanted to do something, so they tended to err on the side of asking *everybody* for permission. As a result, it could take a long time to get final approval for anything—a year or more was not uncommon. This contributed to the stall-and-delay mentality that permeated the top ranks of GM. This matrix effect showed itself in a variety of ways. One example: Engineering projects were regularly vetted by the board—why, I have no idea. But that's how it was when I showed up, and it had been that way for years.

In early 2010, an engine program called Ecotec needed $400 million in additional funding to take it to the next level—these engines deliver superior efficiency for gas engines. The Eco engineering team had already made multiple presentations to the board, but still did not have final approval. Every time they showed up, directors would ask questions; then the engineers would come back to the next board meeting with answers, only to get more questions. This had been going on for months. Meantime, the engine program was basically idled.

Tom Stephens, senior engineering manager, called me one day and said he was ready to come back to see the board; he had answers to questions that had been asked at the previous board meeting.

I told him he didn't need to do that.

"I'm giving you authorization, Tom," I said. "You don't have to come to the board anymore."

Tom was astounded, and also a little nervous. "You sure?"

Two beats.

"We're going to get in trouble."

"No, we're not," I said. "This management team is trusted by this board—I'll tell them what you're doing. Go ahead and get this thing done—*now*."

The engine program got put into effect a month later.

As promised, I informed the board at the next meeting. Nobody had any questions, or issues.

Weaning senior management off the board, and the board off the senior management team, was another focus of mine. Because of all the dysfunction at General Motors, the board had gotten into a habit of micromanaging management, to some extent— the engine program is a good example. By the same token, the former management team had done nothing to instill confidence, so the board understandably felt compelled to step in.

But now it was a new day, and a new management team. Changes were in order, I decided.

Before board meetings, I started pulling senior managers aside, one by one, and coaching them on presentations. No PowerPoints (of course). No long presentations or explanations. I told them to prepare short—ten minutes, max—presentations that covered need-to-know information only: how many cars we sold, by type, what the average price was, how much money we made—those things that directly related to GM's business and the bottom line. I wanted that information communicated with military-like precision, and delivered with confidence. And stop asking board members for direction and opinions as to what they thought senior management should be doing. That's not the board's function or job—that's *your* job, I told them, to figure all that stuff out.

I had an ulterior motive in all this: building confidence in the senior management team. Instead of leaving the impression that this was the same old GM—unsure of itself, low confidence, unfocused—I wanted management to show authority and confidence so the board could begin to trust them, and believe in them. And in the process, I hoped, senior managers would start to believe in themselves, start to understand the power of their authority, the importance of their purpose and messaging. This was all part of creating a focused, effective management team, one that could carry GM far and high. That was my ultimate objective: securing GM's future.

At first senior managers were a little uncomfortable with this highly streamlined format—they were used to walking into board meetings with armloads of charts. But after a few meetings they started to get the hang of it. They also started building some inner confidence. Some board members noticed the change in tenor right away. And they liked it, for the most part, because they no longer had to sit through fifty-slide PowerPoints and explanations that went nowhere. Board meetings that used to last all day got pared to a couple of hours. And I was pretty happy about that, because that gave me more time to devote to other things.

Like car dealerships.

Every week, I set aside a half day to do nothing but talk to car dealers. This was a big commitment of time, yes. But I also considered it time well spent because dealerships are the main point of contact GM has with the car-buying public. If those relationships weren't right, we wouldn't sell as many cars, which meant GM wouldn't make as much money. So the state of those relationships was a point of great interest to me. GM, internally, had armies of people devoted to the care and support of dealers. But I am a big believer in getting things straight from the horse's mouth, so to speak. So I decided to go straight to the horse.

I got a list of every franchise owner in the country. From there, I'd randomly pick out names and start calling—Carmel, California; Washington, DC; Portland; Atlanta; you name it. Cadillac, Chevrolet, Buick, that didn't matter to me, either.

My usual drill was this: I'd call up and say, "This is Ed Whitacre, I'm with GM and I'd like to talk to so-and-so, would you please ask this person to call me back." They'd usually call me back pretty quick. And I'd ask them questions:

Well, how is it out there?

How is your relationship with GM?

What do you think of our products?

Things like that. And I got a great response out of most dealers, I will say. They seemed to appreciate that I was calling, and they were very willing to tell me exactly what they thought. Some dealers also called me.

I remember one guy: He was in a small town in Central

Texas, and he was pretty upset. He'd been a Chevy dealer for fifty years, he told me, and GM was trying to shut him down. And I said: "Tell me more." So he did. The guy told me he'd had some ups and downs in recent years, but he was dedicated to GM, and dedicated to his community as a local car dealer. He was not bad-mouthing GM, but he was direct: "I just don't think it's right that your people are trying to shut me down."

He was sincere in his voice, I could tell. I hung up, called Mark Reuss, and said I wanted information on this dealership—sales history, franchise status, whatever he could tell me. So Mark went to his people and of course they had it all figured out: This guy's numbers had not been so good for two years in a row. But he'd also been a loyal GM dealer for *fifty years*, and he'd had lots of good sales years over that long period of time.

So I asked Mark, "Do you think that dealership's performance the last two years had anything to do with the products we had out there?" Well, Mark's people started hemming and hawing, said they were economically forced to shut down so many dealerships, and this guy was part of that group. And I said, "Well, that's not in concrete"—I was referring to the actual dealerships that were being shut down; some of those decisions were subjective. "So what do you think?"

And they said, "We ought to go ahead and shut this guy down." In so many words.

And I said: "I don't think that. I think you ought to call this guy up today and tell him that we've changed our mind."

Mark's group called him back that day and told him he was no longer being shut down. And that was the right answer, as far as I was concerned. I just didn't think it was right, or made any business sense, to terminate a guy who'd been with us for fifty years just because he'd had two lousy sales years. That dealer called me back, profusely thanking me. And he went on to have some good sales months.

I considered dealer feedback very important, so I was always looking for opportunities to sit down and talk with them. One time, I was out in Cleveland doing a plant tour—that's where the Chevy Cruze was being made. Steve Girsky, our vice chairman, was with me. We thought it might be a good idea to meet with local dealers, just to see what they were thinking. So we put together a dinner at the last minute.

As soon as Steve and I walked in—there were fifteen, twenty dealers in this room—these guys pounced. They were upset about every sort of thing you can imagine: can't get enough cars, not enough money to stay in business, can't deal with this, can't deal with that. They were pretty wound up. Steve and I just sat there listening to all this stuff.

So I sort of put it back to them: "Yes, we have some problems, but you've got some problems, too: You've got these salesmen who lie to people and don't tell the truth, or who are just too slick for their own good. You're not pushing us enough, or advertising us enough," things like that. I started out by saying I'd never met a car dealer who didn't own a private airplane, "so you guys are just crying poor mouth with a ham under each arm." They laughed when I said that, but I was halfway serious. Some of these big dealers do real well, and that's a good thing, because that means they're selling a lot of cars—I just wanted them to start selling more of *ours*, that's all.

We wound up having a great meeting. Not too long after that, sales around Cleveland picked up a little, which I thought was interesting. I've no idea if our meeting had anything to do with that, but I figure it didn't hurt. I did those sorts of meetings all over the country. After a while, I started getting a lot of invitations from dealers to attend their meetings and dinners. I tried to go as often as I could, and if I couldn't make it I'd ask Mark Reuss. I did that to help send a signal, to dealers as well as to our employees: This was a new GM.

I learned a lot by attending those meetings. And one thing I learned was that they had become very dependent on incentives—the discounts dealers offer people when they're buying a car. GM had a reputation for offering the biggest and best incentives. Dealers got used to that, so they kept pushing for more, and more. And GM kept giving them more and more. That might have made sense when GM had subpar products that nobody wanted, but now that we were building the world's best cars—we were winning all kinds of design awards—that made no sense.

My logic was pretty simple: If you've got the best, believe you've got the best, and want other people to believe you've got the best—you've got to treat your product that way. Deep discounts sent the exact opposite message. And employees are quick to pick up on those sorts of signals. So I started putting pressure on Mark to reduce those incentives. I told him, in effect, "If you think you are bad then you are bad—and customers will think that, too."

The matrix extended, in a big way, to GM's relationship with the United Auto Workers (UAW). About 60 percent of its 79,000 employees in the United States are active members of the union. (GM has 207,000 workers globally.) The company also supports 375,000 UAW retirees and surviving spouses. The large number of retirees has to do with the age of GM itself—more than a hundred years.

At GM, the UAW relationship had always been managed by a chain of command that started a few levels below the CEO's office. Because of the nature of the UAW relationship—relations have always been a little tense, and got more so after the bankruptcy—people inside GM were highly sensitive about anything that had to do with the union. All communications and correspondence were closely managed by the people in charge of them. So that was the status quo, if you will.

And you know how I feel about the status quo.

At AT&T, I'd always had a good relationship with the Communications Workers of America (CWA), which was our biggest union. I didn't see any reason why GM couldn't do the same with its union. The president of the UAW was Ron Gettelfinger. I'd heard about Ron but did not know him personally. I wanted to meet and get to know him. So I decided to go over to the union hall in Detroit and introduce myself. I did not have an appointment, or even bother to call ahead. I figured that would just attract attention. So I just showed up.

Tom—he's a GM driver, sometimes took me to places around Detroit—drove me the forty blocks to the union hall and dropped me off. Big, pretty nice building; not like any union hall I'd ever seen before. Lots of steel and glass, it's known as "Solidarity House." So I walked in the front door and found my way to reception. There was a young lady at the desk, so I went over to her and said: "I'm Ed Whitacre. I'm new in Detroit and I'm with GM. I'd like to meet Ron Gettelfinger." Just like that, in a friendly way.

She looked at me sort of strangely, then picked up the phone and called Gettelfinger's secretary: "There's a Mr. Whitacre here who says he'd like to meet with Ron." A few minutes later, Ron came walking down the steps. He looked straight at me and said: "Mr. Whitacre?"

And I said something like, "Yes, I'd just like to sit down and talk with you if you have a minute."

Ron had this look of surprise on his face when I said that. But he was friendly and said okay, so we headed on back to his office—just the two of us—and sat down.

"Ron, I don't have anything on my mind, in particular," I told him. "I'd just like to get to know you and meet you."

And Ron—he'd been pretty quiet the whole time—looked straight at me and said: "I can't believe you're here."

And I said, "Well, I *am* here, and somehow we're going to have to work together and figure all this stuff out"—or words to that effect.

Ron made it clear he was not a fan of GM's senior management. GM and the UAW didn't have much of a relationship, and

GM's management had never really tried to change that—this was Ron's view. I didn't doubt anything he was saying, but I also thought the past didn't have to dictate the future. "I'm here to see if we can help improve things," I told him. And I meant that most sincerely. I had a lot of respect for the UAW and the people it represented, and I felt certain we could get along going forward—that was my view.

So that's how it started. We sat there and talked—about our families, his background, my background, how long he'd been at it, things like that. I told him I hoped to learn from him. I also considered the union to be a big factor in GM's turnaround—we could not do it without them, and they could not do it without GM, but together we could accomplish a lot. I felt we needed to know each other, because we were clearly going to have to work together to make this thing a success. Ron seemed pleased by that.

I liked Ron instantly. He had no airs. Ron was dressed in blue jeans, very casual. And clearly devoted to the union: he'd been a union guy since the 1960s, started out as a chassis repairman for Ford in Louisville, Kentucky, and worked his way up from there. I could tell that this was a sincere, smart guy, and that he knew what was going on. He'd had to testify before Congress, and didn't like the experience. He also didn't like what had happened to General Motors, and wanted to get things on a better track. After an hour, I had to go. I gave Ron every one of my numbers, told him to call me anytime. He did the same thing.

"I'm looking forward to working with you," I told him as I was heading out the door, "and you and I have to work together to make this work."

Ron sort of smiled and nodded in agreement. I felt good about that, good about Ron; good about the prospect of a new working relationship with the union and what it might mean for General Motors.

Then I got back to the office.

By then word had gotten around that I'd been down to meet with Ron, and the GM matrix was not too happy about that. Turned out I had violated every protocol GM had by doing that. What I had done, I was told, was next to the worst sin you could do, and the sin was this: I had gone on my own, without telling or even checking with GM's union person—who was two levels down—that I planned to meet with the president of the UAW. This was simply *not* done. At GM, these meetings were always highly managed and staged events, and the CEO never got involved directly.

Steve Girsky—he was the union's rep on the board before I made him vice chairman—came running into my office: "Oh my God," he said. "Ed, you have done it now. You have violated everything that has been put into place with the UAW for the past thirty years—you wiped that out in one hour." Steve was pretty wound up.

What it all came down to was this: I upset the matrix, big time. Did this concern me? Not one iota. I was the new guy; I was responsible for General Motors, and I wanted to know Ron Gettelfinger. So I really didn't care what anybody thought. I was acting on behalf of General Motors, and I'd keep acting on behalf of General Motors as long as I was the chairman and CEO.

On a positive note, Ron was apparently feeling good about our meeting, too, because he called over and asked to meet for breakfast. I said, yes, of course. And no, I didn't ask for permission to do that, either.

Steve and I met Ron—within a few days, as I recall—at the Motown Diner on Jefferson Avenue in downtown Detroit. The area is a little rough, but it's a good diner—the kind with strong coffee and short-order cooks who know how to do eggs right. We had a good time talking over breakfast; that made me feel even better about Ron. He seemed to enjoy the conversation, too, so we started meeting pretty regular for breakfast at that same diner after that. This did not sit too well with GM security—there'd been some drive-by shootings and robberies in the area, I was told. But I wasn't worried. I also wasn't asking for permission.

Ron turned out to be every inch the gentleman I thought. He was also thoughtful, incredibly intelligent, and well spoken. Not too long after that I called Ron and invited him to a board dinner that was coming up—there's usually a dinner the night before a GM board meeting; only directors, senior management, and invited guests attend.

The UAW had never been invited to a board dinner, to my knowledge, so this was not in keeping with GM protocol. I was not concerned about that, as you might expect. I was impressed by Ron's sincerity. His intelligence and passion—not just for the union, but for the welfare and the future success of GM—came through when he spoke. His sincerity touched me, and moved me, in our first meeting, and again over breakfast. I wanted our board members to hear that, and to see that.

Given the rocky state of relations with General Motors, Ron wasn't sure what he'd say, so he was a little reluctant at first. But he finally agreed, and I was glad about that because I thought it would send a strong signal to employees, and to the union, specifically, that this really was a new GM. I also felt GM and the union had an opportunity to start a new chapter together, and I wanted to get that going as soon as possible.

Ron asked me what he should tell our directors.

"Just say whatever feels right to you." That's basically all I told him.

Ron was perfect. He showed up for the dinner, and I personally introduced him to all the board members and senior officers. Right after dinner, Ron rose and said a few words. He started out by acknowledging that his presence "was a little unprecedented"—that helped break the ice, people sort of smiled when he said that. Then he went on to say he was glad to be there, glad to meet everybody, and looked forward to a better future. He closed out on a personal note: "I want everybody here to know that we want to work together" to help make GM strong again—or words to that effect. People around the room appreciated that, I could tell. And so did I.

The next morning at the board meeting, I got a lot of positive comments to the effect that "he's not what we thought he would be"—people had different ways of expressing that, but that was the basic consensus. Eyeball-to-eyeball contact, as I've said, there's just no replacement for that. I got the same feedback from senior managers, and some of these people had been quite critical of the union. I considered this to be another good sign.

On a gut level, I had a good feeling. One board dinner wasn't going to repair the UAW relationship, of course. But it was a start, at least.

CHAPTER 16

Spirit of Hope

It was supposed to be a feel-good message to America, and the message was this: General Motors is back.

Susan Docherty, head of GM marketing, came up with the idea of a TV commercial to get this across. She didn't want to hire an actor to star in it—"that would be fake," she said. And she didn't think longtime GM people had credibility with the public: "We can't stick somebody up there and say, 'I'm part of the management that bankrupted GM.' That just won't work."

So she asked me to do it. My first impulse was to say no. Doing commercials, for me, ranks right up there with fixing a flat tire in a driving rain—not my favorite thing. But I'd also been pushing marketing to get the word out there that GM was going to rally back and make America proud again. I thought it was important for employees to hear that as much as possible, in as many ways as possible. Some people were still predicting that GM might not make it, and our new nickname—"Government Motors"—wasn't helping.

And so I did my first commercial for GM. This was in the fall of 2009, a few months before I got named CEO. The hook was a new sixty-day money-back guarantee: If you bought a new car and weren't happy with it, for any reason, you had sixty days to return it. We'd take it back, no questions asked.

Getting a positive message to employees was my top concern, but car sales were also on my mind. GM had great products in the market, and in the pipeline. But years and years of not-so-great cars had done a lot of damage to GM's reputation. Younger people, for the most part, didn't even consider GM brands when they went looking to buy a car. We also didn't do so well in big cities, like Los Angeles, Boston, New York—foreign carmakers pretty much dominated. GM's bankruptcy was only making that tough situation worse.

Susan and her marketing team were doing the best they could with their advertising budget—it had been cut repeatedly, over a period of time, to help reduce GM's costs. That, to me, was just nuts. We needed to be advertising more, not less—I mean, how else are you going to sell cars? So we increased marketing's budget substantially, pretty much on the spot.

But that big budget also came with a big responsibility: Marketing had to show *results*. That was the accountability part of the equation. And they didn't have forever to do it.

I didn't know if my being in this commercial would help, but I figured it was worth a shot. So I told Susan that if she thought it would be helpful, sure, I'd do it. The conversation lasted all of ten minutes. She said great, and she went off to plan everything.

The day of filming arrived. I showed up at the engineering center in Warren—that's where it was shot—wearing a dark suit, blue shirt, and tie, as requested. I hadn't seen a script or practiced any lines. I also hadn't given this thing a lot of thought, to be perfectly honest. I was working sunup to sundown at that point, had a lot on my mind. I assumed (and hoped) that I could pop in, say my lines, then get on back to work.

Well, it didn't work out like that. As soon as I got there, somebody handed me a new blue shirt and a red tie. I've worn button-down shirts my whole life—still do. This shirt didn't have any buttons. (I like red ties, so that was okay.) And it is now becoming clear to me, from all the people running around, that this was not going to be a quick in-and-out sort of thing. So immediately I was thinking: *Well, this is off to a bad start.*

The director of the commercial, Jeff—nice guy, very competent; he's with a production company out of California—had me walking down these long halls, saying these lines. I was reading off these big cards that somebody was holding while I walked—which was a little tricky, because I don't see so well and the guy holding the cards was about thirty feet out. The text was pretty straightforward:

> I'm Ed Whitacre, the Chairman of General Motors.
> Before I started this job, I admit I had some doubts.
> Probably a lot like you.
> But I like what I found. I think you will, too.
> Car for car, when compared to the competition—
> we win. It's as simple as that.

Then I laid out the sixty-day guarantee and invited America to "put us to the test. Put us up against anyone. And may the best car win."

So I was walking and talking trying to read off these cards, and Jeff kept cutting in to tell me I wasn't "*in-flect-ing* enough!"—and I kept telling him this is how we talk, and inflect, in Texas. So we had this lighthearted banter going back and forth, and meantime we were doing take after take after take because Jeff wasn't happy with something—a person's foot wasn't where it was supposed to be, a door was opening too fast or too slow, I wasn't inflecting right, whatever. Jeff was really good, but man he was picky. This went on for six or seven hours. Lots of GM employees—hundreds throughout the course of the day, probably—were standing around watching all this, and listening.

Two or three hours into this, I could sort of feel the mood shift. People were smiling, laughing; the whole place was pretty energized. Then it hit me: These employees were *really* pumped. You could tell from the vibe in the room that everybody was really glad we were getting this message out there. *GM is coming back; we're going to be okay*—that was the underlying message in the words I was saying. And hearing that, over and over again, had a big impact on people, I think. There was a spirit of hope in the room that you could just feel, and that commercial was the starting point. That commercial, for the first time, made them think that maybe things really were going to be all right.

It was also a moment for me, because it allowed me to stand up there and say, in a very public way: *I'm signed on with this company, and I'll put my face out there for you, you bet I will. Because your chairman is 100 percent behind you; I am with you, big time.* So that commercial wound up being a lot bigger morale builder than what I'd thought going in. And Susan gets credit for that, because it was 100 percent her idea. I have yet to watch that commercial in its entirety. The people in marketing tried to show it to me. I said if you think it's okay go ahead and run it—but I'm not looking at it. I cannot stand to see myself on TV, makes me feel funny. But I did keep that shirt and tie, as a reminder of that day.

The following spring (2010), GM decided to do a second commercial. This one also got a lot of attention, but for different reasons.

By then I was CEO, and closely tracking our internal sales figures. The first month of the year, we actually made a little money—not much, but a little. The next month we made a little more. And March was looking really good. Those three months,

January to March, constitute the first quarter, as you probably know. Normally you'd report financial results in April, right after the quarter ends. But because of the bankruptcy, we'd pushed that to May, so we couldn't talk about our sales figures publicly. But we were telegraphing as best we could, within the bounds of law and common sense.

Because things were going so well, we decided to repay our outstanding loans to the United States and Canada. Total amount of the two loans was around eight billion; GM got the money as it emerged from bankruptcy. We'd already repaid some of that, but had another $5.7 billion to go. The repayment wasn't due for another five years. But we thought it would send a positive message to the market—and to our employees—if we paid it off early, in full, with interest. So that's what we did. Even with that repayment, the US government would still own a big piece of GM, around 61 percent. But like I said, we had no control over that ownership stake.

We decided to do a commercial to announce the news. The ad ran in April 2010, just ahead of our earnings report. The first ad had been well received, so I was asked to be in this one, as well. I'm not a front man, by any stretch. But everybody seemed to think it was important, so I said okay. This time I showed up with the right shirt and tie.

The message was pretty straightforward: GM is making good on these loans. But the far more important message, and the real reason we decided to do the commercial, was to send a very solid signal to America: GM is back. We're not just *coming* back; that was the thrust of the first commercial. *We're back.* And we're confident about our future, which is why we can afford to repay these loans a full five years ahead of schedule. That was no small thing, especially when you consider that GM, just one year earlier, was flat broke.

By then another outsider had joined GM's upper ranks: Selim

Bingol. He was an outsider to GM, I should say, but not to me: Selim and I had worked together at AT&T for many years; he ran our corporate communications group. GM's public relations department badly needed an overhaul. So I called up Selim—got him on the cell, he and his wife were in the car heading to a San Antonio Spurs game—and asked him to come help. Selim, at the time, was a senior executive with a big public relations outfit. But he also understood, instantly, the greater importance of getting GM back on a good track. A week later, he was in Detroit.

Selim arrived just in time to help us deal with fallout from the second commercial, which stirred up a little controversy. Some people said GM misled people by saying we'd paid off our loans "in full," without mentioning the government's 61 percent stake. Well, okay. But the fact of the matter is we paid off the only debts we had control over at that point in time. And technically speaking, that 61 percent stake was not a loan; it was an ownership stake, and as I have noted only the government could decide when and in what quantity those nine-hundred-million-plus shares got sold. People also said we were just giving the Treasury back its own money, the suggestion being that our early repayment was no big deal. Not fair. What we were doing was no different from what homeowners across America do every day: borrow money from a lender, and pay it all back, over time, with interest. In our case we were repaying five years ahead of schedule. But so it goes.

That spring, GM made another decision that got some attention: We parted ways with our longtime ad agency. The firm had a good relationship with GM, also a long one—more than ninety years. Ad agencies come and go all the time in the corporate world; it's the nature of the business. But this one got a lot of attention because of the legacy issue. On that narrow subject—legacy, as a management consideration—I'd like to share a view.

History is something to be rightly proud of—it speaks to longevity, and sometimes the history is also pretty interesting. My old company, AT&T, is a good example. Alexander Graham Bell was one of the forefathers of the company; he invented the telephone, of course. Just like General Motors, AT&T's roots run deep—the company's been around more than a hundred years. During that time, AT&T had a lot of historical firsts, things that literally changed the world. People at AT&T are rightly proud of that. GM has long roots, too, so lots of interesting history there, as well. Not to mention all the cool car stuff—every stand-out ever produced by GM, from the big-finned Caddies of the 1950s to the Volt, has loads of facts, figures, and gee-whiz trivia attached to it.

But all that said, legacy should never be the first consideration in a business discussion. History can be interesting, and past glories are always fun to talk about. But all that matters, when you peel back the onion and get right down to it, is *today*. And the second most important thing after today is tomorrow—the future. Because the world changes constantly, and if you're not changing with it, and adjusting your business plan—making sure that you have the right people in the right places, that employees are feeling confident and inspired, and all the other things that go into day-to-day management—then you're just asking for trouble, big time.

That brings me to the reassignment of Susan Docherty, the head of US marketing, to our overseas marketing operations. The reason was pretty simple: Mark Reuss, the head of North America, decided a new leadership direction was in order. The reporting arrangement between Susan and Mark was not working as well as everybody had hoped. And when that happens in business you have to deal with it, and Mark did—he was Susan's boss. And so, just as Susan and her team had decided on a new advertising direction for GM, Mark decided on a new leadership direction for marketing. At that point we'd moved or reshuffled most of the top management team at GM, and those tweaks would continue for the duration of my stay at GM.

The net of it: Susan moved to Shanghai to oversee sales, marketing, and operations in China and other major markets. These markets accounted for a large percentage of all new vehicle sales, so this was a huge job. The position reported to international, which was then being run by Tim Lee. Tim was doing an outstanding job, I would add. He was a big fan of Susan's, so when she became available he asked her to join him overseas and help him run things.

I had no instructions, or even suggestions, as to who Mark should get to lead marketing. This is a plum job at GM, also very high-profile, and it was especially high-profile during this period because every single thing GM did—product announcements, personnel changes, you name it—was being examined by the microscope of the global media. Marketing had an annual budget of around $3 billion at the time, making it one of the largest in corporate America. So agencies were also keeping a close watch. And consultants, as always, were circling on the edges. Like every other group at GM, marketing had been rocked by a series of changes, so employees in that department were a little nervous, too.

"So long as it doesn't make me throw up I'll say okay," I told Mark.

I wasn't trying to be cute, but I was making a point: Mark had decision-making authority, so he could bring in anybody he wanted. With one caveat—if the person he had his eye on was so unsuitable that even I, who knew next to nothing about marketing, could see it, then we might have to talk about it. But absent that, he had my full support. The only thing I asked was to be kept informed.

Mark found a very good person: Joel Ewanick, the former head of marketing at Hyundai. I did not know Joel personally, but I certainly knew him by reputation. Joel is the guy behind the "Hyundai Assurance" program. It came out in 2009, when the US economy was in a bad slump and car sales were way down. Joel rightly assessed that job security was a big issue with the car-buying public, so he came up with the Assurance Program—it allowed people who'd lost their jobs to return their new cars, with no penalty whatsoever. It was a bold move, very against-the-grain. GM and all the other carmakers were cutting advertising—they were trying to wait out the storm until things perked up again, basically. Joel followed his gut and did the exact opposite: He doubled down on advertising, announcing Assurance during the Super Bowl that year. That's one of the most popular televised events in America, which is one reason it's one of the most expensive buys in advertising. So Joel was rolling the dice in the most visible way possible. If the gamble didn't work, Hyundai would have had egg on its face, big time.

The result? America responded, and Hyundai sales went up. Pretty amazing, especially when you consider that industry-wide sales that year did a nose dive. Joel's Statue of Liberty move—that's a trick play in football, a little outrageous but it sometimes works—got Hyundai tons of attention, which helped raise brand awareness across America. And Hyundai has been benefiting from that lift ever since. I met Joel right before we hired him, nice guy. (Joel left GM in 2012.)

My message to Mark and other senior managers throughout this period was pretty consistent: "If you don't have the right organization and right people, you aren't going to make it." This is most important, because morale flows from the vibe inside an organization, and that has a big impact on how people feel about their jobs. Efficiency and production will improve, or suffer, accordingly. If things are off or just not working—for whatever reason—it's up to management to fix that. Just hoping and wishing aren't going to help.

GM had never given its senior managers the freedom to run their businesses before—they were always having to check with people before they did anything; this was the matrix effect— so it took a little nudging to get them to use their decision-making authority. But I could also see that people were getting more confident, and getting a lot more focused because of the accountability they now had. So things were finally starting to click.

Around this time, more good news came out: The Obama administration released a report saying forty-five thousand jobs had been created by the auto industry since GM emerged from bankruptcy. According to the report, it was the strongest nine-month period of job growth in the industry since 2000. That's a huge turn from 2008, when we lost four hundred thousand jobs—that's when the industry was in a free fall. Release of the report coincided with the announcement that GM was paying back its loans. Some people were quick to point out—rightly— that the government still owned a big piece of GM. But these critics missed the larger point: GM was clawing its way back, and fast.

At least that's how the Obama administration saw it:

"The prospect of a faster-than-anticipated exit from gov-ernment involvement and a return of most of the taxpayers' investment in these companies has materially improved," Larry Summers, director of the National Economic Council, wrote on the White House blog. He had overseen the auto bailout, and was closely tracking our improving financial condition.

Treasury Secretary Timothy Geithner also had a few words to say:

"We are encouraged that GM has repaid its debt well ahead of schedule and confident that the company is on a strong path to viability," he said in a prepared statement. "This continued progress is a positive sign for our auto investment—not only more funds recovered for the taxpayer, but also countless jobs saved and the successful stabilization of a vital industry for our country."

I could not have been prouder. GM, which started out on the ash heap, was doing exactly as it had promised: It was using that taxpayer money to help build a stronger GM, which over the long haul was going to help build a stronger America. We still had a lot more work to do, but we were light-years ahead of where we'd started out. In a conference call with reporters, Mark Reuss put it like this: "We have a long road back in terms of what people think of us and buying our cars again," he said. "We're going to keep our head down, be humble forever, take it one day at a time, and build it back."

All this stuff had a big impact on morale. And all of it was positive. The contrast was striking. When I first got to GM the RenCen was like a big black hole of despair—you could feel it in the air. Now, less than a year later, the mood was lighter, bordering on cheery some days. People were still a little nervous, which was understandable—once you've been to hell and back, the experience tends to change you. But the signs of optimism were everywhere. People were smiling, focused on work, and getting the job done. One day at a time, like Mark said, but we were clearly moving in the right direction.

A lot of that had to do with senior management. These folks still had a tendency to hole up in their offices way too much—everybody was just really busy. But I could also see that they were making more of an effort to mix and mingle. I'd occasionally see them in the Food Court, the halls, other places, just talking to people casually. Employees were picking up on that, so the whole atmosphere was a lot more relaxed, and the tension level started going down. And that was a very good thing, because that allowed people to start working harder and better.

And the happy result of all this: We were starting to sell a lot more cars. For the first time in years, revenues were higher than expenses, and that trend line was getting stronger by the month.

We reported first-quarter results on May 17, 2010. And what a quarter: We posted our first unadjusted profit in *six* long years, $1.2 billion, up from a loss of $3.4 billion in the year-earlier period. We had the benefit of a lighter debt load—GM shed 70 percent of its debt during the bankruptcy. We also sold Saab, so we got a little lift from that, as well. We weren't out of the hole, at least not yet. But we were finding daylight fast. That was the message we sent with that earnings report, and we reinforced that every which way we could.

Chris Liddell, our chief financial officer, put out a statement that day. It was crafted with a lot of constituencies in mind: the car-buying public, Washington, Wall Street—and our employees, especially.

"In North America, we are adding production to keep up with strong demand for new products in our four brands," he said, drawing a bead to GM's core strength—designing, building, and selling the world's best vehicles. "We're also steadily growing in emerging markets, keeping our costs under control, generating positive cash flow and maintaining a strong balance sheet. These are all important steps as we lay the foundation for a successful GM." In other words, GM was standing strong, and moving forward.

Chris went on to say that the rebound was directly attributable to our operations in North America, which Mark Reuss was overseeing—he did a great job, and under the most difficult of circumstances. Other senior managers were also stepping up—in manufacturing, design, marketing, and international. And our financial results were clearly starting to reflect that. Things were definitely looking up.

CHAPTER 17

A Very Public Offering

GM's IPO

Right after the first quarter, we started talking about the possibility of an initial public offering.

The board's intent was to get the government out of GM's business, and get off the taxpayer dime, as soon as possible. This was in keeping with the stated objective of the US Treasury—they'd made it clear to us they didn't want to be in the car business. They wanted out of GM quickly, assuming conditions were right.

And now the conditions were right.

Morale was building, sales were improving, and we'd just posted our first profit in six years. We also had good products in the market, and good products in the pipeline. Originally, the board thought an IPO could occur no earlier than 2011—a lot of people even thought that was too optimistic. But by the end of the first quarter it was clear to me that GM was recovering faster, in terms of profitability. So we started looking seriously at the possibility of moving up the IPO date.

Getting the government out of GM's business was important

for a couple of reasons. For starters, that "Government Motors" name continued to linger out there, and as I've mentioned it was just terrible because it constantly reminded people that we were not independent. It meant we weren't capable of doing business by ourselves; it meant we had failed. That's how employees looked at it—we all did. So it had a negative impact on our people, and a negative impact on our psyche as a company. We were most anxious to shuck that label.

Emotions aside, there were also some practical reasons for wanting to move ahead. So long as the government was in there, we were subject to TARP rules. TARP was a bureaucratic morass of rules and regulations, subject to the interpretation of one person who is responsible for administering it. This is not a criticism of that person, or the program, certainly—without TARP funds, GM would have collapsed in bankruptcy. The only reason GM didn't get liquidated was because the government stepped in with $50 billion in TARP funding. That's all taxpayer money, so the government, understandably, wants to be careful about how it's spent.

But the rules, in my view, were also a little excessive. If you wanted to give somebody a raise, for example, you had to get approval, because salaries, under TARP rules, are capped. Ford and other companies didn't have these limits, so that put GM at a serious disadvantage in terms of competing for, and retaining, top talent. At other car companies, you might get a nice bonus if you met your annual objectives. But because of the TARP rules, we could pay almost nothing. And when we did pay we had to pay in "salary stock," which is stock that you get at some future point if and when GM started trading on the public market again. So we had low salaries, low bonuses, and no ability to maneuver because of TARP.

And I was most concerned about this. I believed compensation was going to become a big factor for GM at some point down the road. The car business turns on your ability to come up with car designs that grab people. Cars like the Cadillac CTS and Chevy Camaro only happen because some designer dreams it up in his or her head, and has the ability to translate that creative vision into something that GM can actually build and manufacture on a mass scale. But before that can happen, you also have to engineer the car so it looks good and performs well—a whole lot goes into that. Then you have to sell it, which is where your marketing and salespeople come in. And so on. So if you don't have the right people in the right places to pull all this stuff off, then it simply won't happen. Business is all about people, as I keep saying. This is just another example.

GM has some of the most talented designers and engineers in the world—absolutely top-notch. But a lot of these people were being seriously underpaid. Part of that had to do with the bankruptcy; GM kept cutting people's salaries in an attempt to cut costs. Then TARP came along and, boom, all of a sudden GM also had salary caps, making a bad situation worse. And those caps were pretty low by industry standards. Yes, GM had enough loyalty among its employees that they were willing to work for less than they were worth. But common sense will tell you that can't and won't go on forever.

On the plus side, these salary caps made it pretty easy to figure out who was really committed to GM, and who really wasn't. Even though there was no compensation in it for them, Mark Reuss and Tom Stephens stepped up right away. They wanted to show the world that they could pull this company back, and I thought that was a real testament to their loyalty to GM, and their strong commitment to making this thing right. A lot of other people did the same thing. So in an odd way TARP made it easy for me, as CEO, to figure out people's loyalties and level of devotion pretty quickly.

In the spring I started talking to the Obama administration about the possibility of pushing up the IPO. By then Steve Rattner was no longer the Car Czar; he left for personal reasons a few

months after I arrived at GM. Ron Bloom, a former labor nego-
tiator, had stepped in, so that's who I interacted with mostly. I
didn't know Ron personally, but liked him a lot. We had a good
rapport, and we seemed to be on the same page with most
things. We both wanted a positive outcome for GM, that's basically what it came down to. To be clear, nobody in the administration exactly asked for GM's advice on any of this stuff—but
I had some strong opinions, so I offered my two cents anyway.
I had a list of reasons as to why I thought an early IPO made
sense: Sales were good, employees were good, dealers were
good, and every month that went by our earnings were getting
better. Ron didn't give me a thumbs-up right away, but he didn't
try to dissuade me, either. That's all I needed.

In late May, things got rolling. We engaged Roger Altman,
the co-founder and chairman of Evercore Partners, a private
equity investment firm in New York. I've known Roger for years.
He was an assistant secretary of the Treasury under President
Bill Clinton, and had a very successful career on Wall Street—
that's where we first met, and we've been friends ever since. We
also brought in Felix Rohatyn, another longtime friend, to help
out. I was convinced that an IPO before the end of the calendar
year—all this happened in 2010—was reasonable. Also advis-
able, as I said, because the faster we could get back to normal,
the better off everybody was going to be.

Staging an IPO is always a big deal. A company only has one
IPO, so these are also historic events. But this IPO was going to
be especially historic—a once-in-a-lifetime opportunity to repo-
sition a hundred-year-old automobile company that had been a
blue-chip stock for most of its life. And we had exactly one shot
to get it right.

As with any IPO, we'd be required to make a lot of financial
information available to potential investors. Due to the gravity of our situation, there was no room for anything that might
mislead, misdirect, or otherwise give the wrong impression.

Every assertion, projection, and number had to be 100 percent accurate, right down to the last line of the last footnote. This would be the normal course for any IPO; there are lots of rules and regulations around these things to protect investors. But this wasn't just any stock sale, as I mentioned. This was a referendum on the auto bailout, and GM's coming-out party to the financial markets. So a lot was riding on this.

To stage a successful IPO, we'd have to show that GM was profitable, and show a trajectory that looked pretty good. We'd also have to have enough information in hand to go on a road show and convince investors that we're for real. But we couldn't be carnival barkers. The bottom line: We'd have to make our stock attractive to the investing public, but do it in a way that didn't overreach.

Most important for GM, we'd have to be able to raise enough money to make a substantial dent in what we owed everybody, otherwise what's the point? Chris Liddell, our chief financial officer, was working hard to pull it all together. That's a huge undertaking for an offering of this size; the paperwork is unbelievable. Chris was all over it.

The government was our main focus. We'd already paid back our loans, but Treasury had another $43 billion or so tied up in the government's 61 percent ownership stake. We had no control over how much stock the government sold. That was up to the administration, which was ultimately running the show, and rightly so, given its big ownership position. But the more they sold, the quicker we could part ways for good.

Some people thought investors might shy away from GM stock because of the bankruptcy. Bankers, in particular. I did not share this concern. There are always people around who want to make a buck, and GM had a very convincing story. We had great products that people liked, and the sales numbers to prove it. We also had a lot of enthusiasm around some new models that were coming out—like the Cadillac CTS, Chevy

Cruze, and Volt. The Volt wasn't going to be a moneymaker for us for years. But it was proof positive that GM really was designing, building, and selling the world's best vehicles—that was sending a powerful message to the market. Some press reports were still a little down on us, yes. But more and more people were talking about how well GM was going to do. And I knew, internally, how enthusiastic employees were, and how focused management was on getting GM turned around—everything was clicking. So I was highly confident we could overcome any negativism we might run into in the market—and I actually didn't think we were going to run into much.

My biggest concern, to be honest, was the Treasury Department. I felt strongly that the government should sell 100 percent of its portfolio on Day One of the IPO—just sell it all at the go-down. It would be best for GM, and best for America. Taxpayers get paid back, the administration can declare victory on the auto bailout—and GM can get back to normal.

But I was very much in the minority on this.

Lots of hand wringing: *We can't do that! It's not possible, no way, never been done before!* That was the basic pushback. Nobody had ever tried to sell that much stock—around 912 million shares—in a single pass. And nobody wanted to try it for fear that it might collapse the stock price, or not draw enough interest from the investment community, which could also impact the stock price. And a couple of other Chicken Little excuses, but the bottom line was this: Nobody wanted to try, mostly because an offering of that size had never been attempted before.

My response: "Well, there's always a first time."

And I was very serious about that; just because something's never been done before doesn't mean it's not possible. All that means is that nobody's ever tried. And there are lots of examples in history of people doing things nobody had ever attempted before, and succeeding. I mean, nobody had ever climbed Mount Everest—until they did. Or landed on the moon, or figured out that people actually would pay $4 for a cup of coffee—Starbucks hit on that one, made a mint doing it. A lot of people thought Apple was nuts to get into the wireless business, said they had no experience, no track record; predicted certain failure. But the iPhone turned out okay, don't you think?

And I have experienced this a number of times myself. Every time we did a big deal at AT&T, people invariably predicted failure—they did that when we bought that stake in Telmex, when we bought Pacific Telesis, Ameritech, AT&T Wireless, lots of other deals. In fact, I can't think of a deal where that didn't happen. That's not what you want to hear when you're making a big acquisition, but you also can't run your business by taking a straw poll. You just have to use your best judgment and make your call. And that's basically what I did at AT&T for the seventeen years that I was chairman and CEO—I made my calls. And our track record was pretty good, because we closed every big deal we ever announced.

I made my call on GM's stock, too, and my best judgment said we should sell the government's slug—every last share—on Day One, because there was never going to be a more optimum time, or environment, to do that. There's a certain enthusiasm that surrounds big IPOs, but that lift can go away pretty quick. To take advantage of that halo, I thought it just made sense to sell it all at once.

I also had a Plan B in mind if the stock didn't raise enough money to repay the government in full. If that happened, we'd pony up the rest of the dough some other way—GM had the cash, so this would not have been a problem for us. And more important, it would have allowed us to repay American taxpayers in full. That had two big benefits: The government could get out of GM, and GM could get out from under TARP and get back to being a normal business.

But the bankers didn't like that idea, either. The thing that seemed to bother them the most was the volume of shares. They kept pulling out a lot of statistics and past history on IPOs to make the argument that it was not possible to sell nine-hundred-million-plus shares in one big slug. And I kept saying—"Yes, we can"—that was President Obama's line, you know—because we needed to be all the way out. The fact that nobody had ever tried to sell that many shares in one shot meant zero to me, and nothing the bankers were showing me was convincing me otherwise. My plan had conjecture wrapped up in it, sure. But so did everybody else's. If something's never been done before, there's really only one way to find out if you can do it, friend: Try it.

That summer, GM had an annual meeting, our first since bankruptcy. All of our stockholders showed up: a total of three people from the Treasury, a representative of the Canadian government, somebody from the union, and me. We treated it like a regular stockholders' meeting, with adjustments in recognition of the small number of shareowners—it was held in a conference room at the RenCen. I got up and talked about GM's current status and what we expected in the future. At the end of my comments, I thanked the people for being owners of our stock and offered to answer any questions.

I was used to conducting annual meetings with three or four hundred people; this was more like a coffee klatch. Everybody was sort of smiling at each other—like, *Why are we doing this?* The meeting underscored GM's unusual situation—not quite a public company, not quite an arm of the government. It also strongly reminded me, once again, that the sooner we could get back to normal, the better off we'd all be.

My growing internal concern, to be perfectly honest, was that the government was getting a little too comfortable with having a grip on GM. I didn't see any big rush on their part, down in the bowels of TARP and the Treasury, to move that along. They said all the right words. But that was not being backed up with action. What I didn't want to happen was for TARP to become a permanent fixture at GM, because that was going to handicap the company, big time, over the long term. Government programs, once they're established, have a way of taking root, and those roots tend to get longer with time. I'd watched that sort of behavior for years when I was at AT&T, which used to be heavily regulated at the state and federal levels. The climate got better over time, but regulators were loath to give up their control—it took us years to convince them to let go. TARP, it seemed to me, had all the earmarks of a long-term problem in the making.

So we kept going round and round like this. Bankers kept telling me that nobody had ever tried to do a stock sale that large before, and you know my answer to that: "Well what the heck, let's give it a try." I probably expressed it a little stronger than that; I was pretty fired up because I felt strongly that this was the best course for GM, and the best course for America. So I was pretty much a dog with a bone on this IPO. I did not let up.

We continued to wrangle over this into the summer. But I still managed to find time, here and there, to mix and mingle with our employees. Sometimes I'd be riding the elevator with somebody and get into a conversation—sometimes there'd be two people; other times four or five. A lot of times, people would ask me who I was—sometimes they seemed to know, other times they didn't. Other times I'd ask them. And we'd just start talking. If I had the time I'd invite them to come on up to my office on 39, where all the executive offices are located. I'd tour them around, I'd say: "This is where Mr. Liddell sits, this is where Mr. Girsky sits," and so on. Then we'd all go back to my office and sit and talk for a few minutes. That was my way of saying to these employees: *This ain't no ivory tower.* And it's not, you know. At the end of the day we're all employees; we all get our paychecks from the same place. Before people left,

I'd always invite them to come back and visit. A couple of times they did.

And I guess word got around, because after a while I started getting invited to all sorts of employee functions: birthday parties, going-away parties, retirement parties, other things. I really enjoyed doing that, and got to meet a lot of people that way. I always tried to go to those things whenever I could—I got to cut the cake at a few birthday parties, that was nice. GM has some of the greatest people you'll ever meet.

I was basically working nonstop. Downtime was rare—but I had my moments. I'm a big fisherman, as I have mentioned. I was always staring out my office window at the Detroit River—it's part of the Great Lakes System, serves as the international border between the United States and Canada. I'd been told it's a good fishing river—lots of walleye, they can get pretty big, up to twenty pounds. So I decided to go see for myself.

Steve Girsky was always bragging about how good a fisherman he was; he's from New York and had spent some time fishing off Long Island. So one afternoon I said, "Okay, Steve, let's go see about that." We hired a boat to come pick us up right by the RenCen—the building sits right along the river edge, so we could walk out and get on the boat from there. We didn't tell anybody we were going—stuff like this used to drive GM security crazy. But I did tell Vivian, my assistant; told her to get a pair of binoculars, because we were going to be floating by the building.

We spent a couple of hours out there. I caught three or four walleye, pretty nice ones, too. Steve got one trash fish—might've been five inches long. After that, he piped down about his fishing skills.

The captain of the boat figured out who we were, I guess, because he put something on his website the next day. We didn't think that was sending the right message to employees—that the CEO and his number two were out fishing in the middle of the workday. So we asked him to please take it down. But word must've gotten around, I guess, because I later got two invitations to go fishing, from employees. I went with one of the guys, an engineer. We went to Lake Saint Clair—a freshwater lake with a lot of smallmouth bass. They weren't biting that day so we didn't catch much. (Well, I didn't, anyway.) But we had a good time talking and throwing lines, so it was a fun couple of hours.

Discussions around the IPO continued into the summer. Each week there seemed to be new considerations and concerns.

As we got down to the nitty-gritty of assessing the market for an IPO—the economy was perking up, but far from recovered—politics came into play. One of the main issues was how much stock we could sell to foreign investors. Since the government owned us, and essentially controlled us, the government wanted a big say in how much stock was sold to the global community. The feeling I got was that nobody wanted the American people to think that General Motors, which had been saved by the generosity of US taxpayers, was now a financial instrument of foreign competitors. Nobody said this directly to me, I would emphasize—that's just my take on the messages and directions we were being given during this period. To be fair, and to repeat, the US Treasury was our biggest investor, with 61 percent ownership, so it had every right to assert its preferences with respect to our IPO. But the net effect is that we had to cut down the size of the IPO almost immediately. I pushed back, of course, but it was abundantly clear to me that this was a line we would not be able to cross. My hopes for a 100 percent government sell-off, at that point, pretty much bit the dust.

I personally thought this was a mistake. And here's why: As I said a little earlier, the sooner GM and the US Treasury could part ways, the better off everybody was going to be. China and other global investors were flush with money and would have been potential purchasers of the stock, so I had no concerns about our ability to attract buyers. Plus, it seemed to me that if foreign investors owned GM stock, they'd want us to do well. They'd be less likely to wage war against us economically, or any other way. This, to me, was just common sense: If somebody has a huge investment in GM—billions of dollars—why would that country do anything to trip us up? I thought an investment of that sort could even bring us closer as friends— that just seemed logical to me. I made this argument to everybody I could. But not everybody agreed.

By July, planning for the "road show" was in full swing— that's where you tell your story and try to convince investors to buy your stock. These are serious dog-and-pony shows. The chief financial officer usually takes the lead, but other senior managers, most times, are there, too. Investors are counting on management to deliver on whatever it is they promised to do in the IPO "prospectus"—the official document that lays out your strategy, future prospects, risks, other things. So they usually want to talk to managers, to get some assurance that they can deliver on their promises. There are lots of rules and regulations around IPOs, so if investors feel they've been misled in any way, they can come back later and sue. That's why IPOs typically have a lot of lawyers attached to them—so no one accidentally says something that gets them into trouble later. As you might expect, GM lawyers were all over this thing, because we couldn't afford to mess it up.

That same month, we also announced plans to buy an auto-finance company, AmeriCredit, for $3.5 billion in cash. Ameri-Credit specialized in loans to car buyers with less-than-perfect credit scores—these are known as subprime loans in the car business. GMAC, our main lending arm, wouldn't deal with these sorts of customers. As a result, only 4 percent of GM sales were in the subprime category, compared with roughly 20 percent for other big car companies. We did a little research and discovered that people were more prone to default on their home loans than they were on their car loans—I guess people figure you can live in your car if you really have to, but you can't drive to work in your house.

So we decided to fix that. In a period of thirty days or so, we identified potential lenders to buy, picked our target, negotiated terms, and did the deal. Steve Girsky did most of the legwork, did a great job, too. We got some blowback initially—people complained that we were using taxpayer money to buy Ameri-Credit. And in a way I guess we were, but we were also running as hard as we could to increase car sales, and the AmeriCredit deal was a big help in that regard. Around this time we also set up a venture capital fund—GM's first—to help back start-ups working on things related to the auto industry, like electric cars. We made the decision to do that one in about ten minutes, liter-ally: Steve came into my office, said he thought we should do this and I said okay—"Go do it." Steve thought I was kidding; I wasn't. We put out the announcement within a few days.

In late July, President Obama paid a visit to the Volt assem-bly plant in Hamtramck, Michigan. The president wanted to see the plant and talk with employees, we were told, so we built a stage in the middle of the factory floor. Management was not invited to participate in the program, but we were all eager to hear what President Obama had to say, so several of us went out there. We were in the audience, stood shoulder-to-shoulder with hundreds of GM employees. People were pretty pumped, you could tell. It was like, *By God, we feel good about this com-pany.* The president seemed pretty pumped, too. He was very complimentary of GM, and had nice words to say about Ameri-can workers: "Don't bet against them," was his basic message. I could not agree with him more. All you had to do was look around that room to know that.

Afterward, I got invited to meet with President Obama. I was shown to a conference room to wait until the president was ready to see me. Transportation Secretary Ray LaHood was there, too. We'd met a few times before, so we sat around talking for a few minutes. About that time, somebody came and got me, said the president was ready to see me.

It was very informal. He didn't have a coat on, just a shirt and tie. It was the first time we'd ever met—just the two of us, nobody else was in the room. We shook hands, sat down in a couple of metal folding chairs. No airs at all. I liked him right away.

First thing, he said something to the effect of: "Things seem to be going well; we sure hope you'll be staying for a while."

"Well, it's been a good ride," I said. "I'm contemplating all those things, and I appreciate you saying that."

His comment surprised me a little, to be perfectly honest. Up to that point, I'd never had a single conversation with anybody truly in the White House. I'd met Tim Geithner (US Treasury secretary) and Larry Summers (director of the White House's National Economic Council), just quick hellos. But my day-to-day contact was always with the Auto Team—never any higher. (Team Auto reported to Treasury, and Treasury reported to the White House, which had ultimate authority over GM and the auto bailout.)

On one hand I was grateful for the management freedom we had, TARP notwithstanding. On the other hand, I was always a little surprised that nobody in the White House ever tried to engage us more directly. I was always volunteering—"If you need me to come to Washington to talk, to make an argument..." But that didn't happen; nobody ever asked.

I told the president we were deeply appreciative of his support for GM; also let him know I thought he did the right thing by bailing us out. "I think you can tell from the enthusiasm of the crowd that it was the right thing to do," I told him.

I was not committal one way or the other about staying at GM, and the subject never got brought up again. About five minutes into it, somebody came into the room. The president stood up and said he had to go.

By this point we were knee-deep in bankers. Our IPO was shaping up to be pretty big. Millions in banking fees would be paid out to the winners—that's like blood in the water to these guys. Every big name you can think of was circling—JPMorgan Chase, Morgan Stanley, Citigroup, many others. That's when we hit on an idea: If they were going to help us sell America the idea that GM was a good investment, why not make these banks demonstrate a little support by buying our products? So we put the arm on them—bankers at the winning firms had to agree to go out and buy new GM cars. This was not a contractual obligation—just a good-faith request. But if we could help our dealers sell a few hundred more cars, why not? I relayed our request in a lighthearted way; people got a good laugh every time I did that. But I also got my point across—I was dead serious.

There was a lot of speculation about the size and timing of the IPO around this period. Federal rules put a lot of limitations on you, in terms of what you can say, in advance of an IPO, so GM wasn't saying anything publicly. But the financial press was all over this thing. Some people were suggesting we might raise as much as $10 billion—this was based on the assumption that the government sold half its shares. That would have made it one of the largest in history. Treasury people were still debating internally at this point, so they weren't talking, either. We still did not have a firm date for the IPO, but we were zeroing in on November.

That would coincide with the launch of the Volt, which was getting a lot of positive press, as well as a fair number of pre-sales—requests were coming in to dealers at a pretty good clip. Our engineers still didn't have the Volt's algorithms quite right, but they also knew delay was not an option. The attitude shift was apparent throughout the organization: Morale was better, dealers were happier, management was focused and working harder than ever. In other words, GM was finally getting back to what it does best: designing, building, and selling the world's best vehicles.

Looking back on this period, it's difficult to convey the sense of joy and satisfaction I felt—here was a grand American company that had been on the absolute brink. A company many had predicted would never come back; never regain its financial health again. Now, six months into my term as CEO, we were poised to stage one of the biggest IPOs in history. We had good products, and more were in the pipeline. Employees were feeling focused and enthusiastic; management was clear about our business objectives and hitting on all cylinders. I felt fortunate and humbled to serve as GM's CEO; not a day went by when I didn't find myself being reminded, in big and small ways, of how talented and essential the employee body was. *They* were the reason GM was profitable again. Not me; them. As CEO, I'd had their backs every step of the way. But they had mine, too. Together we'd managed to accomplish something that was important for America: the turnaround of General Motors.

All of which made my personal dilemma during this period even more crushing.

Should I go, or should I stay?

To be really clear here, I *wanted* to stay—I loved being at GM, loved working with employees. I was genuinely having a good time and wanted, very much, to play a part as GM continued its rapid climb back to the top. But my personal preferences were not the issue; the IPO was the issue.

As I mentioned earlier, you have to be very careful what you say, and promise, in connection with an IPO. If I stayed on as CEO through the IPO but left afterward, GM could be accused of misleading people. Management is a big consideration for many investors, and the exit of a CEO is considered a "material" or significant event—so GM could be sued if people felt like they got duped. That begged another question: How long would I need to stick around after the IPO, then, to avoid that legal exposure? Some lawyers thought I'd need to stay two to three years. Others said a year might be okay, but might not. In other words, nobody knew for sure. But one thing we all agreed on: We could not do anything that might disrupt the IPO. It was too important for GM, and too important for America.

I also thought about the perception of GM: the company, at that point, had gone through three CEOs in very rapid fashion— Rick Wagoner, Fritz Henderson, and me. If I stuck around for another year and left, it would give the appearance that GM can't hold on to a CEO. But if I left sooner, then it would be more of a non-event, I figured. I'd said all along that I was short term, so I'd just be making good on that. There was also my age: sixty-eight. As a practical reality, I couldn't stay long term. If I'd been forty-five or fifty, this wouldn't have been a debate. But I wasn't. I'd put in forty-four years at AT&T, and had a wife and family waiting for me back home. So it wasn't appropriate for me to move to Detroit full-time, but flying in and out every week was also stressful, and a little lonely, too, to be honest. Working sunup to sundown, living in a rented apartment full of furniture that wasn't mine, shopping for food by myself at nine o'clock at night—not exactly the way I wanted to spend my life, you know? So while I was feeling very fulfilled, I also knew in my heart that I couldn't do this forever. And the people of GM deserved the best leadership they could get.

Adding to my misery around all this, I wasn't feeling too good about my conversation with the president. I was feeling pretty awful, in fact. He'd graciously asked me to stay on, which I really appreciated. But I never really answered him—because in truth I was already thinking about leaving. After that meeting, I headed to a conference in Traverse City. On the plane, all I could think about was—*The president of the United States just asked me to stay, and I've already made up my mind.* What a terrible dilemma. I felt like a traitor. But I also knew that it wasn't right for me to stay another two or three years—I just couldn't do it.

And that was the answer: *I had to leave.* There was no other answer, or outcome. And so, after a lot of thought and deliberation, and a lot of lost sleep at night, I told the board that I would leave in August, ahead of the IPO. I did not debate it with people, or even ask for their personal opinions—this was my decision alone, based on the line of thinking I just laid out. I made it clear I would not reconsider, or extend my stay as CEO.

The board was a little surprised, I think. But everybody could see that I was serious, so they accepted my decision, pretty much on the spot. So the next logical question after that, of course, was: Okay, then who's going to be the CEO of General Motors?

CHAPTER 18

The Last Chapter

I had somebody in mind to take my place as CEO: Mark Reuss.

Mark, of course, was president of GM's North American operations—that put him in charge of the US, Canadian, and Mexican markets. It's a big job, and a big responsibility. He was growing into it well, I thought. Mark had zoomed up the executive chain in record time; he went from midlevel engineer to the number two person in the company in the space of a year, more or less. The plus was that Mark was showing a lot of poise and management potential. The downside was that he hadn't been in the job long enough to prove himself as a CEO. Normally, people in the number two position stay there a few years, at least, before they get moved up to the top job.

But there was nothing normal about this situation. I'd been brought in as CEO under a unique set of circumstances, and the circumstances were still a little unusual: I was leaving in advance of a once-in-a-lifetime IPO, and we needed somebody to step into the top job immediately. GM could not afford to be without a CEO for even an hour, and an interim CEO was not an option—the company had already been through that gut-wrenching experience.

This was around the first week of August. We—I am referring

to myself and the other GM directors—immediately began to discuss our options. They were pretty limited. There was no time or ability to try to recruit a CEO from outside, for all the reasons I have enumerated.

The first question on the table concerned structure: Did we want to have a non-executive chairman, who's not an employee of the company? That was the arrangement I'd had as chairman. That way, if we decided to go with Mark, or another candidate, that person could serve as CEO, with the understanding that he or she would get a little seasoning before assuming the chairman's title. A lot of companies do that these days, though I'm not a fan, myself. I'd always been chairman and CEO; I just think it works better that way. In GM's situation, in particular, I thought it was a bad idea. Whoever replaced me needed to have the responsibility, accountability, and authority to act fast. Split-title arrangements—giving one person the CEO's job, and somebody else the chairman's title—just slows things down. And slow was not a good thing for General Motors.

Views on the board were split. Some people thought a non-executive chairman wasn't a bad idea. Other people really didn't care. A few didn't like the idea at all.

One thing everybody agreed on: Mark had a lot of potential. He's a good car guy, has charisma, also has leadership ability— he'd demonstrated that in a number of ways, and people were impressed by this. Employees liked him—people tend to work better and harder for people they like, so this was no small thing. The only concern was his short time in the job. If we asked him to step into the CEO's job, and it didn't work out, that would be a disaster for Mark—and an even bigger disaster for General Motors. The company needed stability. The revolving door in the CEO's suite had to stop.

It would have been a big step for Mark, no question. But it was my personal assessment that he could do it. I also thought it would be a good signal to the people of GM. Mark was known as a car guy, and GM was a car company—there were a lot of car nuts throughout the organization, and Mark could talk their language, you know? So he was credible in a way that a non-car-guy never can be. Plus, Mark was the right age—late forties—so he could provide continuity. For all those reasons, I thought it was the best thing for GM long term. But this was ultimately the board's decision.

So that's basically what I told everybody:

"I just told you what I would do, so if you have another candidate let's talk about it now, because I'm leaving and we have to make a decision." Whatever the board wanted to do, I was willing to do—I made that clear, too.

At this point Dan Akerson basically volunteered to do the job. Dan had joined the GM board in July 2009; at the time he was with The Carlyle Group, heading up the global buyout business. Dan had held the CEO title at a number of companies: XO Communications, Nextel, and General Instrument. Earlier in his career, he worked at MCI, Phillips Petroleum, and even AT&T, but we'd never crossed paths personally until he came to GM. Dan was a former chief financial officer (at MCI) and had lots of experience dealing with investor types, so the IPO was right up his alley. He also had firsthand experience with bankruptcy, so he had that perspective, as well.

Dan wanted to be chairman and CEO from Day One, had no interest in being a non-executive chairman, or a split title. And I could certainly understand, because that's what I would have wanted if I'd been in his shoes. Dan was sixty-one at the time, so like me he wasn't exactly a spring chicken. But he said he'd do the job for a limited period of time. And the board was okay with that because our back was basically against the wall. There was a lot of talent and experience on the GM board, but nobody else was in position to step up, or wanted the job. The board decided it did not want to go with the split title arrangement, or a non-executive chairman arrangement, or Mark, at least right then, because of the lack-of-experience issue. So when Dan put his hand up, that took care of the problem. Not very elegant, I will admit. But that's basically how it played out.

The board asked me to stay on as a board member. I declined. I didn't think it would be fair to Dan. I had pretty clear opinions on GM and how it should be doing things. Trying to step back and be a regular board member, with no direct accountability or authority to get things done, just wasn't going to work; not my temperament. I did agree to stay on as chairman until the end of the year. Everybody thought that would send the right signal through the IPO—that I'm still there. And I could not disagree with that.

The news of my departure was announced on August 12, 2010. We put the news out concurrent with second-quarter results: GM earned $1.3 billion, making it our best quarter in *six* years. Earnings per share: $2.55. It was our second consecutive quarter of growth, and the trend line going forward was overwhelmingly positive. A big driver of the comeback was GM North America—that was Mark's group. Strong sales of the Chevy Equinox, GMC Terrain (truck division), and Cadillac SRX, a crossover vehicle—all these cars were flying off dealer lots—contributed. We also let people know that our S-1 document—that's what you give the Securities and Exchange Commission in advance of an IPO—would be filed shortly. Our message to the market, and to America, was pretty clear: *GM is back.*

But I, sadly, was leaving.

I didn't say much publicly, just not my way. But I did say a few words at the end of the earnings call. I pointed out that I'd never joined GM with the intention of staying a long time. My goal all along, I said, was to help GM restore profitability, and get back to a strong market position. "Today, we are clearly on that path," I said—and back-to-back earnings results were a pretty strong indicator of that. "We have put a strong foundation in place, so I am very comfortable with my timing."

But that didn't mean I was happy about the timing—I wasn't. I put on a good front for everybody, but privately I just felt terrible. Really terrible, because I felt like I was letting down the people of GM by leaving; we had this great interaction with each other, and here I was walking out the door, you know? I knew in my heart I was doing the right thing, but I was also incredibly sad. I felt very conflicted, emotionally. And I still have ambivalent feelings to this day.

Nobody from the White House called, and I guess I could understand. They had their hands pretty full—the economy, a couple of wars, the Wall Street mess. Plus, I recalled that I didn't exactly distinguish myself in that short conversation with the president. He asked me to stay on, and I basically mumbled my answer and then quit. That still bothers me. Hopefully, one day he'll know my reasons, and understand. I did hear from Ron Bloom, with the Auto Team. He seemed disappointed, like maybe I was letting down the country by leaving. Or at least that's how it felt to me. I hope that is not the case; I did my best. Before we hung up, Ron said "thanks for your efforts" at GM. And that was pretty much that.

After the news went out, I got a lot of emails from employees—hundreds. *Why are you leaving? We're so disappointed—please don't go. We need you.* That made me feel even worse, not that I needed any help with that. A lot of people also came up to my office to see me—by now people were not so reluctant to come to the thirty-ninth floor.

One person who came by was Tony. He's the manager of the Jos. A. Bank clothing store in the RenCen, over by the Food Court. I used to swing by pretty regularly, just to see how things were going. He came up and very emotionally said: "I really hate to see you go." Then he thanked me again for not moving GM out of the RenCen—they were still in business because of that. The Food Court people also came to see me. Or rather, they grabbed me when they saw me down in the Food Court—I was still going there every day, pretty much, to get my lunch. They didn't want me to go, either. So this was a very emotional time.

One of the first calls I got was from Mark Reuss. Told me I'd connected with people at GM like nobody ever had. "I wish you could stay," he said, "because we're just on the verge of being incredible." I will always remember that line, and he was right about that—we were. That made me even sadder. Tom Stephens, head of engineering, also called: "You've done more in a few months than anybody's done in the history of the company." I don't know if that's true or not, but I did appreciate him saying that.

Management had a little going-away party for me, just me and the senior management team. Mark brought me a clock that the engineers had put together, the face is a disc brake—it's cool as can be. Somebody else brought me a little model car with a note: "We're back in business because of you." CFO Chris Liddell read a list of the "10 Reasons We're Going to Miss Ed":

10. Mexican food
 9. How to pronounce "VeHicles"
 8. My monthly copy of *Cattle Herder*
 7. The first 5 minutes of the Monday morning meeting
 6. Road trips
 5. Constant e-mail traffic
 4. CEO drive-by's
 3. Your simplicity and directness
 2. Your leadership
 1. Your friendship

Hearing Chris say those things really moved me, because it reminded me of how far we'd come as a management team. One company, one goal, one team. That was us. But it also made me smile. Chris is from New Zealand, and he'd never quite gotten the hang of Mexican food. And believe me, I tried.

GM tried to throw a going-away party for me in the RenCen—

planned to invite all the employees, people at the Food Court, anybody else who wanted to show up. It was a nice idea, and I did appreciate the thought. But as soon as I found out about it, I shut that down. I didn't want a party. I wouldn't know what to say to all those people—I was a traitor, for God's sake. How can a traitor have a party? It was an emotional time for me; a very emotional time.

I stopped going to Detroit. Dan was now in charge; I didn't want to do anything that might distract from him, or the IPO. So I cleared out my office, and cleared out of the RenCen as fast as I could.

I had a rental apartment not too far from the RenCen, so I had to clear out of there, too. None of the furniture was mine— I had rented it fully furnished. But I'd managed to accumulate a lot of stuff, so Linda, my wife, flew up to help me. We got a GMC van, nothing fancy. The plan was to load it up and drive back to San Antonio, by way of Nashville—I have a sister there, thought it might be nice to swing by and see her on the way back home. On moving day, Tom Carpenske, a GM driver and friend, came over to help out. He'd printed me out a map of my route back home. We were going right by Bowling Green, Kentucky. I decided, on the spot, to swing by the GM plant there—it's right off I-65. That's where all the Corvettes are made. I figured I was still GM's chairman, you know, so why not stop by?

So Linda and I showed up at this plant. I didn't call ahead, as usual, or tell anybody I was coming. It was a Saturday. The plant was closed, but I figured there were people inside, so I found the front door and banged on it. Nobody answered. We took the van around the side—past all these signs that say "Unauthorized Vehicles Not Allowed"—and I started knocking on doors. The whole scene was pretty funny, now that I think of it. We were in this black panel truck, no windows, looked like something the Secret Service might use. And we were driving into all these restricted areas, banging on all these doors.

I finally came across a security guard. So I went up to him and said, "Hi, I'm Ed Whitacre, I was in the neighborhood and I'd like to come in because I'd like to meet some people here." I didn't introduce myself as "chairman"—I feel funny saying things like that, as I have mentioned. He looked at me like I was nuts—I was dressed in blue jeans, really casual. No business card, no nothing. I'm sure the black van didn't help. He was sort of staring at me, not sure what to do. I could see that this was going nowhere. So I asked to see the plant manager. The guard sort of grumbled, walked over to a security station, and called some lady: "There's a guy here who says his name is Ed Whitacre, says he needs to talk to somebody from GM."

I was standing ten feet or so away, and I heard her say: "I'll be right there."

A couple of minutes later, this woman came down, and she had a bunch of plant managers with her—they had some sort of special meeting going on, apparently. So they brought us inside—Linda and me—and we started walking around talking to people. They took me to all the different stations where Corvettes get made, which was fun to see. They also talked about their proud heritage—the Corvette came out in 1953, lots of history with that car—and how good they were feeling about the way things were going. And Corvettes were selling again, so they were feeling pretty good about that, too. By now we had twenty or twenty-five people around us, and we were just having a great time chatting.

People had a lot of nice things to say: *We are so appreciative of what you've done. Thank you for making us a company again. Thank you for this. Thank you for that.* It made me feel good, on one level, but it also made me feel like a traitor all over again. So it turned out to be a lot more emotional than I expected. But I was glad we went. Some people made a point of letting me know that no GM chairman had ever stopped by like that, and it seemed to mean a lot to them. And that meant a lot to me. Linda had a good time, too. She said a couple of people came up to her and said: "We heard he does this"—referring to my habit of dropping by to see people unannounced. She got a big kick out of that.

We must've stayed there two or three hours. Then we got in the van and drove on to Nashville to see my sister. Got back home to San Antonio the next day.

On the day of the IPO—November 18, 2010—I watched the ringing of the bell on Wall Street, which signals the beginning of trading. GM invited me to attend the bell ringing, but I declined. I would have felt funny doing that. I didn't participate in the road show; I was gone. So, to me, that just would not have been appropriate.

But I watched the whole thing from my home office, in San Antonio. A lot of GM people kept calling me—everybody was pumped, because the stock was selling like crazy. On the morning of the IPO, demand so far exceeded what the bankers had predicted that they wound up expanding the number of common shares for sale by a full third—to 478 million. The opening share price was also healthier than anybody had expected: $32 to $33 a share. Original projections had been in the $26 to $28 range.

By the end of the first day of trading, GM raised $20.1 billion—more than double the amount bankers and other people had expected. Including an option that would allow underwriters to sell more shares, GM was on track to top $23 billion—making it the biggest initial offering ever. After the sale, the government's stake in GM dropped to 33 percent, almost half the 61 percent stake it had prior to the IPO.

The level of commitment to GM was even more impressive when you consider that this company, just a year and a half earlier, was fresh out of bankruptcy. Bloodied and beaten down, GM didn't have a chance according to a lot of "experts." Now here it was, just sixteen months later, laying claim to the biggest IPO in US corporate history. And here's the kicker: By the time the bell rang on Wall Street that morning, GM already had orders worth *$86 billion* for the common stock part of the sale. So it could have easily repaid the government the entire $43 billion it owed, and given taxpayers a nice profit for their time and trouble on top of that. Now, I'm not one to say "I told you so," but, geez, what a wasted opportunity.

But on a positive note, the stock sale was a tremendous success. And the reason it succeeded, ultimately, was because of GM's employee body: the two hundred thousand men and women who design, build, and sell the world's best vehicles. They are the reason GM made it; they are the reason GM came back. I helped as best I could, but the only reason GM is with us now is because those employees rose to the challenge, and they did so under the darkest and most difficult circumstances imaginable. Lots of people thought GM didn't have a shot; wrote it off as DOA, ain't coming back, you know? But those employees never stopped believing, never stopped trying. And as a result one of America's proudest and most important companies, General Motors, came swinging back hard, stronger and more tenacious than ever.

And that's why that blue shirt and red tie, the ones I wore in that first TV commercial, still hang in my closet, never to be worn again. They're in a very special place; I see them every time I walk into that closet. And it always makes me smile and feel good to see them hanging there, because they symbolize a terrific period of my life, when what we accomplished exceeded my expectations in ways I never could have imagined or dreamed. Together management and the employees of General Motors brought back a company that America needs, and depends on, and we brought it back *big*.

That shirt and tie remind me, in a very poignant way, that anything is possible—that if the people are with you, and they're feeling motivated and inspired, you can accomplish just about anything. The possibilities are limitless. I saw that at AT&T—what we created there together was also quite special. And the people of GM proved that to me again. As I've said before, I had their backs every step of the way, and I hope they know that. But they had mine, too—I always felt that. And that's why that shirt and tie hang in my closet to this day, and always will.

Reflection

Texas—A (Management) State of Mind

I have been asked, from time to time, if I think my Texas heritage had any influence on my management style, or on my approach to business in general.

Well, the fact of the matter is, I *was* born and raised in Texas, so I have no context or experience base to say how I might have turned out, as a person and manager, if I'd been born in, say, Memphis or New York City.

But my gut says yes, Texas did influence my management style—I mean, how could it not?

Texas is unique, no question. The state is quite large, as you probably know—more than 260,000 square miles. That's bigger than France and Denmark *combined*. A lot of it is not particularly hospitable to man or beast—temperatures tend to be extreme, especially in the summer, and the terrain is pretty rugged in many parts. Our history is colorful; it's full of cowboys, ranchers, good guys, bad guys, a whole cast of characters—so that tends to influence you, too.

As a kid, I was fascinated by the Texas Rangers—they were basically the law back in the early days, when Texas was still pretty wild. Those guys were tough, also legendary. There's a famous story: The mayor of Dallas called in the Texas Rangers to help calm down an angry mob. One Ranger showed up. The mayor didn't know what to make of this, said: "Where are the others?" And the Ranger said: "There's only one riot, right?"

Fearlessness has always defined Texas. It's just in our blood, I guess, and that has a way of showing up in all sorts of ways—from how people talk to how they deal with a business challenge. To those who weren't born and raised here, this can sometimes come across as a little overly self-assured, even arrogant. Which I guess I can understand, because people in Texas are a little different. But in a good way: Texans, at their core, are just fundamentally optimistic about the possibilities in life. As a result, they tend to think big and aren't afraid to give things that matter to them a real shot. *I believe in what I'm doing, and I'm going to hang in there until I accomplish what I'm trying to do. Or die trying.* That second part—hanging in there—is the true measure in Texas. The thing most people truly respect isn't whether you were successful or not—it's that you gave it all you had.

I mean, think about it. One of Texas's proudest moments is also one of its biggest failures, technically: the fall of the Alamo, which is in San Antonio. And it is a pretty dramatic story: More than two thousand Mexican troops surrounded the Alamo; inside, there were around 186 guys, and they were poorly armed. They were led by a young lieutenant colonel, William B. Travis, just twenty-six at the time. The Mexican Army thought it was a done deal, so the commanding general demanded a full surrender. Travis responded by firing a single cannon shot. In other words: *No way.* It was a fight against overwhelming and impossible odds, and Travis lost—every single man died, and the fort was ultimately overrun and captured. And yet, the fall of the Alamo is remembered to this day as one of our finest moments—as a state and as a nation. So it's not the failure that people remember, but the courage and strength of heart.

Rugged individualism and bravery are things that Texans have always admired, and respected. So does the rest of America, I think—we are simply unable and unwilling to let anybody tell us what we can and can't accomplish. If you can dream it, you can do it; that, in so many words, is what America is all about. Resiliency is our shared DNA. So when you get right down to it, a Texas-tough attitude isn't just limited to Texas—people from every state in the union have it.

All of which is a long way of saying—to go back to where I started—that I do think my management style and general outlook on life have been greatly influenced by the fact that I am a Texan. At least I'd sure like to think so.

Epilogue

There's a lot of talk these days about how America has lost its competitive edge; that we're falling behind in the global economy that we helped birth and have spent the past forty years promoting. We've lost our way, in other words—as an economic power, as a cultural force, and as a political leader in the world.

You know what I think?

I think people who say things like that are pontificating about things they know nothing about. They've never worked in industry or been around people, I guess, so they don't know what a valuable asset we have out there in terms of the spirit, depth, and capability of the American worker. And my recent experience at General Motors underscores that for me, big time. Here was a company a lot of people had written off for dead. But as we've discussed in this book, GM did manage to get itself turned around. GM emerged from bankruptcy in July 2009. Sixteen months later, in November 2010, that formerly bankrupted company staged the largest IPO in history. By the time the opening bell rang on Wall Street that morning, we had more than *$86 billion* in orders from people who wanted to buy GM stock. At that level, GM could have paid back every last nickel it owed American taxpayers—around $43 billion at that time—and had another $43 billion left over. The US Treasury decided not to sell all of its shares at the IPO, as we all know, so that didn't happen. But that's the only reason.

My larger point is this: General Motors didn't just come back from the ashes in sixteen short months, it came back strong. Brings to mind that famous line by Winston Churchill: "If you're going through hell...keep going." GM did, and now it's selling a lot of cars and trucks. In 2011 General Motors recorded an all-time record profit of $7.6 billion. That tops GM's old record of $6.7 billion, which was recorded in 1997 at the height of the pickup truck–SUV craze.

What caused GM's miraculous revival, and comeback?

That's an easy one: employees. The people of GM came together, as one, and brought that company back from the brink. Management helped, as we have discussed, in terms of creating an environment that allowed good things to happen. And management was 100 percent responsible for the outcome. But nothing management did, or tried, would have made a shred of difference if the men and women of GM had not been willing to put their shoulders to the wall and push; and they kept pushing until General Motors got its heartbeat back again.

Is GM perfect? No. Is there still a lot to do? You bet. GM still has a lot of fat that needs to be cut out, and its heavily matrixed bureaucracy still has a strong hold on parts of the organization. One of my biggest regrets is that I didn't get rid of more of that; maybe future leadership will take an ax to all that stuff. (I hope so.) Meantime, life goes on. The global car business is as tough as ever, and the current economic swings aren't helping. As this is being written, gas prices are hitting $4 a gallon, a US presidential election is looming, and the global debt crisis is continuing to rattle the financial markets.

Nobody's found a crystal ball yet that can accurately predict how all this stuff turns out. But I personally have no doubt that GM will do okay. The source of my optimism, as always, is the two-hundred-thousand-plus men and women who show

up for work every day so that General Motors can do the one
and only thing it does in life: design, build, and sell the world's
best vehicles. Just think how much better and stronger General
Motors can become over time if in sixteen months it could go
from "dead and never coming back" to the biggest IPO in history. And two years later, to record profitability.

American spirit.

That's what we're really talking about here. It's a bold way
of looking at life, and at life's possibilities; a uniquely American
attitude that says: *We can do anything. We're the best. We're the
most innovative. We're the most enthused, the most capable.*

That can-do spirit, ultimately, is what gives me so much hope
about the future of this country, because if it can happen at GM
it can happen all over America. American workers really are the
backbone of this country: They may fuss, they may moan, but
they come back to work every day to do their jobs so they can
do right by their companies, do right by their families and themselves. There is a spirit of persistence there, and that tells me that
things are pretty good. The majority of days I believe that. Other
days I'm as pessimistic as everybody else, to be perfectly honest.
But that never lasts too long because of what I've seen, and personally experienced, throughout my many years in business. And
what I've concluded, after almost fifty years of chipping away at
this stuff, is this: If we stick together, as a nation and as a people,
we can do anything. There are no obstacles we can't overcome.

The people of General Motors reminded me of that in a
big way. So did the people of AT&T. Unlike GM, AT&T was
never bankrupted, but the transformation, in many ways, was
just as dramatic. We turned a regional phone company, Southwestern Bell, into the largest telecommunications enterprise on
the planet. When we started, Southwestern Bell had annual revenue of $9 billion; by the time we got done AT&T was right
at $120 billion. I had a front-row seat to all that as the CEO,
and even now, looking back, I still can't believe we did all that.

But we did. And by "we" I'm referring to management and the employee body of AT&T. We were one company, united around one goal: to turn our company into a strong competitor that could survive and thrive in the global economy. And keep going for years—decades—to come.

There's an old cowboy saying: "Do it right or get off the horse." Focus and common sense. Don't ever underestimate the value of either in a business environment. Persistence, that's another important ingredient. You just hang in there; you don't give up. Before you can get to that point, of course, you have to be willing to stand up and say—to yourself or to an entire employee body: *Let's go do this.* Because if you never give it a shot, never push outside your comfort zone to at least try, you'll never get to the point we're talking about. That's how I always saw my role as CEO: as the guy who was always willing to stand up and say to everybody: "Let's give this thing a shot." I never knew for sure how things were going to turn out when I did that. But I was always hopeful. And I *always* believed in my people. I just fundamentally believed that so long as the people were with us, we could do and accomplish just about anything. Maybe I was just lucky. But it worked for me.

I'm retired now, but still pushing it because I do believe in the American business model that I've sketched out here: If you give people the authority to go out and do something, let them be accountable and responsible, and provide an environment that allows people to feel confident and be the best they can be, amazing things can happen. I also believe in the timeless draw of the American Dream; it's a uniquely American idea that says, basically, no matter who you are, or where you come from, you can have a shot at success in this country—and success can be defined any way that makes sense to you.

I'm living proof that the American Dream is alive and well. Still can't believe I got to be the CEO of one big company, much less two—I'm Edward from Ennis, you know? I'm still not exactly sure how that happened, and if you can come up with an answer to that after reading this book then you're ahead of me on that one. But my basic point is that America really is the land of opportunity. That's not just a saying, that's a fact.

Nobody does this stuff alone, and I didn't, either. Somebody gave me a chance way back when; several chances, in fact. I am trying to return the favor, in my own, small way, by creating opportunities for some people who might not have a shot otherwise. That was my goal when I bought a little water-well company in 2007, McKinley Drilling; it's in South Texas, about an hour's drive from the Gulf of Mexico. The business had four employees when I bought it; today we've got about twenty.

So far, things are working out pretty good. Our revenues have increased substantially, and are still growing. I am not rewarded by the money; most of that is going to our workers. I've also set up a performance-based compensation system for management. So if the business does good, they do good. Meantime, we're vertically integrating other businesses to supplement our core water-well-drilling business. People have clear areas of responsibility and decision-making authority; they're also accountable for results. This extends to welders, pipe fitters, bulldozer operators, and management. I am encouraged by this. I've always believed that the same management principles I used at AT&T and GM could be applied to a business of just about any size, and my experience with McKinley Drilling water well business is hard confirmation of that. I never really doubted that, but like President Reagan used to say: "Trust but verify." Consider it verified.

While I am very pleased by the performance of the business— I'm a businessman at heart, what can I say—I will also tell you that the real joy, for me, is seeing these people grow and learn. The community where the business is located is largely Hispanic, mostly lower income. My goal, over time, is to get across the idea to our employees that a better life is possible; that trust, loyalty, and respect are things that you should aspire to have in life, and that these things are actually achievable in America, no matter who you are, or what your circumstances in life might be. And that, ultimately, is what the American Dream is really all about.

As for all those eternal pessimists out there, the ones who keep saying that America is falling behind, that's just a lazy way of looking at things, in my view. Anybody can be pessimistic. It's the easy way out; no heavy lifting required. Just pick up a newspaper or turn on the news these days and the headlines will do your thinking for you, if you're inclined in that direction. On the contrary, it takes conviction and strength of heart to create your own luck and breaks—whether you're talking about General Motors or backhoe operators for a local water-well company. The common trait between those two groups of people? They have an innate optimism about the possibility of a better tomorrow.

Pessimists don't have that burden; they tend to plant their feet like signposts and don't move around a lot. With optimists, it's just the opposite. They're in constant motion, always thinking, creating, and trying to figure out a better way. I'm with the optimists, and always will be. I just fundamentally believe in the power of the American worker to change things for the better, and when I say that I'm definitely referring to the entire melting pot that is our America—Hispanics, Asians, African Americans, Caucasians, Indonesians, Indians, or pick an ethnic group or persuasion. We're all Americans, and when we put our hearts and minds into something, the possibilities are truly limitless.

The remarkable revivals and turnarounds of General Motors and AT&T are prime examples of the sort of can-do American spirit I am talking about. Absent the support and enthusiasm of those two employee bodies, it wouldn't have mattered how smart or gutsy management was; neither company would have ever been too successful, or profitable. But the people were with us every step of the way, and that made all the difference.

Snapshots

General Motors

Annual revenue (2011): $150.2 billion
Number of employees: 207,000 worldwide
Year founded: September 16, 1908; reincorporated on November 18, 2010, in the world's largest initial public offering
Name of founder: William C. Durant
Number of countries in which GM operates/does business: More than 120
Headquarters city: Detroit, Michigan
Historical highlights:

- During World War II, GM produced $12.3 billion worth of military supplies, including airplanes, tanks, engines, trucks, and weapons.

- GM developed and produced the two-stroke diesel loco-motive engine, which revolutionized the railroad industry (GM Electro-Motive division, 1930–2005).
- GM manufactured the guidance and navigation systems that guided *Apollo 11* astronauts to Man's first successful landing on the moon in 1969.

GM was also the first to develop and introduce:

- Electric self-starter (1912)
- Mass-production V-8 engine (1915)
- Ethyl gasoline (1923)
- Shatterproof safety glass (1928)
- Fully automatic transmission (1940)
- High-volume production sports car (1953 Chevrolet Corvette)
- Small-block V-8 engine (1955)
- Catalytic converter (1974)
- Extended-range electric vehicle (Chevy Volt, 2010)

(Source: General Motors)

AT&T

at&t

Annual revenue (2011): $126.7 billion

Number of employees: 256,420 worldwide

Year founded: 1877—then called American Telephone & Telegraph Co.; reemerged as a stand-alone long-distance company after the 1984 breakup of Ma Bell

Founders: Alexander Graham Bell, Gardiner Hubbard, and Thomas Sanders

Number of countries in which AT&T operates/has networks: Just about every country on the planet

Headquarters city: Dallas, Texas

Historical highlights:

- AT&T Labs traces its roots back to Alexander Graham Bell's invention of the telephone in 1876. The Labs today are home to twelve hundred scientists and engineers.
- AT&T completed the first transcontinental telephone call in America in 1915, and the first mobile call in 1946. AT&T also had the first commercial modem (1958) and figured out how to get a live TV image from earth to outer space and back (1962).
- In 1927 AT&T presented the first public demonstration of television in the United States. Secretary of Commerce

Herbert Hoover was featured; his image was transmitted via cable to New York.

- In 1965 two AT&T researchers heard unexplained noises during a radio astronomy exercise. They later figured out that they had heard the "Echo of Creation," related to the Big Bang theory of creation, and were awarded the Nobel Prize for their discovery.
- AT&T has been awarded seven other Nobel Prizes over the years. The company has thousands of patents, and continues to issue new ones at a steady rate: about two a day.
- The Internet's beginnings can be traced to the Labs' development of UNIX, a computer operating system, in 1971.

(Source: AT&T)

Acknowledgments

With most accomplishments in life, it takes an army of people to get there.

This book was no different.

I'd first like to thank Rick Wolff, the editor of this book, for the opportunity to commit my two cents about business and life to paper, and for thinking that maybe some people out there might find some value in that. I hope he's right. I'd also like to thank the publisher, Grand Central—Rick was the guy who founded the imprint (Business Plus) that is publishing this book, so I guess that means he's a pretty smart businessman on top of being a pretty good editor. I also want to send along my thanks to Rick's team, including Meredith Haggerty, Dorothea Halliday, Flag Tonuzi, and Mark Fortier, for doing such a great job. And thanks to Joe Veltre, my literary agent. Joe is with the Gersh Agency (New York); he put us together with Rick and Grand Central—good move, Joe. And a special thanks to Alison Wright—she took the cover photo, and a few others you'll see inside. I am not too fond of having my picture taken—just not a camera-ready kind of guy. But Alison was a good sport, and I do think she did a pretty good job, especially considering the material she had to work with. I'd also like to thank my collaborator, Leslie Cauley, for hanging in there with me. Leslie helped me figure out a way to turn seventy years of living into this three-hundred-plus-page book. And I am not a big talker, even on a good day. So that took a little doing—thank you, Leslie.

And to Selim Bingol of General Motors, and Larry Solomon of AT&T—thanks, guys, for helping us out.

This book would have never happened, most likely, had it not been for the support and encouragement of my wife, Linda, and our two daughters, Jessica and Jennifer. I wasn't convinced that I had a story to tell, to be honest. But they thought different. So thank you, girls, and thank you, Linda.

Last, but certainly not least, I'd like to offer my personal thanks to the employees of AT&T and General Motors. Not just for working so hard and for accomplishing so much—and you certainly did that—but for doing it in a way that made your CEO, and your country, proud. It's people like you who make people believe in the goodness, and greatness, of America— and I'm one of them. Thank you all.

Index

About the Author

Ed Whitacre is the former chairman and CEO of two major American corporations: General Motors and AT&T. At GM, he set a clear vision and mandate—"Design, Build, and sell the World's Best Vehicles"—that continues to this day. As the chief executive of AT&T, Whitacre applied a set of management principles and disciplined growth strategy that would turn the company, originally known as Southwestern Bell, into the largest telecom company in the world

Born and raised in Ennis, Texas, Whitacre attended Texas Tech, earning a bachelor's degree in industrial engineering. He began his career with the phone company in 1963, as a student engineer in Dallas. In 1990 he was named CEO, and he remained in that leadership position for seventeen years. In 2009 the White House appointed him chairman of GM, and he became CEO later that year.

Whitacre is actively involved in a number of organizations, including Boy Scouts of America, the United Way, and Texas Tech. He is a current or past member of several boards, including ExxonMobil, Burlington Northern Santa Fe, and Anheuser-Busch. He is married to Linda Whitacre, and they have two daughters, four grandchildren, and a really great dog, Lucille.

**BUSINESS
PLUS**

Recognized as one of the world's most prestigious business imprints, Business Plus specializes in publishing books that are on the cutting edge. Like you, to be successful we always strive to be ahead of the curve.

Business Plus titles encompass a wide range of books and interests—including important business management works, state-of-the-art personal financial advice, noteworthy narrative accounts, the latest in sales and marketing advice, individualized career guidance, and autobiographies of the key business leaders of our time.

Our philosophy is that business is truly global in every way, and that today's business reader is looking for books that are both entertaining and educational. To find out more about what we're publishing, please check out the Business Plus blog at:

www.bizplusbooks.com